# Enforcement of Actions in Corporate Law by Non-Shareholder Constituencies

# Enforcement of Actions in Corporate Law by Non-Shareholder Constituencies

## Lessons for the Common Law World from South Africa

Tshepo Herbert Mongalo

LEXINGTON BOOKS
*Lanham • Boulder • New York • London*

Lexington Books
Bloomsbury Publishing Inc, 1385 Broadway, New York, NY 10018, USA
Bloomsbury Publishing Plc, 50 Bedford Square, London, WC1B 3DP, UK
Bloomsbury Publishing Ireland, 29 Earlsfort Terrace, Dublin 2, D02 AY28, Ireland
www.rowman.com



British Library Cataloguing in Publication Information Available

**Library of Congress Cataloging-in-Publication Data**

Names: Mongalo, Tshepo, author.
Title: Enforcement of actions in corporate law by non-shareholder constituencies: lessons for the common law world from South Africa / Tshepo Herbert Mongalo.
Description: Lanham: Lexington Books, 2025. | Includes bibliographical references and index.
Identifiers: LCCN 2024048823 | ISBN 9781666922585 (cloth) | ISBN 9781666922592 (ebook)
Subjects: LCSH: Corporation law—South Africa. | Business enterprises—Law and legislation—South Africa. | Stockholders—Legal status, laws, etc.—South Africa. | Stockholders' pre-emptive rights—South Africa. | Minority stockholders—Legal status, laws, etc.—South Africa.
Classification: LCC KTL1040 .M66 2025 | DDC 346.68/066—dc23/eng/20241017
LC record available at https://lccn.loc.gov/2024048823

For product safety related questions contact productsafety@bloomsbury.com.

∞™ The paper used in this publication meets the minimum requirements of American National Standard for Information Sciences—Permanence of Paper for Printed Library Materials, ANSI/NISO Z39.48-1992.

*For Ernest Ralph ('Raphadu') Mongalo (May his soul continue to rest in peace). Your seeds of success planted in me are beginning to sprout in earnest.*

# Contents

# Preface

Because of the recent corporate law developments in the United States and the United Kingdom – often characterised as a single 'Anglo-American' system – the type of corporate law enforcement model in operation in these jurisdictions can justifiably be referred to as 'conventional, shareholder-focused enforcement'. This approach propagates for the enforcement philosophy focused on enabling only the beneficiaries of directorial duties to bring corporate actions under applicable corporate statute and the common law.

Within the United Kingdom, this form of corporate legal enforcement regime is commonly referred to as 'the Enlightened Shareholder Value Approach' (ESVA). The similar ultimate goal of the corporate legal enforcement framework notwithstanding, the variations within the corporate law statutes of these two major jurisdictions point to the danger of generalisations, which essentially obfuscate immense differences across applicable corporate statutes in different state jurisdictions of the United States and in the United Kingdom.

This book presents the existence of a different form of corporate legal enforcement regime in South Africa, which is characterised by actionable remedies in corporate law, designed for the benefit of both shareholder and non-shareholder constituencies. Initially termed the 'Actionable Enlightened Shareholder Value Approach' (AESVA), recent research points to the preference of the term 'Structural Stakeholderism', as it is characterised by measures aimed at increasing stakeholder power, such as extended legal standing to bring actions in corporate law and the authorisation of stakeholder representation in corporate boards. By considering different approaches to corporate law enforcement, this book argues that the Anglo-American jurisdictions may learn something from South Africa with regard to corporate legal enforcement model. Although the country does not (yet) mandate stakeholder representation in corporate boards, making such eventuality only a possibility, it nevertheless affords non-shareholder constituencies the opportunity to access remedies in pursuing corporate actions, in a manner originally reserved for corporate entities themselves and their contributors of financial capital (i.e., equity investors or shareholders).

Fundamentally, this book argues that in bringing about regulatory measures in an attempt to reform the corporate legal enforcement framework in a way that gives consideration to the interests of non-shareholder constituencies is a worthy improvement in corporate law. Nevertheless, it argues, doing so without providing for a complementary enforcement framework for these constituencies is, unfortunately, a futile exercise.

Tshepo Herbert Mongalo is a Professor of Corporate Law at the University of the Witwatersrand's School of Law in Johannesburg and a Sessional Lecturer at Wits Business School in the same university. He is also the Chairperson of the Legal Entities' doctrinal study group of the International Association of Law Schools. His teaching and scholarship focus on corporate law, corporate law regulatory framework design, securities regulation, corporate governance, and leadership studies. He is the current faculty member of the global Advanced Leadership Academy (ALAC Global), the Deputy Chairperson of the Specialist Committee on Company Law in South Africa (SCCL), and the life member of the Pan African Lawyers Union, based in Arusha, Tanzania. He was recently appointed commissioner of the South African Law Reform Commission.

## THE PROBLEM

The problem of corporate constituencies, other than shareholders, being powerless to monitor or challenge corporate actions that are purportedly taken in their interests has always been part of corporate law attempts in Anglo-American jurisdictions, particularly within the United Kingdom and the United States, since the mid-1980s. These efforts have intended to address the concerns raised by Adolf A. Berle in his objection to E. Merrick Dodd's seminal arguments in favour of the need for corporate constituencies' considerations in corporate decision-making in the early 1930s.

In other words, the long-standing corporate law hindrance to the full enjoyment of the benefits of corporate actions by these corporate constituencies is the corporate law assumption respecting the corporate balance of power, which is to the effect that the law focuses directorial duties on – and limits enforcement powers to – shareholders. This is more so where the enjoyment of such benefits of corporate actions by non-shareholder corporate constituencies is directly mandated by the specific statutory corporate constituency measure to which the company is subject, such as the corporate constituency statute or the benefit corporation statute, as enacted in many states of the United States.

The statutory corporate constituency measure notwithstanding, it has also been observed in the 2014 US Supreme Court case of *Burwell v. Hobby Lobby* Stores Inc. 513 US (2014), 1, 23, that there are many examples of circumstances (other than the obvious case of a contract) in which the interests of non-shareholders may be considered regardless of the impact that such consideration may have on the profit motive of the corporation. The Court concluded that a for-profit corporation may, for example, take costly pollution-control and energy conservation measures that go beyond what the law requires or may exceed the requirements of local law regarding working conditions and benefits (without having to consider the impact on profit motive of the corporation, particularly when the non-profit motive is relatively easy to identify by reference to the wishes of those in control of the corporation).

As much has been said about whether companies, particularly directors, should legally be entitled or compelled to consider the interests of corporate constituencies in addition to those of shareholders, this book provides an in-depth critique of corporate law's design of the corporate legal enforcement scheme, solely on the basis of the conventional assumption that directorial responsibilities are exclusively or primarily owed to shareholder constituencies in companies. After a critical analysis of the latest corporate law developments in the United States, the United Kingdom and South Africa, the book concludes that such a link between the corporate legal enforcement regime and the questionable exclusivity or primacy of shareholder interests in corporate decision-making, particularly in public companies, is bound to perpetuate a conventional legal enforcement framework which ultimately disregards corporate law's attempts to accommodate the role of non-shareholder corporate constituencies in corporate decision-making. The book concludes that Anglo-American jurisdictions implicated in this research should seriously consider the policy wisdom of enacting extended legal standing statutory provisions to satisfactorily accommodate the transition in corporate law, particularly in connection with public companies, from the conventional association of directorial responsibilities exclusively with the shareholder corporate constituent group. While it is acknowledged that such extended legal standing will imply the granting of the right of action to the non-shareholder corporate constituent groups, the determination of whether the provision of that right is a good idea is, of course, a decision for policymakers. The book proposes that it is a good idea. The book argues that such a lack of extended standing provision in the statutory corporate constituency mechanisms discussed herein is a weakness primarily because it is jurisprudentially and pragmatically unsound to make non-shareholder corporate constituencies the apparent beneficiaries of the relevant statutory corporate constituency mechanisms but still continue to provide shareholders with the exclusive right of action over corporate law remedies, regardless of whether they are the beneficiaries of the particular statutory corporate constituency mechanism or not.

In his treatise published in the Harvard Law Review in 1932, an eminent Harvard University Law scholar, E. Merrick Dodd, emphatically and poignantly insisted that business had responsibilities to the community and that it was expected of corporate managers, without waiting for legal compulsion, to manage their businesses in such a way as to fulfil those responsibilities.

This proposition, which was way ahead of its time, was unsurprisingly objected to by another eminent legal scholar from Columbia Law School, Adolf A. Berle, whose primary argument for disagreement was that the view that business corporations existed for the sole purpose of making profits for their stockholders could not be abandoned until such time as corporate law was prepared to offer a clear and reasonably enforceable scheme of responsibilities to someone else.

Berle's primary objection presented a two-pronged proposition – that is, that corporate law needed to come up with (a) a clear scheme of responsibilities to someone else other than a shareholder, and that (b) such a scheme of responsibilities needed to be enforceable by that other constituency.

While Adolf A. Berle conceded twenty-two years later in an acknowledgement that the argument had been settled squarely in favour of Professor Dodd's contention, he never retracted the second part of his primary objection, which spoke to the need for the scheme of responsibilities to someone else to be enforceable.

It is indeed apparent that corporate constituency measures, which were introduced within the notable Anglo-American jurisdictions of the United Kingdom and the United States from the mid-1980s, attempted to address only the first part of Adolf A. Berle's primary objection by merely presenting a scheme of responsibilities to constituencies other than shareholders. These corporate constituency measures took the form of statutory provisions under the different Companies Acts in the United Kingdom and the corporate constituency statutes in the United States, otherwise known as the Non-Stockholder Constituency Statutes. With regard to the United Kingdom, the first statutory corporate constituency measure was reflected under s 309(1) of the UK Companies Act of 1985, wherein directors of companies were encouraged, but not required, to have regard to the interests of the company's employees in general in the performance of their functions. Meanwhile, starting in the early 1980s, many states of the United States enacted laws known as corporate constituency statutes or Non-Stockholder Constituency Statutes that allow, and in one instance require, corporate directors and executives to consider corporate constituencies' interests without breaching fiduciary obligations to shareholders. The pioneer of such statutory corporate constituency measures in the United States was the state of Pennsylvania in 1983.

With the enactment of the new Companies Act by the UK Parliament in 2006, corporate law developments witnessed the institutionalisation of the Enlightened Shareholder Value Approach in s 172(1), which, unlike s 309(1) of the previous Companies Act of 1985, effectively authorises, without obliging, directors of companies to consider not only the interests of the company's employees in acting, in good faith, to promote the success of the company. Directors are additionally encouraged to have regard to (a) the likely consequences of any decision in the long term, (b) the need to foster the company's business relationships with suppliers, customers, and others, (c) the impact of the company's operations on the community and the environment, (d) the desirability of the company maintaining a reputation for high standards of business conduct, and (e) the need to act fairly, as between members of the company.

Starting at the beginning of the second decade of the twenty-first century, a number of US states started enacting benefit corporation statutes which effectively authorise the creation of general and specific public benefit purposes by corporations, the pursuit of which, as opposed to the pursuit of stockholders' interests, is tantamount to the promotion of the best interests of the corporation and does not subject the corporation or its directors to liability or derivative suits except for specified reasons. Currently, thirty-six states in the United States recognise benefit corporations as a type of business form which may be utilised to allow social entrepreneurs to consider interests beyond those of maximising shareholder wealth without the risk of facing shareholder suits.

Regardless of the fact that some of these benefit corporation statutes expressly contemplate that a 'benefit enforcement proceeding' may be brought against a benefit corporation or its directors or officers by the corporation itself or derivatively by shareholders, directors, persons who hold more than 5 per cent of the equity of a parent entity or other persons specified in the articles or bylaws of the corporation, benefit corporation statutes generally lack enforcement mechanisms for use by or for the benefit of corporate constituencies.

Many commentators are in agreement that such schemes of responsibilities brought about by these corporate constituency measures do not dislodge the traditional corporate law premise that the primary, and perhaps the only, legitimate beneficiaries of directorial duties are the shareholders. While there appears to be acknowledgement among many of the commentators that the exercise of directorial duties in favour of constituencies other than shareholders may excuse directors from being in breach of such directorial duties, particularly in the case of corporate constituency statutes, there still remains an entrenched denial that such schemes of responsibility to constituencies other than shareholders go further – that they question implicitly the underlying precept that directors ought to be accountable exclusively, or at least primarily, to shareholders.

Furthermore, what remains unaddressed is the second part of Adolf A. Berle's objection to Dodd's contention, which loudly calls for the need for such schemes of responsibilities to constituencies other than shareholders to be clearly enforceable.

This lack of scheme of enforcement for the benefit of non-shareholder constituencies has been at the heart of the dismal failure of earlier measures aimed at the protection of employees under the United Kingdom's companies' statute. By the same token, the lack of an enforcement scheme available for use by or for the benefit of non-shareholder constituencies has effectively relegated Non-Shareholder Constituency Statutes in many states of the United States to the abyss of uselessness and impotence.

Given the enforcement framework that characterises the benefit corporation statutes, it can cogently be argued that these statutes will suffer the same fate as the other corporate constituency measures which came before.

## BOOK OBJECTIVES

It is argued in this book that the apparent continued insistence of these corporate constituency measures in linking enforcement powers in corporate law to the conventional understanding of the role of directorial duties and corporate voting as being for the exclusive benefit of shareholders is extremely unsatisfactory, as it is indisputable that the single biggest cause for the failure of these measures is their lack of a clearly enforceable framework for the benefit of non-shareholder corporate constituencies. With the uncertainty in corporate law regarding whether the corporate constituency measures demand a reconsideration of the beneficiaries of directorial duties, the objective of the book is to question whether the current justifications for retaining the traditional position of shareholders as the exclusive beneficiaries of directorial duties can continue to be sustained. The book also considers whether the legislative trend spearheaded by the broadly inclusive enforcement framework under the different statutory provisions of South Africa's 2008 Companies Act (Act No. 71 of 2008) has justifiably called into question the very corporate law assumption that the law focuses directorial duties on – and limits enforcement powers to – shareholders.

This enforcement framework under South Africa's 2008 Companies Act, dubbed the 'Actionable Enlightened Shareholder Value Approach', effectively adopts an all-inclusive enforcement approach by, among other things, empowering constituencies to initiate proceedings to restrain the company from doing anything inconsistent with Companies Act [Section 20(4)]; affording constituencies the opportunity to have a director declared delinquent [Section 162(2)]; empowering constituencies to institute derivative litigation proceedings to recover losses directly from directors on behalf of the company in circumstances where the directors are guilty of wrongdoing against their companies [Section 165(2)]; and affording opportunities for stakeholders acting in the public interest (with leave of the court) to avail themselves of extended standing provisions to apply for remedies under the Act [Section 157(1)].

As much has been written on whether the law should continue to equate the interests of companies with those of shareholders alone, the overarching objective of this book is to demonstrate that the acceptance of the questionability of equating the interests of the company with those of shareholders invariably necessitates the criticism of the general lack of the extension of legal standing to corporate constituencies other than shareholders to bring remedies under corporate law. The book then endeavours to question whether such lack of enforcement mechanisms for the benefit of non-shareholder corporate constituencies under the existing corporate constituency measures as outlined above is capable of being resolved by both the reconstruction of the legal landscape around fiduciary obligations and the acceptance of broadly inclusive enforcement mechanisms, akin to the ones provided for under the 2008 Companies Act in South Africa.

## FINDINGS

The analysis indicates that there is consistent inadequacy across all corporate constituency mechanisms in providing adequate standing for non-shareholder corporate constituency groups in enforcing the consideration of their interests under corporate law.

The analysis further reveals that the continued preoccupation of corporate law with the shareholder-oriented enforcement scheme is predicated on the misconceived assumption that the sole objective of the fiduciary obligations is to elevate the interests of shareholders above those of other corporate constituencies, rather than the prohibition against self-dealing.

## RECOMMENDATIONS

The book concludes by recommending that even though the current corporate constituency mechanisms lack standing provisions for use by – or for the benefit of – non-shareholder constituency groups, some of these mechanisms do not expressly exclude the possible extension of legal standing to such non-shareholder constituent groups, particularly where those mechanisms are not expressly prohibitive of the possible introduction of extended legal standing provisions favouring non-shareholder corporate constituencies.

The book further recommends that the provision of access to enforcement mechanisms by non-shareholder corporate constituency groups in a manner akin to that explicitly provided for under the 2008 Companies Act of South Africa is justified – and, indeed, loudly called for – by the need for corporate law to refocus its attention on the restraint of directorial self-dealing as the legal justification for fiduciary obligations, as opposed to strictly shareholder wealth maximisation.

# Acknowledgements

In the best stakeholder capitalist tradition, this book has been produced as a result of the optimisation of cooperative and productive relationships in the Common Law World, generally, and within my own circles, in particular. Minah Tong-Mongalo, Pholoso Mongalo and Mohau Mongalo all withstood my constant absence from home and from domestic activities in order to see this project through. Pholoso Mongalo bore most of the brunt as I had to constantly excuse myself from 'dad and son' ball activities quite often such that he ultimately gathered his eight-year-old strength (at the time) to ask me how many PhDs I had enrolled for. It was just one, and my apologies for making you think there was more than one. To Dennis Davis, Michael Katz and James J. Hanks Jr., your friendship and camaraderie have shown me that we do not need to always be in agreement to be of assistance to one another. To my late stepfather, Ernest Ralph Mongalo, thanks for planting seeds of self-confidence in me from an early age. To my sisters Jeanette, Asnath and Deborah, you are all saluted for always being my cheerleaders. To my brothers Tshepo and Nico, thanks for always encouraging me without fail. To Sara Noakes and Anna Debiec of Lexington Books, thanks for your persistence in assuring me that the submission of the final manuscript on time was possible. Your persistence has paid off in the end.

Although I have to concede that the burden has yet again been shouldered, sometimes silently, by my wife and children – for whom I owe unlimited gratitude – all of this would not have been possible without the grace of our heavenly Father and saviour, Jesus Christ.

# Introduction

## *Methodology and Background*

### INTRODUCTION

Over a number of years, the Anglo-American corporate law approach of equating the interests of the company with those of the company's shareholders has been a result of a myopic view of the concept of fiduciary obligations, something which has led to the unfortunate perpetuation of shareholder-friendly enforcement mechanisms, consisting primarily of shareholder voting and derivative litigation. This exclusive reliance on the narrow corporate legal enforcement framework, which originated from the parochial and antiquated focus of corporate law on shareholder wealth maximisation, disregards the primary purpose of the directorial common law duties as being the monitoring of the use of corporate power to minimise or eradicate directorial self-serving misconduct. The conventional position on directorial common law duties mistakenly assumes that their role is the exclusive protection of shareholders, who are presumed to be the exclusive beneficiaries of those duties.[1] However, events that took place in the 1930s and the 1980s, particularly in the United States, set in motion corporate law developments that initiated a jurisprudential trajectory that attempted to extend the responsibilities of companies and directors beyond the shareholders to include the recognition of other stakeholders, such as the community, the employees, the creditors, the environment, and other social considerations.[2]

Writing within the context of severe economic disruption during the Depression in the United States in the early 1930s, E. Merrick Dodd of Harvard Law School poignantly surmised that:

> [T]here is . . . a growing feeling not only that business has responsibilities to the community but that our corporate managers who control business should

> voluntarily and without waiting for legal compulsion manage it in such a way as to fulfill those responsibilities.[3]

Although this proposition was almost instantaneously objected to by an equally eminent scholar from Columbia Law School, Adolf A. Berle, who cautioned that '[y]ou cannot abandon emphasis on "the view that business corporations exist for the sole purpose of making profits for their stockholders"',[4] the latter scholar subsequently conceded that '[t]he argument has been settled (at least for the time being) squarely in favor of Professor Dodd's contention'.[5] This concession by Adolf A. Berle was, however, qualified, as the initial primary objection by the author was that a clear and reasonably enforceable scheme of responsibilities to constituencies other than shareholders was needed before the proposition that business corporations should be run solely for shareholder wealth maximisation could be departed from. This primary objection by Adolf A. Berle is essentially two-pronged; first, it advocates for a scheme of responsibility to constituencies other than shareholders and, second, it propagates for that scheme of responsibilities to other constituencies to be clear and reasonably enforceable. It was in response to Adolf A. Berle's first part of the objection as stated above that a number of subsequent judicial decisions, coupled with legislative reactions, made it clear that the legal position is no longer that companies should pursue the interests of shareholders to the exclusion of other stakeholders, but that stakeholder interests should also be regarded as the interests of the company to the extent that such interests are related to the long-term interests of corporate shareholders.[6]

In addition to the events set in motion by the Depression in the 1930s, the widespread prevalence of hostile takeovers, at least in the United States, led to the reinvention of non-shareholder constituency considerations 'as a defense against hostile takeovers'.[7] What started off as a mechanism for directors or corporate managers to use as a defence against hostile takeovers led to judicial decisions[8] and statutory formulations – first in the form of Non-Shareholder Constituency Statutes[9] and, lately, through benefit corporation statutes – which effectively provided formal recognition to non-shareholder constituency considerations as a matter of law.[10]

These judicial and statutory interventions in the United Kingdom and the United States clearly indicated the acknowledgement by both the courts and the legislatures that the model of shareholder primacy no longer accommodates the realities of a typically large public company, and thereby attempting to introduce a scheme of responsibilities to corporate constituencies other than shareholders in the case of statutory interventions,[11] and explicitly acknowledging that directorial primacy is the central concern in corporate decision-making, particularly in both control transactions and derivative litigation.[12] While both these judicial and statutory interventions started the crusade to outline a scheme of responsibilities to non-shareholder constituencies, an enforcement framework favourable to such non-shareholder corporate constituencies continues to elude corporate law developments to this day.

It is argued in this book that although these statutory formulations, both in corporate statutes and in Non-Shareholder Constituency Statutes, generally present an all-inclusive normative statement suitable for the protection of non-shareholder constituencies, the main weakness is in the enforcement framework. It is argued that a forward-looking normative statement which has no enforcement mechanisms is effectively not worth the paper it is written on.

The primary reason why Adolf A. Berle initially took issue with Merrick E. Dodd's proposition regarding the existence of a duty to non-shareholder constituencies was the lack of an enforcement scheme. He observed that '[y]ou cannot abandon emphasis on 'the view that business corporations exist for the sole purpose of making profits for their stockholders' *until such time as you are prepared to offer a clear and reasonably enforceable scheme of responsibilities to someone else*'[13]. [Emphasis added].

In commenting on earlier corporate social responsibility formulations expressed by legal scholars, Margaret M. Blair emphatically stated that

> [t]he idea never had much theoretical rigor to it, failed to give clear guidance to help managers and directors set priorities and decide among competing socially beneficial uses of corporate resources, *and provided no obvious enforcement mechanism to ensure that corporations live up to their social obligations.*[14] [Emphasis added].

Within the context of the sentiments expressed by the above two scholars, it is therefore still lamented that normative statements expressed as schemes of responsibilities to non-shareholder corporate constituencies in a number of statutory formulations in the Anglo-American jurisdictions of the United Kingdom and the United States are still not appropriately backed up by an effective enforcement framework. While these statutory interventions may be addressing the first part of Adolf A. Berle's objection to Merrick E. Dodd's contention for greater corporate social responsibility, they nevertheless fall short of addressing the second part of Berle's objection, as they fail to extend legal standing to non-shareholder corporate constituencies in ensuring a clear legal enforcement framework of corporate law for all corporate constituent groups.

It needs to be emphasised that regardless of Berle's concession that '[t]he argument has been settled (at least for the time being) squarely in favor of Professor Dodd's contention',[15] he never retracted his contention for a clear and reasonably enforceable scheme of responsibilities to corporate constituencies other than shareholders. It is this part of Berle's contention that this book attempts to consider, by investigating the justifiability of the extension of legal standing to non-shareholder corporate constituencies to bring remedies traditionally reserved for shareholders.

Even in the context of the institutionalisation of the 'Enlightened Shareholder Value Approach' as reflected in s 172(1) of the UK Companies Act of 2006, it is still observed that its major weakness is with regard to enforcement, because regardless of the fact that directors are encouraged to take account of a wide range of non-shareholder considerations,[16] the duty is still owed to the company, which appears to imply that only the shareholders can enforce the duty, thereby nullifying the possible existence of any 'reasonably enforceable scheme of responsibilities to enumerated non-shareholder constituencies'.[17]

The book presents a critical trajectory of the Enlightened Shareholder Value Approach, apparently aimed at the recognition of non-shareholder constituency interests, by presenting the existence of what is referred to as the Actionable Enlightened Shareholder Value Approach (AESVA), brought about by a variety of enforcement provisions enacted under the 2008 Companies Act in South Africa.

## INADEQUACY OF EXISTING CORPORATE CONSTITUENCY MECHANISMS TO PROVIDE FOR THE ENFORCEMENT FRAMEWORK FOR THE BENEFIT OF NON-SHAREHOLDER CORPORATE CONSTITUENCIES

The book proceeds from the premise that regardless of the introduction of corporate constituency statutory mechanisms in both the United Kingdom and the United States in recent years to endeavour to clarify schemes of responsibilities to non-shareholder corporate constituencies, these mechanisms still fall short of adequately empowering those non-shareholder corporate constituencies, in that they fail to grant legal standing to those identified non-shareholder corporate constituencies to bring remedies. To the extent that these statutory mechanisms spell out schemes of responsibilities to specified non-shareholder corporate constituencies, they provide normative statements without the appropriate legal enforcement framework for the benefit of those corporate constituencies. It is the lack of a legal enforcement framework that this book argues to be the single greatest deficiency of the corporate constituency statutory mechanisms. Since the fundamental justification for corporate law remedies is arguably the supervision of the use of corporate power to minimise or eradicate self-serving misconduct on the part of corporate controllers, the benefits of such supervision cannot only be exclusively enjoyed by a single corporate constituent group but can and must, be afforded to other corporate constituencies as a matter of law.

Writing recently on the appropriate enforcement scheme under company law, Dennis Davis lamented the fact that '[t]raditionally, company laws have left the enforcement of their provisions to shareholders [and directors], the liquidator in winding-up, and the Director of Public Prosecutions'.[18] He observed that:

> Experience has shown that these methods of enforcement are inherently defective.[19]
>
> He further observed that '[a]nother type of regulatory intervention is enforcement of corporate and security laws through a [*sic*] supervisory agencies and criminal sanctions'.[20] Yet he conceded: 'Little evidence exists that public enforcement matters.' He concludes that regardless of the apparent disregard for public enforcement as another type of regulatory intervention, it 'may be the most effective tool to prevent specific forms of expropriation'.[21]

What appears to be indisputable is the fact that the traditional enforcement scheme under company laws, as referred to by Dennis Davis above, typically interprets the 'duty to promote the interests of the company' as being owed only to shareholders[22] *qua* shareholders,[23] as a general body.[24] This justifies the above traditional bias for the enforcement of company law provisions in favour of the shareholders, even though the primary justification for corporate law remedies is the supervision of the use of corporate power for the wider benefit of all corporate constituent groups.

Writing about a theoretical and practical framework for enforcing corporate constituency statutes in the United States, Lawrence E. Mitchell argued twenty years ago that the very corporate law assumption upon which a shareholder-oriented focus of directorial duties and enforcement powers relies and has evolved has been called into question by the judicial and legislative trends which began in the 1980s.[25] These trends led to the questioning of the underlying precept that directors ought to be accountable exclusively to shareholders.[26] He concludes that because of the questioning of this corporate law assumption, there seems to be no basis for the maintenance of the assumption in corporate law circles that corporate law enforcement should be limited to shareholders.[27]

Those who are opposed to an enforcement model which is accessible to corporate constituencies over and above shareholders have argued that the current enforcement model is justified by shareholders' position as residual claimants, who are generally entitled only to what is left of the corporation after all other contracts are fulfilled.[28] They base this conclusion on the argument that employees, suppliers, creditors, and others are free to contract with corporations to achieve their desired results.[29]

The rationale for this derives from the assumption that a free market will lead to the efficient allocation of resources so long as companies are motivated by profit maximisation.[30] It is argued that because market processes will restore equilibrium, in the sense that all participants will realise fair value, there is no need for any legal infrastructure other than one that facilitates contracting and market efficiency.[31]

To assume that contracting and market processes are adequate to address claims resulting from corporate actions which end in injury to non-shareholder corporate constituencies is, in the words of Lawrence E. Mitchell, to allow the law to abdicate 'its function as a socializing tool . . . [and] leaves the redressing of individual and societal wrongs to the forces of competition'. This method of redress is presumptuous and is oblivious to the peculiar circumstances of certain corporate constituencies whose violations at the hands of corporate controllers may be incapable of being resolved by contracting and market processes. To put this in perspective, take the example of the defunct WorldCom which, in the year 2000, opened the door to a world of opportunities for dozens of minority engineering students. The company pledged $10 million to help pay for the college tuition of engineering students chosen by the National Action Council for Minorities in Engineering ('Council'). However, WorldCom had made only one instalment on its pledge before the company went bankrupt. Subsequently, WorldCom informed the Council that it would not provide the rest of the promised funds. As a consequence, approximately sixty minority engineering students did not have the means to pay for the rest of their college education.[32]

As corporate constituencies whose financial well-being was tied to the company's success, these minority engineering students had little, if any, influence in the company and they could only hope corporate leaders would consider their company's extensive effects and act responsibly toward all affected groups. Without much that could be accomplished by relying on contracting and market processes in the example given, it would have been different if corporate law afforded these corporate constituencies an opportunity to access legal remedy in the same manner as the shareholders, particularly if the consideration of their interests constituted the subject matter of a statutory framework to which the company was subject, such as the corporate constituency statute or the benefit corporation statute. This book proceeds from the premise that corporate law remedies are underpinned by the primary function of supervising the use of corporate power for the main purpose of minimising or eradicating directorial self-serving misconduct and not the exclusive protection of shareholders. Thus, it accepts the need for the consideration of non-shareholder corporate constituencies' interests in corporate law on that basis.

Therefore, except for the assumption that there are instances in which the interests of non-shareholder corporate constituencies are enumerated in specific statutory corporate constituency mechanisms, the book does not attempt to justify the need for consideration of non-shareholder corporate constituencies' interests except on the basis of the overarching purpose of corporate law remedies as set out above, particularly in large public companies.

As regards the enforcement of company law provisions 'by liquidators in winding-up', there are some authorities that support the proposition that in the event of the company's insolvency, the interests of the company are not those of the shareholders but of the creditors.[33] The justification in this regard is that although directors owe no fiduciary duties to the company's creditors as such,[34] when a company is in insolvent circumstances,[35] and, consequently, its creditors' money is at risk rather than the shareholders' proprietary interests,[36] the duty to promote the interests of the company is owed in favour of the company's creditors,[37] or, at least, requires their interests to be taken into account.[38]

It is in the context of this state of affairs with regard to the traditional scheme of enforcement under company law that it is argued that for the purposes of accommodating the corporate statutory dispensation, which deliberately protects the interests of non-shareholder constituencies, a new model of enforcement is not only desirable but is demanded by the intricacies of a modern public company. This is based on the appreciation that the continued scheme of enforcement, based on the one traditionally adopted under company law, will effectively render the normative statements advancing the interests of non-shareholder constituencies nugatory.

## PRINCIPAL THEORIES UPON WHICH THE BOOK IS BASED

Chapter 1 shows that the scheme of enforcement applicable for the normative standards in judicial and statutory interventions formulated for the benefit of any corporate constituency is primarily dependent on the theoretical foundation in application. The chapter shows that there are basically three categories of theoretical approaches in corporate law, which determine the type of enforcement scheme that may be adopted for the practical application of the normative standards determined. These theoretical approaches are divided into (a) those that perpetuate the traditional view of the company being tantamount to the interests of the shareholders, (b) the alternative theory accommodative of non-shareholder corporate constituencies, and lastly (c) those that support the extension of legal standing to allow non-shareholder corporate constituencies to have access to corporate law remedies. Those that fall into the first category include (i) the shareholder primacy or the Shareholder Value Approach and (ii) the Enlightened Shareholder Value Approach. The second category is made up of the Pluralist or Stakeholder Theory, while the last category consists of (a) the Entity Maximisation and Sustainability Model and (b) the new theoretical approach called the Actionable Enlightened Shareholder Value Approach (or the so-called Structural Stakeholderism), which is documented hereunder.

This new theoretical approach is said to be apparent from the provisions of the South African Companies Act of 2008 (Act No. 71 of 2008). It has also been explained in detail by Paine in a recent Harvard Business Review article.[39] It is argued that the traditional company law enforcement scheme originates from the application of the shareholder primacy or the shareholder value theory. It is further argued that regardless of the general acceptance that the 'Enlightened Shareholder Value Approach' provides a significant new development in corporate law, it is nevertheless fundamentally indistinguishable from the shareholder primacy theory, as its major weakness lies in the fact that the duty imposed on the directors is still ultimately owed to the shareholders. It is also argued that because of the possible extension of fiduciary obligations of directors to corporate constituency groups other than shareholders, the silence of the Pluralist or Stakeholder Theory on extended enforcement is inconsequential as enforcement is often an important aspect in Stakeholder Theory and, as such, the possibility of extended corporate law remedies to those constituencies is more real than imagined. Even if enforcement may not be an important aspect in Stakeholder Theory, the theory lends itself to such extended enforcement, particularly with regard to derivative litigation. The chapter concludes that even the Entity Maximisation and Sustainability Model, although useful, does not go far enough. This is because, under this model, possible access to remedies by non-shareholder corporate constituencies is limited only to derivative actions. Chapter 1 concludes that the Actionable Enlightened Shareholder Value Approach is best suited for the advancement of the non-shareholder corporate constituencies' interests, as it is characterised by extended legal standing rules in the general enforcement of corporate law normative standards and in instituting derivative legal suits or procedures. This approach enhances the inadequate 'Enlightened Shareholder Value Approach' by clearly authorising members of each relevant constituent group to have standing to challenge corporate actions that they claim have injured them. On the latter approach, the chapter concludes that there are still shortcomings as the only version of the approach, as demonstrated under the South African Companies Act of 2008, still lacks the substantive normative basis to complement the undeniably extensive legal enforcement framework.

## CHAPTER OUTLINE

The book starts off by laying out the basis for the study by providing a diagnosis of the inadequacy of the corporate constituency mechanisms in providing a credible legal enforcement framework for the benefit of non-shareholder corporate constituencies in the Introduction.

In chapter 1, the book lays out the jurisprudential foundation for both the judicial and legislative corporate constituency mechanisms aimed at non-shareholder corporate constituency protection. The chapter does this by setting out the categorisation of corporate law theories into those that perpetuate the traditional corporate law view of equating the interests of the company with those of the shareholders, that which is arguably accommodative to non-shareholder corporate constituent groups and the alternative theories that support the extension of legal standing for non-shareholder constituencies to access the conventional corporate law remedies. While the theory that is accommodative to non-shareholder corporate constituencies does this only by extending fiduciary duties to these non-shareholder corporate constituencies, its continued failure in addressing the issue of legal standing makes the theory ineffective as a viable jurisprudential basis for the extended legal enforcement framework. This chapter concludes that while the introduction of corporate constituency judicial and statutory interventions may have theoretically extended the ambit of corporate constituent groups to be considered in corporate decision-making, their continued reliance on theories that are still anchored on the legal enforcement framework which focuses directorial duties on – and limits enforcement powers to – shareholders is still highly problematic and is the central cause for the failure of such interventions.

In chapter 2, the book sets out both the judicial and legislative corporate constituency mechanisms aimed at protecting non-shareholder corporate constituencies, and it reviews their jurisprudential justification. The chapter observes that these judicial and legislative corporate constituency mechanisms are not complimented by an extended enforcement framework but are still based on the conventional enforcement framework, which is primarily anchored on shareholder wealth maximisation, rather than the restraint of directorial self-serving misconduct, which should be the only justification for the enforcement framework under corporate law.

The analysis of the statutory corporate constituency mechanisms indicates that not all of these mechanisms are inimical to the interpretation which allows for the extension of legal standing to non-shareholder corporate constituencies. That said, the mere compatibility of some of these statutory corporate constituency mechanisms with the interpretation favouring the preferable legal enforcement framework is not enough. The chapter specifically demonstrates that the failure of corporate constituency statutory mechanisms in explicitly granting legal standing to recognised non-shareholder constituency groups perpetuate the current corporate law enforcement framework.

In the chapter, a comparative analysis of the different judicial and statutory corporate constituency mechanisms in the United Kingdom is undertaken by:

Analysing similarities between each of the corporate constituency mechanisms;
Highlighting the differences between those mechanisms;
Drawing attention to the significance of such differences in justifying the need for the introduction of an enforcement framework favouring non-shareholder corporate constituencies;
Drawing conclusions on the viability of introducing enforcement measures favourable to all corporate constituency groups, and not only shareholders, in respect of each of the corporate constituency mechanisms.

With regard to the United States, different comparative analysis methods are used, depending on whether the analysis relates to corporate constituency statutes or benefit corporation statutes. Concerning corporate constituency statutes, distinct relevant features of the statutes form the basis for the comparative analysis. The main point of comparative analysis regarding benefit corporation statutes relates to their treatment of the corporate objective and legal standing. Again, the analysis in this regard zeroes in on the two pre-eminent states from the corporate law perspective, namely, Delaware and Maryland.

In this chapter, the corporate constituency mechanisms considered for the comparative analysis include (a) the relevant statutory provisions under the two successive UK Companies Acts of 1985 and 2006, respectively; (b) the corporate constituency statutes enacted in most of the states of the United States since 1983; and (c) the relevant statutory provisions of the benefit corporation statutes currently in force in a number of states of the United States. The chapter concludes that while the general criticism against these statutory corporate constituency mechanisms – that they perpetuate the shareholder primacy norm – may not be accurate with respect to all these mechanisms, their wholesale deficiency in extending legal standing to all corporate constituent groups for the purposes of accessing remedies remains their single most problematic aspect.

In chapter 3, the doctrinal foundation of non-shareholder constituency protection mechanisms is traced and critically analysed, with a view to determining whether such doctrinal foundation offers the appropriate jurisprudential basis for such protection mechanisms. The chapter concludes that the continued insistence of traditional corporate law in anchoring its enforcement framework on the basis of shareholder wealth maximisation is oblivious to the importance of restraining directorial or managerial self-dealing as the proper basis for the enforcement framework.

In chapter 4, the enforcement framework under the 2008 South African Companies Act is set out, with an analysis of the jurisprudential foundation of each of the enforcement mechanisms thus set out. The chapter concludes that there is a jurisprudentially justifiable and rational basis for each of those enforcement mechanisms under the Act. The chapter concedes, however, that notwithstanding the justifiability of such enforcement mechanisms, their deficiency in lacking the complementary substantive normative framework cannot be ignored.

In the Conclusion, a review of the research is conducted, and findings and conclusions are reached on the consistent inadequacy across all corporate constituency mechanisms in

providing adequate standing for non-shareholder corporate constituency groups in enforcing corporate law;

failing to appreciate the supervision of the use of corporate power as the fundamental justification for corporate law remedies;

reinforcing, through their enforcement schemes, the assumption that the entitlement to enforce corporate law is based exclusively on fiduciary obligations that are mistakenly assumed to be owed primarily, or exclusively, to one corporate constituency group, i.e., the shareholders.

The Conclusion further recommends that the provision of access to enforcement mechanisms by non-shareholder corporate constituency groups, in a manner akin to that explicitly provided for under the 2008 Companies Act of South Africa, is justified and indeed loudly called for by the need for corporate law to refocus its attention to the restraining of directorial self-dealing as the legal justification for corporate law remedies instead of, strictly, shareholder wealth maximisation.

The Conclusion also recommends possible ways in which some of the existing corporate constituency mechanisms can be salvaged and be made relevant for the extension of legal standing to non-shareholder corporate constituencies. The Conclusion finally wraps up by considering the exportability of the South African corporate law enforcement framework as enacted under the 2008 Companies Act.

On the issue of reference techniques, the terms 'company' and 'corporation' are used interchangeably in the book to refer to a corporate form of business entity, even though the latter is the terminology used primarily in the United States and the former is used in the United Kingdom and South Africa. Although it is acknowledged that the aim of footnotes is to ensure that the reader obtains a full citation to the source and knows the precise place in the source to which reference is made, the book adopts the *South African Law Journal* (*SALJ*) method of footnote referencing, which excludes the publisher and the place of publication in respect of books and reports. The full references are contained in the bibliography at the end of this book.

In the bibliography, under the heading 'Further Readings', other relevant sources are listed. These sources are valuable as they provide background to the topic of this book but are not directly relevant.

## JUSTIFICATION FOR THE CHOICE OF COMPARATIVE JURISDICTIONS

The reasons for comparing the South African legal enforcement framework under corporate law with those of the United Kingdom and the United States, and the reasons for identifying the particular statutory provisions within the United Kingdom's corporate statutes and the United States' Non-Stockholder Constituency Statutes, benefit corporation, and flexible purpose corporation statutes for the purpose of the comparative analysis, are discussed hereunder.

Based on Montesquieu's observation that 'each legal system presents a different vision of justice', Richard Hyland argues that taking into account 'families of law' remains the dominant method for classifying diverse systems for the purposes of comparison.[40] It is within the context of this widely accepted statement that it is argued that the main reason for choosing the jurisdictions referred to above is that, at least in corporate law, South Africa resides within the same family of law as those jurisdictions. That family of law is referred to as the 'Common Law' family, and English law is the prime example thereof. Common law is ordinarily distinguished from the 'Civil Law' family, in respect of which France and Germany are the central examples.

While Hugh Collins does not dispute the existence and the importance of the different families of the legal systems in existence, he nevertheless places different approaches to comparative law in the context of broader legal theory and also provides a taste of micro-comparison and its interaction with macro-comparison. Collins's central emphasis appears to be that comparative law should be underscored by a better understanding of one's own system.[41]

Hugh Collins' observation regarding comparative law, including his approach to the importance of understanding one's own system better, has also motivated the choice of jurisdictions for comparison with the South African approach. In particular, the understanding of the original justification for the traditional company law scheme of enforcement[42] as being anchored on the interpretation of 'the company' (within the context of the duty to promote the interests of the 'company'), as defined since nineteenth-century

Anglo-American cases provide an excellent example of a comparative analysis based on 'a better understanding of one's own system', as eloquently motivated by Hugh Collins. This reason is particularly apt, as the recent corporate constituency statutory interventions in both the leading common law and Anglo-American jurisdictions of the United Kingdom and the United States are clearly not accommodated by this conventional interpretation of the 'company'.

While belonging to the same family of legal systems may be reason enough for justifiable comparative analysis, another important question to answer is whether it can ever be justified that rules, principles and legal institutions can be divorced from their cultural context. This is at the heart of Pierre Legrand's argument, which emphasises that 'all legal representations are immersed in a cultural context', and therefore, objective comparison is impossible since cultural prejudice can never be overcome.[43]

Pierre Legrand's 'cultural context' arguments notwithstanding, it remains questionable whether the purposes of comparative law (in contrast to, say, comparative sociology or anthropology) really necessitate attention to cultural contexts. What is ultimately clear is that the traditional, and the most common, method for examining differences and similarities among legal systems, at the micro as well as the macro level, has been to focus on families of legal systems.[44]

In addition to sharing similar legal traditions, the United States and the United Kingdom have much in common with South Africa, in that they all share similar sophisticated economic, financial and market systems.[45] The United States and the United Kingdom are also listed as South Africa's major trading partners[46] and some South African companies also have a United States or United Kingdom listing, thereby being subjected to the regulatory regimes of those countries in some way.[47]

In view of the above commonalities, and from the perspective of international trade, and the influence of the Model Business Corporation Act (MBCA), the Delaware General Corporation Law (DGCL), the Maryland General Corporation Law (MGCL) and the UK Companies Act of 2006 in the development of the recent South African Companies Act (Act 71 of 2008), comparing the corporate enforcement framework of South Africa with those of the United States and the United Kingdom is both relevant and instructive.

## DEFINITION OF KEY TERMS AND FOCUS AREA

In the definition of key terms and the delineation of the focus area of the research, the first term to be defined and put in context is 'Corporate Law'. In this context, the term 'corporate law' is not limited only to the domestic area of substantive law which regulates how companies or corporations are regulated within the context of the relevant national statutory instrument and common law. The term is extended to include judicial and statutory corporate constituency interventions expressed in the form of court judgments and legislative instruments from Anglo-American jurisdictions of the United Kingdom and the United States, with which South Africa shares company law traditions. Again, the term 'corporate constituencies', as used in this book, refers to corporate constituent groups, with the exception of shareholders, whose financial well-being is tied to the corporation's success, such as employees, suppliers, charities and communities.

The expressions 'non-shareholder corporate constituencies', 'non-shareholder constituencies' and 'stakeholders' are used interchangeably to refer to all corporate constituency groups whose financial well-being is tied to the corporation's success, with the exception of shareholders, whom the law already recognises as residual claimants in corporate entities. Except where specifically otherwise indicated, the expression 'corporate constituencies' refers to all corporate constituent groups, including shareholders.

The expressions 'Non-Stockholder Constituency Statutes', 'Non-Shareholder Constituency Statutes', 'Corporate Constituency Statutes' and 'Stakeholder Statutes' refer to statutory enactments adopted by more than half of the states of the United States since 1983 in an attempt to permit (or, in the isolated case of Connecticut, to oblige) corporate directors to consider the interests of, or the effects of their corporate decisions on, specified corporate constituencies in their corporate decision-making. These statutory measures, discussed in chapter 2, were initially adopted as another form of defence to allow directors to thwart an intended corporate hostile takeover which posed a threat to a constituency interest. It is interesting to note that some of these statutes are still limited to instances of takeovers or change of control transactions.

The terms 'corporate constituency statutory mechanisms' and 'statutory corporate constituency mechanisms' refer to legislative instruments, either in the form of corporate constituency statutes or another form of corporate legislation such as the Companies Act, which specifically recognises the need for corporate directors to consider constituency interests, in addition to those of shareholders, in corporate decision-making. By identifying the relevant constituent groups in their respective corporate constituency statutory mechanisms, the relevant legislatures signal that the specified corporate constituent groups are owed at least some level of corporate protection. The book accepts this assumption on the basis that the promotion of the supervision of corporate power is a fundamental justification for corporate law remedies. Such supervision of corporate power, for an overarching purpose of minimising or eliminating directorial self-serving misconduct, benefits not only the shareholders but all corporate constituent groups. Finally, the term 'judicial corporate constituency mechanisms' refers to court judgments or pronouncements which signify a departure from the traditional common law position of regarding shareholders as the only corporate constituency group to be considered in corporate decision-making.

## CONCLUSION AND CHAPTER SYNOPSIS

This Introduction provides a preliminary framework of the issues discussed at length within the body of this book. The Introduction starts off by presenting an account of the emergence of the corporate constituency statutory mechanisms in the United States as having been triggered by a limited need to provide companies with a legally acceptable defence for the purposes of warding off unwanted hostile takeovers. It is observed, however, that such mechanisms have since been extended, in a majority of cases, beyond the original justification for their introduction into the corporate regulation milieu. With the emergence of the general application of these corporate constituency statutory mechanisms, the Introduction observes that the continued reliance upon the traditional company law enforcement scheme is quickly becoming unworkable, if not obviously untenable.

The Introduction indicates that the initiation of the forward-looking enforcement scheme, which accommodates non-shareholder constituencies' interests, underscores the significance of the study undertaken in this book. The Introduction also presents the primary research question as being, in essence, whether the traditional company law enforcement scheme is suitable to accommodate the normative underpinnings of the corporate constituency statutory mechanisms. It is highlighted in the Introduction that the traditional shareholder primacy and the enlightened shareholder value theories are not suitable for the accommodation of the legal enforcement framework propagated in this book. The Introduction further brings to light that the 'Actionable Enlightened Shareholder Value' theory, similar to the one adopted under the South African Companies Act of 2008, may be suitable for accommodating the proposed enforcement framework. Finally, the Introduction underscores that the choice of jurisdictions identified for comparative analysis was based primarily on the considerations of 'the family of legal systems', 'a better understanding of South Africa's own legal system', the sophistication of the economic, financial and market system, trading relationships, and the influence of the statutory instruments on the recent corporate statutory law reforms in South Africa.

## NOTES

1. This Anglo-American approach was elucidated as far back as the late nineteenth century, particularly in the 1883 English decision of *Hutton v West Cork Railway* (23 Ch. D 654, at 672–673), where the court stated that: 'the test . . . is not whether [the action] is bona fide, but whether, as well as being done bona fide . . . it is reasonably incidental to the carrying on of the company's business for the company's benefit', with 'the company's benefit' being interpreted as the benefit of the company's shareholders. Even in the United States, the celebrated 1919 case of *Dodge v Ford Motor Co* (1919) 170 NW 668 made it emphatically clear that ' A business corporation is organized and carried on primarily for the profit of the stockholders', at 684. Even after these decisions of the late nineteenth and early twentieth centuries, subsequent court decisions and statutory provisions in both England and the United States continued to restate this legal position without any sign of an apparent contrary intention. Some of these judicial pronouncements are found in cases which include *Percival v Wright* [1902] 2 Ch 421 and *Multinational Gas & Petrochemical Co v Multinational Gas & Petrochemical Services Ltd* [1983] Ch 258 in England, and *Revlon Inc v MacAndrews & Forbes Holdings Inc,* 506 A 2d 173,179 (Del. 1986) and *Polk v Good,* 507 A 2d 531,536 (Del. 1986) in the United States. This position has even been codified in statutory provisions such as § 8.30(a) of the Model Business Corporations Act (Official Text with Official Comment and Statutory Cross-References Revised through 2012). This approach influenced corporate law developments not only in England and the United States but also in jurisdictions such as Australia, Botswana, Canada, New Zealand and South Africa.

2. Prior to the clear recognition of non-shareholder constituency interests through statutory provisions from the middle of the 1980s, the position adopted by a number of judicial decisions in the United Kingdom and the United States moved from a strictly shareholder-centric model to one that recognised consideration of stakeholder interests only to the extent that such interests are reasonably connected or linked to the pursuit of shareholder interests.

3. Dodd EM, 'For Whom Are Corporate Managers Trustees?' (1932) 45 *Harvard Law Review* 1145, at 1153–1154.

4. Berle AA, 'For Whom Corporate Managers Are Trustees: A Note' (1932) 45 *Harvard Law Review* 1365, at 1367–1368.

5. Berle AA, *The 20th Century Capitalist Revolution* (1954), 169.

6. Primarily, as a result of a general acceptance that 'traditional profit maximization theory does not amount to rejection of modern-day notions of corporate responsibility . . ., [but provides] ample opportunity for expenditure of corporate funds upon worthwhile public welfare measures [with the only] limitation [being] that corporate policy must be reasonably related to long term corporate benefit' (see, in particular, Ruder D, 'Public Obligations of Private Corporations' (1965) 114 *University of Pennsylvania Law Review* 209, at 223). A number of judicial pronouncements adopted this position, notable of which include *Pepper v Litton* 308 US17 295 (1939); *Unocal Corp. v Mesa Petroleum Co*493 A.2d 946 (Del. 1985); and *Revlon, Inc. v*

*MacAndrews & Forbes Holdings, Inc.* 506 A.2d 173 (Del. 1986), which made it clear that there is no obligation to consider the interests of stakeholders in the absence of 'some rationally related benefit accruing to the stockholders'. It is worth mentioning that even in the aftermath of Professor Dodd's insistence that there existed a purely stakeholder-oriented notion of corporate governance, this notion spectacularly failed to receive embrace by the courts and the legislature in Britain and the United States. (See Vagts DF, 'Reforming the Modern Corporation: Perspective From the German' (1966) 80 *Harvard Law Review,* at 37. See also Mitchell LE, 'A Theoretical and Practical Framework for Enforcing Corporate Constituency Statutes' (1992) 70 (3) *Texas Law Review*, at 580–581 and 610 (arguing that in addition to the corporate constituency statutes, the common law, as well, has been moving toward a recognition that the model of stockholder primacy no longer accommodates the realities of the large public corporation).

7. See Hanks Jr. JJ, 'Playing with Fire: Nonshareholder Constituency Statutes in the 1990s' (1991) 21 *Stetson Law Review* 97 (hereafter Hanks 'Playing with Fire', at 98).

8. In *Unocal Corp. v Mesa Petroleum Co.* 493 A.2d 946, at 955 (Del. 1985), the Delaware Supreme Court made it clear that in determining the reasonableness of a takeover defence in relation to the threat posed, the directors may consider 'the impact on "constituencies" other than shareholders (i.e., creditors, customers, employees and perhaps even the community generally)'. James J. Hanks Jr. asserts that as the court cited no case in support of this proposition, it left open the possibility that the 'impact' on non-shareholder constituencies is limited solely to the impact of the offer during takeover negotiations and not in other circumstances. (See Hanks, 'Playing with Fire', op cit note 7, at 100).

9. Non-Shareholder Constituency Statutes made their first appearance in 1988 in the ten US states of Arizona, Kentucky, Maine, Minnesota, Missouri, Nebraska, New Mexico, Ohio, Tennessee and Wisconsin. Ever since then, these statutes have spread like wildfire across the United States. Currently, 31 states have adopted some form of Non-Shareholder Constituency Statutes (See https://stanford.edu/dept/gsb-ds/Inkling/CSI_Legal_Structures/ops/s9ml/chapter04/constituency_statutes.xhtml, accessed on 4 May 2024; Tyler J, 'Negating the Legal Problem of Having "Two Masters": A Framework for L3C Fiduciary Duties and Accountability' (2010) 35 *Vermont Law Review* 117, at 132). These are (1) Arizona, (2) Connecticut, (3) Florida, (4) Georgia, (5) Hawaii, (6) Idaho, (7) Illinois, (8) Indiana, (9) Iowa, (10) Kentucky, (11) Louisiana, (12) Maine, (13) Maryland, (14) Massachusetts, (15) Minnesota, (16) Missouri, (17) Nevada, (18) New Jersey, (19) New Mexico, (20) New York, (21) North Dakota, (22) Ohio, (23) Oregon, (24) Pennsylvania, (25) Rhode Island, (26) South Dakota, (27) Tennessee, (28) Vermont, (29) Virginia, (30) Wisconsin and (31) Wyoming.

10. The substantive normative statement of the responsibilities of corporate controllers towards a wide range of corporate constituencies is well established in both the United States and the United Kingdom.

11. Starting with the first attempt under the UK Companies Act of 1985, almost all subsequent statutory interventions in both the United Kingdom and the United

States were primarily aimed at providing a voluntary scheme of responsibilities by companies to corporate constituencies other than shareholders alone.

12. The leading cases coming out of the leading corporate law jurisdiction of Delaware, which signify this important shift, include *Zapata Corp. v Maldonado* 430 A.2d 779 (Del. 1981), *Unocal Corp. v Mesa Petroleum Co* 493 A.2d 946 (Del. 1985), *Grobow v Perot* 539 A.2d 180 (Del. 1988), *Paramount Communications, Inc. v Time Inc* 571 A.2d 1140 (Del. 1989), and *Spiegel v Buntrock* 571 A.2d 767 (Del. 1990).

13. Berle, 'For Whom Corporate Managers Are Trustees', op cit note 4, at 1367–1368.

14. Blair MM, *Ownership and Control: Rethinking Corporate Governance for the Twenty-First Century* (1995), at 203.

15. Berle, *The 20th Century Capitalist Revolution* (1954), op cit note 5, at 169.

16. Infra, note 114.

17. This is also endorsed by, among others, the findings of John Kong Shan Ho, who argues that '[A] careful examination of section 172 of the [UK] Companies Act 2006 shows that it simply reflects existing law and modern business practices. Therefore, the purpose of implementing such duty on directors does no more than reinstate the practical reality.' (See Ho JKS, 'Director's Duty to Promote the Success of the Company: Should Hong Kong Implement a Similar Provision?' (2010) 10 (1) *Journal of Corporate Law Studies*, 17.)

18. Dennis M Davis, 'Dealing with Corporate Defaulters: Curbing the Unfettered Exercise of Criminal Law' in Tshepo Mongalo (ed.), *Modern Company Law for a Competitive South African Economy* (2010), at 411.

19. Ibid. See also the Department of Trade and Industry, *South Africa: South African Company Law Reform for the 21st Century: Guidelines for Corporate Law Reform (May 2004),* at 45. (Referred to hereafter as Guidelines for Corporate Law Reform).

20. Ibid., at 413.

21. Ibid. See also Luca E & Volpin P, 'Corporate Governance Reforms in Continental Europe' (2007) 21. *Journal of Economic Perspectives*, at 117.

22. *Harris v North Devon Railway Co* (1885) 20 Beav 384; 52 ER 651; *Coronation Syndicate Ltd v Lilienfeld and the New Fortuna Co Ltd* (1903) TS 489 497; *Australian Metropolitan Life Assurance Co Ltd v Ure* (1923) 33 CLR 199 217 (HC of A); *Parke v Daily News Ltd* [1962] Ch 927 963; [1962] 2 All ER 929 948; *Russell Kinsela Pty Ltd v Kinsela* (1983) 8 ACLR 384 402–404 SC(NSW); *Kinsela v Russell Kinsela Pty Ltd* (1986) 10 ACLR 395 401–402 CA(NSW); *Brady v Brady* [1988] BCLC 20 40 (CA); *West Mercia Safetywear Ltd v Dodd* [1988] BCLC 250 252–253 (CA); *Australian Growth Resources Corporation Pty Ltd v Van Reesema* (1988) 13 ACLR 261 268 SC(SA); *Lee Panavision Ltd v Lee Lighting Ltd* [1992] BCLC 22 31 (CA). 'In considering whether the actions of directors were *bona fide* in the best interests of the company as a whole, the court is not obliged to look at the company as in some way disembodied from its members', *per* Kirby P, *Darvall v North Sydney Brick & Tile Co Ltd* (1989) 15 ACLR 230 248 CA(NSW).

23. *S v Hepker* 1973 (1) SA 472 (W) 484, where it was pointed out that even when directors hold all the shares in a company, they cannot exercise their powers to serve

their own private ends. In *Kinsela v Russell Kinsela Pty Ltd* (1986) 10 ACLR 395 401 SC(NSW) Street CJ said: 'In a solvent company, the proprietary interests of the shareholders entitle them, as a general body, to be regarded as the company when questions of the duty of directors arise.' This was quoted with approval by Dillon LJ in *West Mercia Safetywear Ltd v Dodd* [1988] BCLC 250 252–253 (CA). In the *Kinsela* case, Street CJ followed, with one minor possible reservation, the reasoning of the New Zealand Court of Appeal in *Nicholson v Permakraft* [1985] 1 NZLR 243. Clearly, what is meant here is not any propriety interests of the shareholders in the company's assets but their 'proprietary' interests *qua* shareholders in the company.

24. See *Greenhalgh v Arderne Cinemas Ltd* [1951] Ch 286 291; [1950] 2 All ER 1120 1126 (CA). It was established early on that 'the interests of the company' are the interests of all the shareholders. Thus, in *Harris v North Devon Rail Co* (1855) 20 Beav 384 387–388; 52 ER 651 652 Sir John Romilly MR, dealing with a power vested in the directors to direct a forfeiture of shares, said:

> [T]he forfeiture of shares in this case is . . . a power and discretion in the directors, who are trustees for the benefit of all the shareholders, which is to be exercised for the benefit of all the shareholders in the company; and it is the duty of the directors to direct a forfeiture when it is for the benefit of all the shareholders, and to refrain from doing so when it is not for their benefit.

25. Mitchell, 'A Theoretical and Practical Framework', op cit note 6, at 581–582.

26. Ibid.

27. Ibid., at 635–636. He argues that, under the preferable approach, '[m]embers of each . . . constituent group [not only shareholders] would have standing . . . to challenge corporate actions that they claim have injured them'.

28. See generally Playing with Fire, op. cit. note 7, at 108 and 111.

29. Ibid. See also DeBow ME & Lee DR, 'Shareholders, Nonshareholders, and Corporate Law: Communitarianism and Resource Allocation' (1993) 18 *Delaware Journal of Corporate Law*, 393.

30. See, for example, Cabot WM, 'The Free Market Promotes Long-Term Efficiency that Benefits all Stakeholders' (1991) 21 *Stetson Law Review*, 245 at 252.

31. Ibid.

32. Robert Ingrassia, 'They Gave and It Hurts' *Daily News*, Sept. 24, 2002, at 9. This story is also related by Hale K, 'Corporate Law and Stakeholders: Moving Beyond Stakeholders Statutes' (2003) 45 *Arizona Law Review*, 823, at 823–824.

33. Barrett RI, 'Directors' Duties to Creditors' (1977) 40 *MLR* 266; Dawson F, 'Acting in the Best Interests of the Company – For Whom are Directors Trustees?' (1984) 11 *NZULR* 68; Hill J, 'Duties of Directors towards Creditors' (1986) 60 *ALJ* 525; Sealy LS, 'Directors' Wider Responsibilities-Problems Conceptual, Practical and Procedural' (1987) 13 *Monash ULR* 164; Heydon JD, 'Directors' Duties and the Company's Interests' in PD Finn (ed.), *Equity and Commercial Relations* (1987), at 120; Dabner J, 'Directors' Duties-The Schiziod Company' (1988) 6 *C&SLJ* 105; Sealy LS, 'Directors' Duties-an Unnecessary Gloss' (1988) *CLJ* 175; Finch V, 'Directors' Duties Towards Creditors' (1989) 10 *Company Lawyer* 23; Riley CA, 'Directors' Duties and the Interests of Creditors' (1989) 10 *Company Lawyer* 87;

Baxt R, 'A Senior Australian Court Gives the Thumbs Up to the *Winkworth* Principle' (1989) 7 *C&SLJ* 344; Baxt R, 'Duties of Directors with Respect to Creditors' (1989) 63 *ALJ* 846; Farrar JH, 'The Responsibility of Directors and Shareholders for a Company's Debts' (1989) 4 *Canterbury LR* 12; Hawke N, 'Creditors' Interests in Solvent and Insolvent Companies' [1989] *JBL* 54; Watts PG, 'Directors' and Shareholders' Duties Arising Otherwise than by Contract' [1990] *NZRLR* 192; Prentice DD, 'Creditor's Interests and Director's Duties' (1990) 10 *Oxford JLS* 265; Calnan RJ, 'Corporate Gifts and Creditors Rights' (1990) 2 *C&SLJ* 91; Grantham R, 'Directors' Duties and Insolvent Companies' (1991) 54 *MLR* 576; Grantham R, 'The Judicial Extension of Directors' Duties to Creditors' [1991] *JBL* 1; Wishart DA, 'Models and Theories of Directors' Duties to Creditors' (1991) 14 *NZULR* 323; Fourie OJS, 'Die Plig van Direkteure Teenoor Maatskappyskuldeisers' (1992) 4 *SA Merc LJ* 25; Ziegel JS, 'Creditors as Corporate Stakeholders: The Quiet Revolution – an Anglo-Canadian Perspective' (1993) 43 *UTLJ* 511.

34. See Re Wincham Shipbuilding, Boiler, and Salt Co (Poole, Jackson, and Whyte's Case) (1878) 9 ChD 322 328–329 (CA); Re Forrest of Dean Coal Mining Co (1878) 10 ChD 450 453; *Wilson v Lord Bury* (1880) 5 QBD 518 (CA); Re Horsley & Weight Ltd [1982] Ch 442; [1982] 3 All ER 1045 (CA); *Multinational Gas and Petrochemical Co v Multinational Gas and Petrochemical Services Ltd* [1983] Ch 258; [1983] 2 All ER 563 (CA); *Kuwait Asia Bank EC v National Mutual Life Nominees Ltd* [1991] 1 AC 187 217–218; [1990] 3 All ER 404 420–421 (PC). Of course, in the winding-up of an insolvent company the liquidator must act in the interests of the creditors: *Sammel v President Brand Gold Mining Co Ltd* 1969 (3) SA 629 (A).

35. *Standard Chartered Bank of Australia Ltd v Antico* (1995) 131 ALR 1 66; (1995) 18 ACSR 1 66 SC(NSW); and see *Kuwait Asia Bank EC v National Mutual Life Nominees Ltd* [1991] AC 187; [1990] 3 All ER 404 (PC).

36. Standard Chartered Bank of *Australia Ltd v Antico* (1995) 131 ALR 1 66; (1995) 18 ACSR 1 66 SC(NSW); and see *Kuwait Asia Bank EC v National Mutual Life Nominees Ltd* [1991] AC 187; [1990] 3 All ER 404 (PC).

37. In *Re New World Alliance Pty Ltd: Sycotex Pty Ltd v Baseler* (1994) 122 ALR 531 550 (Fed C of A) Gummow J said: 'Where a company is insolvent or nearing insolvency, the creditors are to be seen as having a direct interest in the company and that interest cannot be overridden by the shareholders. This restriction does not, in the absence of any conferral of such right by statute, confer upon creditors any general law right against former directors of the company to recover losses suffered by those creditors . . . the result is that there is a duty of imperfect obligation owed to creditors, one which the creditors cannot enforce save to the extent that the company acts on its own motion or through a liquidator.' This was quoted with approval by the High Court of Australia in *Spies v R* (2000) 35 ACSR 500 526 (HC of A), where it was said: 'In so far as remarks in *Grove v Flavel* (1986) 43 SASR 410 (see also the remarks in *Nicholson v Permakraft* (NZ) Ltd [1985] 1 NZLR 242) suggest that directors owe an independent duty to, and enforceable by, creditors by reason of their position as directors, they are contrary to principle and later authority (*Kuwait Asia Bank EC v National Mutual Life Nominees Ltd* [1991] 1 AC 187; Re New World Alliance) and do not correctly state the law.' In *Yukong Line Ltd of Korea v Rensburg*

*Investments Corp of Liberia* [1998] 2 BCLC 485 503 Toulson J said: 'Where a director, or a person having the management, of an insolvent company acts in breach of his duty to the company by causing assets of the company to be transferred in disregard of the interests of its creditor or creditors, under English law he is answerable through the scheme which Parliament has provided. In my judgment, he does not owe a direct fiduciary duty towards an individual creditor, nor is an individual creditor entitled to sue for breach of fiduciary duty owed by the director to the company.'

38. *Walker v Wimborne* (1976) 137 CLR 1 (HC of A); *Nicholson v Permakraft* (NZ) Ltd [1985] 1 NZLR 242 CA(NZ); *Kinsela v Russell Kinsela Pty Ltd* (1986) 10 ACLR 395 CA(NSW); *Grove v Flavel* (1986) 11 ACLR 116 SC(SA); *Winkworth v Edward Baron Development Co Ltd* [1987] 1 All ER 114 118 (HL); *Brady v Brady* [1988] BCLC 20 (CA); [1988] BCLC 579 597 (HL); *West Mercia Safetywear Ltd v Dodd* [1988] BCLC 250 252–253 (CA); *Jeffree v National Companies and Securities Commission* (1989) 15 ACLR 217 SC(WA); *Castrisios v McManus* (1991) 4 ACSR 1 SC(Tas); *Lee Panavision Ltd v Lee Lighting* [1992] BCLC 22 31 (CA); *Galladin Pty Ltd v Aimnorth Pty Ltd* (1993) 11 ACSR 23 29–30 SC(SA); *Equiticorp Finance Ltd v Bank of New Zealand* (1993) 11 ACSR 642 680 724–725 CA(NSW). And see *Lonrho Ltd v Shell Petroleum* [1980] 1 WLR 627 (HL). In *Linton v Telnet Pty Ltd* (1999) 30 ACSR 465 CA(NSW) *Charterbridge Corp Ltd v Lloyds Bank Ltd* [1969] 2 All ER 1185; [1970] Ch 62. See also *Colin Gwyer v London Wharf* [2003] 2 BCLC 153 ChD. Moreover, the extension of fiduciary duties to other non-shareholder constituencies under certain circumstances, as indicated herein, is a testament to the reality that the role of fiduciary duties – and by extension, corporate law enforcement regime, is not just for the protection of shareholders but to prevent managerial misconduct or self-interested conduct by directors. See para 4.2, infra.

39. Paine LS, 'What Does Stakeholder Capitalism Mean to You? A Guide to the Four Main Types' (2023) *Harvard Business Review*, 109–119. Paine argues that Structural Stakeholderism, which advocates for the increase of stakeholder power, 'calls for giving nonshareholder stakeholders voting or other powers in the governance process, such as [corporate actions' enforcement powers], a defined role in selecting directors or formal representation on corporate boards'. (at 118).

40. Richard Hyland, 'Comparative Law' in Patterson (ed.) *Blackwell's Companion to Law and Legal Theory* (1999).

41. Collins H, 'Method and Aims of Comparative Law' (1991) *Oxford Jnl of Legal Studies* 396, at 398–403.

42. Which scheme unashamedly favours 'shareholders, [and directors,] the liquidator in winding-up, and the director of public prosecutions' as observed by Judge Dennis Davis (op cit, note 18).

43. See Legrand P, 'Comparative Legal Studies and Commitment to Theory' (1995) 58 *Modern Law Review* 262; Legrand P, 'Comparing Legal Cultures' (book review) (1997) 56 *Cambridge Law Journal* 646–649; and Legrand P, 'Against a European Civil Code' (1997) *Modern Law Review* 44.

44. See, among others, Kotz H, 'The Role of the Judge in the Court-room: The Common and Civil Law Compared' (1987) *Tydskrif van Suid-Afrikaanse Reg (TSAR)* 35 and authorities cited therein.

45. See the document available at http://www.southafrica.info/business/economy/econoverview.htm, accessed on 3 May 2024.

46. See the document available at http://m.state.gov/md2898.htm, accessed on 17 May 2022.

47. Companies such as Sasol Ltd, SAB Miller Ltd, Anglo-American PLC and Old Mutual PLC are examples of companies with listings in both South Africa and the United States or the United Kingdom.

# Chapter 1

# Theoretical Foundation

## INTRODUCTION

There has been, for many years, 'a continuing debate in corporate law circles regarding the precise objective of public companies'.[1] What is clear from this debate is that the corporate objective of a public company in any given jurisdiction is determined by the underlying corporate theoretical foundation in force within that jurisdiction. In the words of Jeswald W. Salacuse, 'Any system of corporate governance must answer a fundamental question: what is the objective of the corporation and for whose benefit is it to be run?'[2] His statement is pertinent to this analysis. Accordingly, the information provided in the Introduction clearly describes the significance of the study: the traditional corporate law enforcement framework does not adequately protect the interests of corporate constituency groups other than shareholders.

It can therefore be cogently argued that the scheme of enforcement adopted at a particular moment will almost invariably be consistently underscored by the theoretical approach followed in the relevant jurisdiction under consideration. The misalignment of the theoretical approach with the intended legal enforcement framework will invariably lead to untenable results. For example, the continued espousal of the shareholder primacy will not support the legal enforcement framework required to empower all corporate constituent groups by granting them legal standing to access remedies in corporate law.

In this chapter, the intention is to critically review the different corporate law theories, which are categorised into those that perpetuate the traditional corporate law view of equating the interests of the company with those of the shareholders, those which are arguably accommodative to non-shareholder corporate constituent groups, and the alternative theories that support the extension of legal standing for non-shareholder constituencies to access the conventional corporate law remedies. While the chapter concludes that the introduction of corporate constituency judicial and statutory interventions may have theoretically extended the ambit of corporate constituent groups to be considered in corporate decision-making, it argues that the continued reliance on these interventions on theories that are still anchored on the legal enforcement framework, which focuses directorial duties on – and limits enforcement powers to – shareholders, is still highly problematic and is the central cause for the failure of such interventions.

With regard to the first category of theories, their linking of the legal enforcement framework characterised by shareholder voting and derivative actions to the corporate law objective of pursuing fiduciary obligations only for the benefit of shareholders makes these theories unsuitable for the legal enforcement framework intended for extending legal standing for non-shareholder corporate constituencies to access corporate law remedies.

On the other hand, the mere accommodation of non-shareholder corporate constituencies by the Pluralist or Stakeholder Theory in making these corporate constituencies beneficiaries of fiduciary obligations of directors is unhelpful if the extension of these fiduciary obligations does not necessarily lead to the extension of legal standing to these corporate constituencies to access corporate law remedies. At best, the only corporate law remedy that may be available for the non-shareholder corporate constituencies under this theory may be derivative action proceedings, as it is the company, and the company alone, which is entitled to the remedy for the breach of fiduciary obligation by the directors.

The last category of theories consists of those foundational theories which expressly envisage the extension of legal standing to non-shareholder constituency groups in certain situations. Of the two theories in this category, only the 'Actionable Enlightened Shareholder Value Theory' is expansive enough to extend legal standing to non-shareholder corporate constituencies beyond the ability to only bring derivative actions proceedings. The Entity Maximisation and Sustainability Model expressly envisages the extension of legal standing to non-shareholder constituencies to institute only derivative action proceedings.

## THEORIES SUPPORTING THE TRADITIONAL CORPORATE LAW VIEW OF EQUATING THE INTERESTS OF THE COMPANY WITH THOSE OF SHAREHOLDERS

It is widely accepted that there are basically two primary foundational theories supportive of the view that shareholder interests are the bedrock of any enforcement mechanism, even if such a foundational theory may be 'considerate' of the interests of other corporate constituency groups.[3] These foundational theories are known as the shareholder primacy theory (otherwise also known as the shareholder primacy norm, the 'Shareholder Value Approach' or the 'Shareholder Wealth Maximisation Approach') and the 'Enlightened Shareholder Value Approach' (otherwise known as a 'Shareholder-First Interpretation or Theory').

## Shareholder Primacy Theory

Except in exceptional instances wherein statutory and judicial corporate constituency measures have been adopted, this approach is generally regarded as applying in relation to companies located in Anglo-Saxon jurisdictions.[4]

### *The Content of the Theory*

This theory is also known as the shareholder wealth maximisation norm, and it primarily advocates the running of a company in such a manner as to maximise the wealth of the shareholders ahead of any other interests, including those of corporate constituencies who may have helped to produce the company's return on its equity. 'The objective of the company, under this principle, is to maximise the market value of the company "through allocative, productive and dynamic efficiency."'[5] The theory is premised upon the age-old problematic belief that directors are solely charged with an unyielding fiduciary duty to the corporation and its shareholders.[6] This theory is succinctly summarised by the United Kingdom's Company Law Review Steering Committee ('the Company Law Steering Committee'), established in 1998 by the Department of Trade and Industry to review UK Corporate Law. The Company Law Steering Committee categorically stated that UK law reflected the fact that companies are managed for the benefit of the shareholders and confer upon the shareholders ultimate control of the undertaking, such that '[t]he directors are required to manage the business on their behalf'.[7] The Committee proceeded to surmise that the ultimate objective of companies is to generate maximum wealth for shareholders.[8] Indeed, this theory asserts that the primary concern of corporate decision-making should be with those who supply finance to companies and, more narrowly, shareholders. The single overriding concern under this theory is, in the words of the Hampel Committee, 'the preservation and the greatest practicable enhancement over time of . . . shareholders' investment'.[9] That, however, does not mean that other stakeholders should be ignored but that shareholders should receive primacy in corporate decision-making.[10] As asserted elsewhere, [through the shareholder primacy theory] 'the interests of other stakeholders can only be advanced through the "prism" of shareholders'.[11] In light of the aforegoing, the essence of this theory can succinctly be encapsulated in the statement made by Dean Robert Clark of Harvard Law School in 1986, when he said:

> [L]awyers, judges and economists usually assume that the more ultimate purpose of a business corporation is to make profits for its shareholders. More precisely, corporate managers (directors and officers) are supposed to make corporate decisions so as to maximize the value of the company's shares, subject to the constraint that the corporation must meet all its legal obligations to others who are related or affected by it. These others include employees, creditors, customers, the general public (as affected by the company's pollution, for example), and governmental units. In other words, although the corporation has numerous and perhaps all-encompassing duties to these others, it is the shareholders who have the claim on the residual value of the enterprise, that is, what's left after all definite obligations are satisfied, and the managers have an affirmative open-ended obligation to increase this residual value, rather than the wealth of some other affected group (including themselves).[12]

### *The Primary Proponents of the Theory*

Andrew Keay observes that the shareholder primacy theory 'has been largely fostered as a leading principle of corporate law . . . in the United States'.[13] Notable figures within this principle – who hoisted the banner of shareholder primacy supremacy – include Professor Adolf Berle, who argued as early as 1932 that directors should not, as managers of companies, have any responsibilities other than to the shareholders of their companies, for whom the return on their investment was to be maximised.[14]

Subsequent to that, perhaps the next leading proponent of shareholder primacy is the Nobel Laureate, Milton Friedman, who famously argued that '[f]ew trends could so thoroughly undermine the very foundations of our free society as the acceptance by corporate officials of a social responsibility other than to make as much money for their stockholders as possible'.[15] Later, scholars such as James J. Hanks Jr.,[16] Jonathan R. Macey,[17] Stephen Bainbridge,[18] Bernard Black & Reiner Kraakman,[19] D Gordon Smith,[20] and Henry Hansmann & Reinier Kraakman.[21] Professor Jonathan R. Macey argued that it is the underlying premise of corporate law that the fiduciary duties should flow only from directors to shareholders (as encompassed within the 'corporation') and that this is the primary, if not the only, rationale for making shareholders exclusive beneficiaries of corporate fiduciary duties from an economic analysis point of view.[22] A similar reasoning was used by Professor Stephen Bainbridge in defending the shareholder wealth maximisation norm.[23] Relying on the reasoning that shareholders remained the primary beneficiary of the enforcement mechanisms for fiduciary duties, Black and Kraakman observed that, in this way, the corporate law model was self-enforcing. D. Gordon Smith reiterated the principle enunciated in the late nineteenth-century English decisions that the law does not say that there are to be no cakes and ale, except such that are required for the benefit of the shareholders.[24]

In both the legal writings of James J. Hanks Jr. referred to herein,[25] he vociferously argued in favour of the shareholder primacy theory on the basis that:

(a) Only shareholders have any property rights in the corporation, and others dealing with the corporation have been left to protect themselves by contract;
(b) Measures aimed at advancing the interests of other stakeholders introduce the possibility of an almost unlimited number of potential new competitors for the residual assets of the corporation and, therefore, for directors' attention;
(c) Directors are charged with an unyielding fiduciary duty to the corporation and its shareholders;
(d) Many of the groups sought to be protected [by these measures] are already protected by other statutes or are parties to contracts defining their rights to the corporation;
(e) The corporation is not the only form of business organisation in which the residual owners benefit from goods and services furnished by others. If the rationale that the return on equity should be shared with all who helped produce it is sound, even if they have already been compensated in accordance with statutory and contractual rights, then why limit it to corporations? Why not extend it to partnerships, trusts or even sole proprietorships?
(f) Protection of other groups other than shareholders through these measures has the potential to deter equity investment.[26]

### *Some of the Documented Justifications of the Theory*

In augmenting the six primary reasons advanced by James J. Hanks Jr. above as the jurisprudential and practical justifications for the continued need for the shareholder primacy theory,[27] in a statement attributed by Dean Clark to Milton Friedman, it is stated that:

> A single, objective goal like profit maximization is more easily monitored than a multiple, vaguely defined goal like the fair and reasonable accommodation of all affected interests. It is easier, for example, to tell if a corporate manager is doing what she is supposed to do than to tell if a university president is doing what she is supposed to do. Since shareholders do have some effective control mechanisms (the proxy contest, the takeover bid, and the derivative lawsuit), better

> monitoring means that corporate managers will be kept more accountable. They are more likely to do what they are supposed to do, and do it efficiently. Better accountability thus encourages people to participate in large organizations, in which claims on the organization and the power to manage it are necessarily separated; it helps such organizations exist and function well. Large organizations are in turn often desirable for everyone. They increase social welfare, because without them certain large-scale business ventures would be impossible or would be carried out in a wasteful way.[28]

Some of the primary justifications for this theory are clearly summarised by Andrew Keay as follows:[29]

> First, and in line with the agency theory,[30] directors are the agents of the shareholders and are employed to run the company's business for the shareholders who do not have the time or ability to do so, and thus it is the shareholders who are best suited to guide and discipline directors in the carrying out of their powers and duties;
>
> Second, it is argued that the principle is based on efficiency. Shareholders have incentives to maximise profits and so they are likely to foster economic efficiency. It is more efficient if directors operate on the basis of maximising shareholder wealth, because the least cost is expended in having this as the object rather than something else; and the directors can work more efficiently if they are focused only on one objective;[31]
>
> Third . . . if directors owe duties to various constituencies, then it would be impossible for directors to balance all of the divergent interests, with the result that directors will make poor decisions.[32] It is said that the principle is certain and easy to administer, especially when compared with the stakeholder theory,[33] under which directors are to act with all stakeholder interests in view. Shareholder value allows, so the argument goes, courts to review managerial conduct with some rationality.[34]
>
> Fourth, it is argued that constituencies other than the shareholders are able to protect themselves by the terms of the contracts that they make,[35] while shareholders do not have this kind of protection.[36] The assertion is made that the shareholders are vulnerable in that they are not, unlike creditors, able to negotiate special terms by way of contract, and are consequently, in many ways, at the mercy of the directors. This is due to the fact that there is an inherent difficulty in monitoring the work of directors.[37]
>
> Finally, it is argued that shareholders are not able to exit a company without considerable sacrifice, because while they can sell their shares to another, the price obtained will not take into account any shareholder exploitation.[38]

Hansmann and Kraakman have also argued that non-shareholder corporate constituencies enjoy the greatest benefits if the company is governed in the interests of shareholders.[39] In supporting their objection to using corporate law to protect the interests of non-shareholder corporate constituencies other than creditors, they argue that the most efficacious legal mechanisms for protecting the legal interests of those constituencies lie elsewhere.[40] For workers, they argue, legal mechanisms for protecting their interests include the law of labour contracting, pension law, health and safety law, and anti-discrimination law.[41] As for consumers, the argument goes that protection lies in product safety regulation, warranty law, tort law governing product liability, antitrust laws, and mandatory disclosure of product contents and characteristics.[42] For the public at large, they argue that protection lies in environmental law and the law of nuisance and mass torts.[43]

### *The Shortcomings of the Theory*

While the argument that non-shareholder constituencies dealing with the corporation are better left to protect themselves by contract appears to lend itself to the conclusion that it is not only shareholder interests which are protected under this theory, it is nevertheless too simplistic. In essence, the argument assumes that non-shareholder constituencies have the same, if not superior, bargaining power when negotiating contractual terms to protect their interests. This apparent assumption is clearly incorrect and is too simplistic, as non-shareholder constituencies such as employees have relatively inferior bargaining power in corporations. Even the assumption that creditors protect their interests better by negotiating favourable contractual terms is not always correct within a corporate setting, as considerations such as the relative financial muscle of a particular corporation may, and usually, necessitate the acceptance of less favourable conditions by creditors in return for a potentially lucrative financial return.

Moreover, the communitarian scholars (i.e. those who have challenged the shareholder primacy principle by focusing on the sociological and moral phenomenon of the corporation as a community, in contrast to the individualistic, self-reliant contractarian stance that dominates academic discourse in corporate law) have forcefully argued that 'effective non-shareholder self-protection through bargain (or contract) often is not practically feasible'.[44] David Millon argues that the reasons for this infeasibility include the fact that '[p]articular kinds of conduct likely to be harmful to non-shareholders may be difficult to foresee and to specify contractually with adequate precision'.[45] It is further argued that even in situations where future contingencies are foreseeable, 'the parties may choose not to bargain about them, believing that the remoteness of the risk does not justify the time needed to decide *ex ante* how the costs should be apportioned'.[46]

Still, it would be presumptuous to assume that the terms of non-shareholders' relationships with the company are subject to individualised bargaining at all times. In fact, the reality is that non-shareholder corporate constituencies often find themselves bound by terms already negotiated by others, such as an investment bank concerning corporate bonds or collective bargaining in the unionised sector in relation to employee compensation, working conditions, and the like. Also, bargaining that is beneficial to non-shareholder corporate constituencies may be frustrated by free-rider problems, that is, when a particular contract term stands to benefit all members of the group regardless of their investment in the bargaining effort.[47]

To argue that the substitution of the shareholder primacy theory by any stakeholder-oriented approach introduces the possibility of an almost unlimited number of potential new competitors for the residual assets of the corporation is to grossly underestimate the contribution of non-shareholder constituencies in providing goods and services in respect of which those residual owners greatly benefit. The contribution of non-shareholder constituencies to the well-being of the residual owners is also acknowledged by some of the ardent proponents of the shareholder primacy theory.[48] Moreover, to defend this theory on the basis that measures aimed at advancing the interests of other stakeholders introduce the possibility of an almost unlimited number of potential new competitors for the residual assets of the corporation appears to suggest the existence of unnecessary and potentially damaging conflicts between the interests of shareholders, on the one hand, and those of other corporate constituencies, on the other hand. This is because, as surmised by Lawrence E. Mitchell, 'to suggest that these conflicts are direct is fallacious'.[49]

Since any possible conflict between shareholders and other corporate constituencies can only be in relation to corporate actions which lead to 'horizontal conflicts' (such as the expropriation of wealth from bondholders by stockholders and the layoff of employees as a cost-cutting measure designed to assure the repayment of debt assumed to finance a leveraged takeover) – which exist among two or more relatively powerless groups that have interests in the corporation – to suggest that this is a concern in respect of which one constituency group has to be preferred over others is unjustified because the shareholders themselves are powerless to effect the corporate actions giving rise to such tensions.[50] Thus, the failure to distinguish between the board's actions (and thus the nature of the conflict) in vertical conflicts and horizontal conflicts is the principal cause of confusion over the functions of various fiduciary duties.[51]

Furthermore, arguing that the interests of non-shareholder constituencies are better protected in other areas of law – for example, consumer law, labour law, and environmental law – and can, thus, not be expected to be protected in company law as well is to unnecessarily overestimate the role of regulatory measures, particularly when it relates to non-shareholder corporate constituencies. This argument fallaciously assumes that, in addition to protecting the beneficiaries of the particular regulatory initiative in the subject matter of the regulation, the regulatory initiative also aims to protect their interests in the context of their participation within corporate relations in a particular company. If this argument is to be accepted in relation to non-shareholder constituencies, it must also be accepted in relation to shareholders, as they are also beneficiaries of regulatory measures such as those concerned with investor protection – including those dealing with the prohibition against insider trading, regulation of public offerings of securities, restrictions on the transferability of securities, and so on. Shareholders also benefit from regulations – such as those on antitrust laws and environmental laws – that are supposedly designed for the benefit of non-shareholder constituencies.

Proponents of the shareholder primacy theory unapologetically assert that directors are charged with an unyielding fiduciary duty to the corporation and its shareholders. In this regard, it is maintained that although the traditional legal viewpoint is to the effect that directors and officers have a fiduciary duty to the 'corporation',[52] 'the corporation' is conventionally interpreted to refer exclusively to shareholder interests. This interpretation, however, is incrementally being jettisoned in a number of jurisdictions which have traditionally espoused this interpretation, particularly those that have adopted the Non-Shareholder Constituency Statutes. Moreover, the indiscriminate blending of the different types of restraint for which fiduciary obligations are targeted – together with limited enforcement mechanisms – has ultimately produced the fiduciary formulation that (incorrectly) focuses directors' duties on shareholders' interests.[53] In other words, treating directors' fiduciary duties as a unitary concept masks the differences in the nature of the underlying conflicts those duties are meant to mediate and leads to a faulty analysis of the purpose and significance of different fiduciary rules.[54] This culminates in a hasty and unjustified conclusion that all fiduciary duties or obligations are owed exclusively to the shareholders.

Further, the argument that non-shareholder constituencies are already protected by contractual covenants, other statutes, and the dictates of the free market is also presumptuous, as it implies that equal bargaining powers exist between contracting parties at all times and also the existence of a wholesale, all-encompassing statutory scheme for the protection of non-shareholder corporate constituencies within a corporation, something which is very unlikely and cannot be conclusively proved. Furthermore, to assume that contracting and market processes are adequate to address claims resulting from corporate actions that lead to injury to non-shareholder corporate constituencies is, in the words of Lawrence E. Mitchell, to allow the law to abdicate 'its function as a socializing tool . . . [and] leaves the redressing of individual and societal wrongs to the forces of competition'.[55]

The argument that the corporation is not the only form of enterprise that should be subjected to non-shareholder protection mechanisms, as it is not the only one benefiting from goods and services furnished by stakeholders, clearly loses sight of the fact that 'corporate activity [particularly of public companies] has broad social and political ramifications that justify a body of corporate law that is deliberately responsive to public interest concerns'.[56] It is therefore unjustifiable to argue that since partnerships, trusts and sole proprietorships are also beneficiaries of goods and services furnished by stakeholders, they too should be subjected to non-shareholder constituencies' protective measures. Moreover, the point made about the company is that it is the only vehicle of its kind that the law clothes with special legal status – it is this property of the law that clearly distinguishes the corporation from other business vehicles. It is surely this foundation that leads to the question about the special status of the company.

Again, while the agency theory, which is used for justifying the application of the shareholder primacy theory, emphatically states that directors are the agents of the shareholders and are employed to run the company's business for the shareholders,[57] the reality of the corporate legal scheme is that the directors are not the agents of the shareholders.[58] In the early twentieth century English decision of *Automatic Self-Cleansing Filter Syndicate Co. Ltd v Cuninghame*,[59] the Court rejected the argument that directors were the agents of the company [or the shareholders] and that, as such, were bound to obey the directions of their principal, the company.[60]

Arguments of 'efficiency' raised in defence of the shareholder primacy theory are, in essence, premised on the reasoning that rules requiring corporate directors to accommodate all affected interests will invariably lead to a multiplicity of lawsuits against the company and the inability of directors to act without the fear of being second-guessed. Proponents of the theory argue that it would be impossible for directors to balance all of the divergent interests, with the result that directors would be subjected to too many lawsuits by multiple stakeholders and would, as such, make poor decisions. The South African statutory framework points to the possibility that this fear is exaggerated. In responding to the misgivings raised against the introduction of class action in South Africa (as mirrored by s 38 of the Constitution, which provides, among other things, for the right of 'anyone acting in the public interest' to approach a competent court in enforcing their rights under the Bill of Rights) on the basis that this would lead to courts being engulfed by interfering busy-bodies rushing to court for spurious reasons – the so-called 'floodgates' argument – Froneman J (as he then was) unequivocally stated that 'the possibility of unjustified litigation can be curtailed by making it a procedural requirement that leave must be sought from the High Court to proceed on a representative basis prior to actually embarking on that road'.[61]

Moreover, the argument that shareholders are not able to exit a company without considerable sacrifice grossly underestimates the sacrifice of other non-shareholder constituencies whose entire livelihoods may, and often are, at the mercy of large public corporations.

Perhaps the best-substantiated critique of the shareholder primacy theory is the one put forward by Professor David Millon of Washington and Lee University when he stated as follows:

> Corporate law might legitimately regulate the shareholder-manager relationship because of the inherent accountability problems that trust relationships present. But the shareholder primacy position implicitly rejected the notion that there was a public welfare dimension to corporate activity; it therefore also rejected any justification for legal regulation based on the idea that activities of large corporations affect in important ways a broad range of constituencies other than shareholders. In this manner, shareholder primacy implied a private conception of corporate law. The theoretical foundation of this shareholder-centered, privatized conception of corporate law included a complete disregard for the entity based idea on which [Professor] Dodd built his corporate citizenship argument. The shareholder primacy conception reduced the corporation to the purely private financial interests of its owners, the 'shareholders'[62]

Arguably, the commonly accepted – and clearly misplaced – justification for the shareholder primacy norm has to do with the unnecessary interaction that is drawn between the role of fiduciary rules – which should ideally serve the purpose of prohibiting directorial self-dealing – and the narrowly conceived enforcement mechanisms of shareholder voting and derivative litigation. It has been observed that the dysfunctional result of this equation is to impose the costs of enforcing self-dealing rules on all corporate constituents except shareholders and directors.[63]

It is submitted that the primary shortcoming of this theory, in the context of this book, lies in its inability to extend the enforcement of corporate law beyond the traditional company law enforcement scheme, which effectively endorses the enforcement of corporate law by the narrow category of shareholder constituencies. It is indisputable that, under this theory, non-shareholder constituencies have little or no power to influence the direction companies take in corporate decision-making. What is very clear is that, under this theory, enforcement lies squarely within the domain of company shareholders, as the excessively narrow interpretation of directors' fiduciary responsibilities exacerbates the continued equation of the 'company' exclusively with company shareholders.

As it is only those persons to whom enforcement powers are vested who can remedy any breach of fiduciary responsibilities, the continued exclusion of non-shareholder constituencies from being the beneficiaries of these fiduciary responsibilities effectively means that, under this theory, any possible departure from the traditional company law enforcement scheme, as observed by Judge Dennis Davis, remains an unattainable dream, particularly for non-shareholder corporate constituencies. It is, indeed, becoming increasingly apparent that by de-associating corporate voting and other corporate governance privileges from the equity investment instruments exclusively, modern corporate law rules are signifying that the long-standing question of 'for whom does the company exist?' cannot be easily responded to by simply hand-picking a single corporate constituency group, merely because that group happens to have preferred to invest in the company by using one of the many investment instruments available for potential investors to choose from.

### *Concluding Observations*

In the final analysis, it would appear that the shareholder primacy norm disregards the possible consideration of non-shareholder constituencies' interests within the enforcement framework purely based on the justification that those interests are better taken care of elsewhere – through legal mechanisms operating outside of corporate law, such as contractual provisions and statutory initiatives. These justifications are clearly unsustainable, as some of those legal mechanisms outside of corporate law are, curiously, designed for the protection of shareholder interests, which continue also to be protected as a matter of corporate law. Moreover, these justifications presume that contract-based and statutory-based mechanisms for non-shareholder interests' protection are concerned with interests within the context of corporate relations, whereas, more often, these measures are aimed at attending to specific interests within contexts that are often unrelated to interests within the corporate law context.

## ENLIGHTENED SHAREHOLDER VALUE APPROACH (AKA 'INSTRUMENTAL STAKEHOLDERISM')

When the United Kingdom's Department of Trade and Industry commissioned the Company Law Review with effect from March 1998, the review was to be overseen by a committee that became known as the Company Law Review Steering Group (CLRSG). The CLRSG clearly saw the issue of the party in whose interest company law should be formulated as a critical one in its deliberations. After acknowledging that the 'Shareholder Value Approach' was in operation in the United Kingdom at the time.[64] The CLRSG then formulated what subsequently became known as the 'Enlightened Shareholder Value Approach' (ESVA) as enacted in s 172(1) of the United Kingdom's Companies Act, 2006.[65] This section came into operation with effect from 01 October 2007.

## Enlightened Shareholder Value Approach

### *The Content of the Theory*

In rejecting the Pluralist or the Stakeholder Approach on the basis that its adoption would invariably necessitate substantial reform of the law on directors' duties (given the possible extension of fiduciary responsibilities of directors beyond shareholders to include stakeholders),[66] the CLRSG justified the Enlightened Shareholder Value Approach on the basis that it was clearly based on the shareholder value and involved directors having to act in the collective best interests of shareholders.[67] Even though the ESVA is based on the Shareholder Value Approach, it nevertheless eschews 'an exclusive focus on the short-term financial bottom line' and seeks a more inclusive approach that values the building of long-term relationships. Paine[68] describes this approach as 'Instrumental Stakeholderism' and describes it as one through which the consideration of stakeholders' interests can assist in the maximisation of returns to shareholders. She argues that the way in which a company treats non-shareholder stakeholders can affect shareholder value.[69] The ESVA involves 'striking a balance between the competing interests of different stakeholders in order to benefit the shareholders in the long run'.[70] Further, the fact that the ESVA refrains from 'an exclusive focus on the short-term financial bottom line' does not mean that the short-term interests of shareholders are completely disregarded. What it means is that the process envisages directors taking a balanced view of the shareholders' interests, where their long-term interests should not be regarded as being more important than their short-term interests, or vice versa.[71]

The core of the Enlightened Shareholder Value principle is embodied in Section 172 of the UK Companies Act, 2006, which defines the fiduciary duties of corporate directors as follows:

> A director . . . must act . . . in good faith . . . to promote the success of the company for the benefit *of its members* [or shareholders] *as a whole, and in doing so have regard to* . . . (a) the likely consequences of any decision in the long term, (b) the interest of the company's employees, (c) the need to foster the company's business relationships with suppliers, customers and others, (d) the impact of the company's operations on the community and the environment, (e) the desirability of the company maintaining a reputation for high standards of business conduct, and (f) the need to act fairly as between members of the company. [Emphasis added].[72]

The ESVA bears some similarity with the provisions of most Non-Stockholder Constituency Statutes[73] that apply in the majority of the American states.[74] A typical Non-Stockholder Constituency Statute permits but does not require, the corporate directors to consider, in addition to the long- and short-term interests of the corporation, the long- and short-term effects upon certain listed constituencies, such as current and/or retired employees, suppliers, customers, creditors, and the local community.[75]

Inasmuch as the ESVA does not extend fiduciary obligations of directors to the corporate stakeholders, the Non-Stockholder Constituency Statutes also allow corporate directors and executives to consider stakeholders' interests without breaching fiduciary obligations to shareholders.[76]

### *The Primary Proponents of the Theory*

As the initial proponents of the ESVA the New Labour Party Government under Prime Minister Tony Blair in the United Kingdom referred to the 'Enlightened Shareholder Value' as 'stakeholder capitalism' and justified it on the basis that 'the value of shareholders could only be maximised if the interests of other stakeholders were also catered for'.[77]

In its consultation document published in early 1999, the CLRSG set out its objectives as being to 'provide straightforward, cost effective and fair regulation which balances the interests of business with those of shareholders, creditors and others'.[78] While the ESVA was still in its recommendation format by the CLRSG, one commentator stated that '[s]uch changes in UK company law would reflect the fundamental assumptions and often long-established principles in company law and practice in Europe, which have yet survived the onslaught of shareholder value ideology'.[79]

As observed by Professor Andrew Keay, '[c]oncern for long-term wealth is something that has been advocated even by those who have been the most fervent supporters of shareholder value',[80] notable of whom are Professors Hansmann, Kraakman and Jensen. In their well-known article, 'The End of History for Corporate Law', Professors Henry Hansmann and Reiner Kraakman insisted that there was 'no longer any serious competitor to the view that corporate law should principally strive to increase long-term shareholder value'.[81] Professor Michael Jensen, a long-time advocate of shareholder value, echoes these sentiments.[82]

The Australian Parliamentary Joint Committee on Corporations and Financial Services stated in 2006 that:

> Progressive, innovative directors, in seeking to add value for their shareholders, will engage with and take account of the interests of stakeholders other than shareholders.[83]

Of late, one commentator who has emerged as a leading proponent of the ESVA is Virginia Harper Ho,[84] who argues that 'an "enlightened shareholder value" vision of the corporate purpose . . . transcends the shareholder-stakeholder divide'[85] primarily because 'in contrast to both traditional shareholder primacy and the approach of most constituency statutes, [it] requires boards to justify their decisions in terms of stakeholder interests and to disclose risks impacting stakeholders'.[86] By doing so, Ho argues that 'the U.K. endorses a multi-stakeholder decision-making rule and makes management at least *indirectly* accountable to stakeholders'.[87] She concludes that 'the goal of the U.K. approach is to "maintain [corporations'] financial accountability to a constituency of dispersed, independent shareholders while *simultaneously* using market forces to nudge companies in the direction of greater social responsibility'. [Emphasis added].[88]

### *Some of the Documented Justifications of the Theory*

Of the main justifications raised by the proponents of ESVA five points stand out to be of pivotal importance: first, as with the Stakeholder Theory, the argument concerns the role that the modern corporation plays in society. In a famous statement by E. Merrick Dodd, Jr., he emphatically stated that:

> [T]he association . . . takes its place in a business world with certain ethical standards which appear to be developing in the direction of increased social responsibility. . . . [W]e may then . . . conceive of it as a person, which, like other persons engaged in business, is affected not only by the laws which regulate business but by the attitude of public and business opinion as to the social obligations of business. If a business is tending to become a profession, then a corporate person engaged in business is a professional even though its stockholders, who take no active part in the conduct of business, may not be. Those through whom it acts may therefore employ its funds in a manner appropriate to a person practising a profession and imbued with a sense of social responsibility without thereby being guilty of a breach of trust.[89]

It is in the context of this reasoning that it appears that the argument stands for the point that many constituencies make up the modern corporation, of which shareholders are just one constituency. It follows that corporations have social, as well as profit-making, responsibilities to all of their constituencies and that the ESVA allows the directors to satisfy these responsibilities.

A further argument raised in favour of the ESVA (and by the same reasoning, the Non-Stockholder Constituency Statutes) is that since non-shareholder constituencies are less able than shareholders to protect themselves from the negative effects of major corporate action (especially hostile takeovers), the ESVA provides much-needed protection and allows a more even distribution of the gains and losses that accompany these situations.[90] This argument begins by recognising that the nature of a shareholder's investment in a corporation is generally short-term, while that of non-shareholder constituencies is long-term.[91]

Again, the ESVA allows directors to take the interests of stakeholders or consider the effects of their decisions on non-shareholder constituencies without the fear of breaching their fiduciary duties to their companies.[92]

Next, the ESVA allows flexibility in management's responses to hostile takeovers, particularly when applying the Non-Stockholder Constituency Statutes (e.g., management is not limited to focusing on the short-term interests of shareholders), which will allow them to compete more effectively with German and Japanese companies, which are focused on the long term.[93] A similar argument is that these statutes will 'help protect the directors from liability and thus encourage them to resist takeover offers'.[94]

Finally, proponents argue that due to the effects takeovers have on all the constituencies of corporations, including the economy and society as a whole, the ESVA reflects a legitimate public policy concern.[95]

### *The Shortcomings of the Theory*

While the importance of non-shareholder constituencies' considerations cannot be gainsaid, they remain mere pies in the sky if the failure of corporations to accommodate them cannot be rectified. The rectification referred to herein requires an enforcement scheme which will ensure, first, the proactive consideration of non-shareholder constituencies' interests by directors and, second, the rectification of any failure on the part of the directors to consider such interests. To withhold either of the means of rectification effectively means that any statutory corporate constituency measures will fall short of being characterised as a clear scheme of responsibility to someone other than shareholders, which is also reasonably enforceable.

Moreover, regardless of the fact that, in terms of the ESVA, directors are allowed to take the interests of stakeholders into account without the fear of breaching their fiduciary duties to their companies,[96] this is still not good enough as fiduciary obligations of directors remain owed to the company and its shareholders. In practice, the impact of this eventuality is that it is the shareholders who will exclusively be vested with the powers to institute proceedings to remedy any breach of fiduciary duties. Professor Andrew Keay observes that the apparent benefit of allowing directors to take into account the interests of non-shareholder constituencies without breaching their (i.e. directors') fiduciary duties to the shareholders 'might well be illusory, for s 172(1) might not assist directors, for if they fail to comply with the ultimate aim of s 172(1), that is, to promote the success of the company for the benefit of the members as a whole, then derivative proceedings could be initiated by members for breach of duty'.[97]

The argument that the ESVA allows directors to compete more effectively with German and Japanese companies, which are focused on the long term,[98] appears to be oblivious to the longstanding judicial acceptance of the view that the consideration of the long-term view by the directors has been the legal position even before the formal adoption of the ESVA. This interpretation has its origin in the 1883 English decision *Hutton v West Cork Railway*[99] where the court stated that: 'the test . . . is not whether [the action] is bonâ fide, but whether, as well as being done bonâ fide . . . it is reasonably incidental to the carrying on of the company's business for the company's benefit'.[100] The court went on to say that '[t]he law *does not say that there are to be no cakes and ale*, but there are to be no cakes and ale except such as are required for the benefit of the company'.[101] [Emphasis added].

Even subsequent to the above case, the UK courts have, on occasion, produced dicta that suggested a broader approach, the application of the shareholder value principle notwithstanding.[102]

To argue that the ESVA will 'help protect the directors from liability'[103] is also myopic, as only the shareholders are able to bring derivative proceedings against directors if it can be proved that they have failed 'to promote the success of the company for the benefit of the members as a whole'.[104]

If, as argued by some,[105] the ESVA reflects a legitimate public policy concern, the general lack of the ability by the non-shareholder constituencies to enforce such a 'legitimate public concern' is a considerable drawback that cannot be easily ignored. Indeed, the move from 'the shareholders alone' philosophy to 'the shareholder first' approach, as reflected by the 'shareholder primacy' and the ESVA approach, respectively, would have been progressive if the latter approach were capable of being enforced beyond the former, with non-shareholder corporate constituency groups not being left to the mercy of the shareholders insofar as enforcement is concerned. The fact that this model of enforcement continues to be perpetuated even under the ESVA approach signifies that this approach achieves the same result as the traditional shareholder model, i.e. that directors invariably will owe duty only to shareholders and not to other constituencies. In other words, the granting of the discretion to directors to consider the interests of non-shareholder corporate constituency groups, without further enforcement, is tantamount to taking two steps forward and one step backwards – the apparent ground made by listing interests additional to those of shareholder corporate constituencies is negated by the law's continued persistence that the pursuance of those additional interests can only be undertaken through the prism of the shareholder corporate constituent group.

*Concluding Observations*

As the fiduciary duties of directors continue to be owed only to shareholders under this theory, any possibility of enforcement of any breach of such duties by non-shareholder constituencies who are expressly mentioned under this theory is virtually non-existent. While it is denied that it is impossible for directors to owe fiduciary obligations to multiple constituencies, failure to provide extended legal standing for the benefit of non-shareholder constituencies in identified circumstances is particularly disempowering.

In the final analysis, both theories in this category are based on the flawed assumption that there is a natural, immutable character inherent in the current ordering of corporate law, which is reflected particularly in the limitation of standing to bring derivative suits to shareholders.

## ALTERNATIVE THEORY ACCOMMODATIVE OF NON-SHAREHOLDER CORPORATE CONSTITUENCIES

### Stakeholder/Pluralist Theory ('Classic Stakeholderism')

The Pluralist Theory, which is also commonly known as the Stakeholder Theory or Classic Stakeholderism, effectively maintains that 'cooperative and productive relationships [within companies] will only be optimised where directors are permitted (or required) to balance shareholders' interests with those of others committed to the company'.[106] What this means is that this theory regards corporate law objective as being concerned primarily with benefiting 'all those who can be identified as stakeholders'.[107] In other words, 'directors are not only to manage the company for the betterment of shareholders, but also in the interests of a multitude of stakeholders (including the shareholders) who can affect or be affected by the actions of a company'.[108] It is commonly accepted that the Pluralist Theory is embraced in many continental European jurisdictions, and most notably in Germany.[109]

*The Content of the Theory*

The Pluralist Theory is predicated on the acceptance that, as the so-called residual owners (i.e. shareholders) benefit from goods and services furnished by other stakeholders, these stakeholders also have claims on a company's assets and earnings because they contribute to a company's capital.[110] The crux of this theory is that [corporate] 'wealth should be distributed fairly to all stakeholders, and that corporations have a social responsibility that goes beyond the mere maximization of shareholder wealth'.[111] According to Paine, this form of stakeholderism holds that 'at least some stakeholders' interests must be respected as well as considered'.[112] Regardless of the apparent departure from the excessively narrow preoccupation with shareholder wealth maximisation that characterises the shareholder primacy theory the Stakeholder Theory's extension of directors' fiduciary obligations to non-shareholder corporate constituencies only offers the potential for non-shareholder corporate constituent groups to enforce the violation of the company's legal interests through derivative actions. This is so because the violation of the company's legal interests invariably concerns the breach of fiduciary obligations which, under this theory, are owed to all corporate constituencies. Other than this potential for derivative litigation remedy, there does not appear to be the potential for non-shareholder corporate constituencies to avail themselves of other corporate law remedies since the theory is not supplemented by the extension of a legal enforcement framework equivalent to that applicable in favour of the shareholders, in relation to the shareholder primacy norm.[113]

This is particularly disturbing as the egalitarian treatment of all corporate constituency groups through the extension of fiduciary obligations is apparently its primary preoccupation.[114] Professor Irene-Marie Esser, quoting a number of commentators on the Stakeholder Theory, submits that '[i]n terms of this approach, directors owe fiduciary duties to different stakeholders'.[115] She concludes that '[t]he interests of employees may in certain instances receive priority over those of the shareholders collectively'.[116] To be lukewarm about whether the Stakeholder Theory, in fact, extends legal standing to non-shareholder corporate constituencies to whom fiduciary duties are owed is unhelpful and, at best, renders virtually futile the directors' ability to take a broader view of their responsibilities, as there seems to be nothing that aggrieved stakeholders can do if directors fail to take such stakeholders' interests into account in corporate decision-making. In the pertinent words of Professor Andrew Keay:

> If the directors fail to take into account a particular stakeholder's interests, what can that stakeholder do? Absent the shareholders, who are entitled to seek permission to continue a derivative claim or present a petition on the unfair prejudice ground, the answer, as far as the law goes, appears to be: very little.[117]

It is, however, too simplistic to quickly conclude that legal standing to bring derivative action does not exist for non-shareholder corporate constituencies under this theory, as the mere fact that those corporate constituencies are owed fiduciary duties, unlike the case of the ESVA approach, automatically creates a presumption that such legal standing exists, particularly with regard to derivative action proceedings, the primary purpose of which is to protect the company against the breach of such fiduciary duties.

In addition to the possibility of derivative litigation proceedings being instituted by non-shareholder constituencies, the apparent accommodation of extended fiduciary duty to other stakeholders under this theory effectively means that these extended duties could have greater value even if they did not grant other remedies to stakeholders. The value that extended fiduciary duties could have if they were combined with adequate remedies is even greater. Unlike the shareholder primacy norm, which radically excludes remedies for stakeholders, the extension of fiduciary duties under this theory creates the possibility of protecting the company's legal interests by non-shareholder constituencies as they are also owed fiduciary duties under the theory.

### *The Primary Proponents of the Theory*

R. Edward Freeman is one of the notable proponents of the Stakeholder Theory.[118] Professor David Millon also identifies another group of commentators who propagated the adoption of the Stakeholder Theory on the basis of Corporate Citizenship arguments, which originated in the wake of the Depression and were spearheaded by Professor E. Merrick Dodd.[119] Other advocates of the Stakeholder Theory who firmly assert that groups in addition to shareholders have claims on the company's assets and earnings because they contribute to the company's capital include Jill Fisch,[120] Kent Greenfield,[121] and Margaret Blair & Lynn Stout.[122]

One of the few Stakeholder Theory proponents who clearly argued for the extension of fiduciary duties of directors to stakeholders is Professor Kent Greenfield.[123] Greenfield forcefully argues that the elimination of the profit maximisation norm and the extension of the scope of fiduciary duties to include stakeholders other than shareholders would increase contributions to social welfare. He argues for the inclusion of stakeholder representatives within boards of directors with a view to meaningfully contributing to corporate decision making.[124] Greenfield concedes, though, that although these proposed radical changes to enable directors to take a broader view of their responsibilities by extending their fiduciary responsibilities are profound, this 'would not require seismic shifts in corporate law'.[125] In this regard, it is clear that Greenfield does not want to interfere with those special characteristics of corporations – perpetual existence, limited liability, specialised management, and share transferability – that create such a powerful ability to generate financial wealth.[126]

### *Some of the Documented Justifications of the Theory*

Early on in 1932, Professor E. Merrick Dodd directly intimated that corporate directors should be able to legally undertake social responsibilities without being guilty of a breach of trust.[127]

It has been said that '[t]he modern corporation, by its nature, creates interdependencies with a variety of groups with whom the corporation has a legitimate concern, such as employees, customers, suppliers, and members of the communities in which the corporation operates'.[128] It has also been argued that 'stakeholders have claims on the company's assets and earnings because they contribute to the company's capital'.[129] At the inception of the Company Law Reform process in the United Kingdom, one of the initial justifications for a need to consider an approach broader than the shareholder primacy theory was that while it was important not to constrain directors to do anything against the long-term interests of shareholders, they should at the same time 'be free from an excessively narrow interpretation of their fiduciary responsibilities which could actually work against the company's interests'.[130]

Arguing in the context of the US Non-Stockholder Constituency Statutes, some commentators observe that [the Stakeholder Theory] validates 'the modern trend of stakeholder management, presents a legal regime consistent with modern theories of the corporation, and promotes a consistent and efficient approach to judicial policing of corporate fiduciary duties'.[131]

Some argue that the Theory exemplifies 'an effective means to ensure that the many varying interests affected by a corporation are given a voice in directors' decisions'.[132] One proponent maintains that:

> The . . . concept . . . has several benefits. First, by requiring directors to act in the best interests of the corporation, it assures shareholders that their money will be invested with the goal of enhancing long-term corporate wealth and the corporation's ability to maximize corporate profits. Second, the [Stakeholder Theory] expressly permits the directors to take into consideration the interests of other corporate stakeholders. This affords directors flexibility to balance the sometimes competing goals and expectations – especially in the takeover context – of those who have invested in the corporation, whether through financial capital or human capital. Finally, and most importantly [the theory] embodies the best standard for director decision-making.[133]

Others go as far as arguing that the relationship between stakeholders and shareholders does not have to be antagonistic.[134]

### *The Shortcomings of the Theory*

Justifying the need for the Pluralist Theory on the basis that the company is endowed 'with certain ethical standards'[135] which demand increased social responsibility from those running the company is to effectively incentivise directors to 'to act opportunistically and then to hide behind an assertion that they acted in order to benefit a particular stakeholder group'.[136] It is to unquestionably and naively trust that the directors are always disposed to doing the right thing, as good stewards. This is referred to as the stewardship theory and, according to Professor Andrew Keay, it is 'embraced by many favouring Stakeholder Theory or something akin to it'.[137] According to this stewardship theory, as a subset of the broader Stakeholder Theory, 'there is a focus on directors' need for achievement, responsibility, recognition, altruism and respect for authority, and as a result, they [directors] can be seen not as opportunistic, but as good stewards who will act in the best interests of the stakeholders'.[138]

One justification for the application of the Stakeholder Theory is on the basis that, as dictated by age-old corporate law rules, the company is a separate legal person and, as such, 'like other persons engaged in business, is affected not only by the laws which regulate business but by the attitude of the public and business opinion as to the social obligations of business'.[139] As discussed below under the Entity Maximisation and Sustainability Model, this reasoning can also be dismissed for the same reasons as the stewardship theory reasoning. Moreover, both these justifications appear to be oblivious to the fact that for the purposes of enforcement, stakeholders' legal standing, or lack thereof, is not at all dependent on the 'good heart', or lack thereof, on the part of the directors. Neither is the enforcement by aggrieved stakeholders dependent on the existence of the company as a separate legal person. As it is argued later, even the possible extension of fiduciary obligations to stakeholders, although a welcome improvement, is somewhat inadequate as it is not supplemented by greater enforcement powers in favour of the stakeholders. Nevertheless, the possibility of the institution of derivative action proceedings by non-shareholder constituencies is a useful step in the right direction.

There is also an argument that the need for the Stakeholder Theory is justified by the fact that '[t]he modern corporation . . . creates interdependencies with a variety of groups with whom the corporation has a legitimate concern, such as employees, customers, suppliers, and members of the communities in which the corporation operates'.[140] Mere legitimate concern for stakeholders, without more, also appears to be a weak justification for the application of the Stakeholder Theory, particularly if the disregard of those 'legitimate concerns', whether deliberate or not, is incapable of being remedied by the affected stakeholders.

For the same reasons, stakeholders' 'entitlement to the company's assets and earnings on the basis that they contribute to the company's capital'[141] sounds good as a platitude, but does not increase the chances of concerned stakeholders' participation in those assets and earnings unless there is a clear and reasonably enforceable scheme of responsibilities to those stakeholders, something that is still lacking under the Stakeholder Theory.

The need to enable directors to 'be free from an excessively narrow interpretation of their fiduciary responsibilities by extending their fiduciary duties to other stakeholders'[142] is practically worthless if, in addition to not providing guidance on how to rank competing stakeholders' interests, there is no enforcement ability by the stakeholders.

To argue that the Stakeholder Theory 'promotes a consistent and efficient approach to judicial policing of corporate fiduciary duties'[143] appears to be oblivious to the reality that corporate law, particularly within most Anglo-Saxon jurisdictions, ordinarily prescribes that fiduciary duties are owed to the company or shareholders and not to other stakeholders. Therefore, the corporate law scheme of enforcement, where fiduciary duties are owed exclusively to the company or the shareholders, will almost invariably not provide an enforcement scheme for stakeholders other than shareholders, unless there is an overhaul of conventional corporate law to require directors to owe fiduciary obligations not only to shareholders.

While some Stakeholder Theory proponents argue that the relationship between stakeholders and shareholders does not have to be antagonistic,[144] there are invariable instances in which a choice has to be made in favour of one constituency over another, and the lack of guidance on the prioritisation of these competing interests may be debilitating to those tasked with the role of enforcing their fiduciary duties.

Regardless of the fact that the Stakeholder Theory is different from the ESVA approach, in the sense that directors clearly owe fiduciary duties to non-shareholder corporate constituencies on an equal footing with shareholder corporate constituencies, the clear presumption that the only possible remedy that can be resorted to by all corporate constituencies is that of derivative action proceedings (as the effect of the breach of fiduciary duties is to deprive the company, and none of the corporate constituency groups, of some benefit to which the company is legally entitled) reduces the utility of the Stakeholder Theory as an alternative to both the shareholder primacy norm and the ESVA approach.

## *Concluding Observations*

The Stakeholder Theory appears to be hesitant on whether legal standing follows fiduciary obligations of directors even to non-shareholder corporate constituencies, unclear on the prioritisation of competing stakeholders' interests, and clearly inadequate in providing for a clear, enforceable scheme of responsibilities in favour of the affected non-shareholder corporate constituencies. In the event that fiduciary duties (under this theory) are indeed owed by directors to all stakeholders, it is doubtful whether any meaningful enforcement of the Stakeholder Theory would result, since the idea of requiring a director to take into account the interests of all constituencies is 'essentially vacuous'.[145] O. Hart based this on the view that directors would be able to justify any decision on the basis that it benefited some person or group.[146] The author was concerned that the directors might be able to act opportunistically and then to hide behind an assertion that they acted in order to benefit a particular stakeholder group. Even the Company Law Review Steering Group, in its review of UK company law, said that there is little sense in requiring a duty to be owed to a group that is unable to enforce it.[147]

In the final analysis, it appears that the theory is incapable of supporting a legal enforcement framework that benefits all corporate constituency groups. Even if the theory can be said to accommodate all corporate constituencies through the extension of fiduciary obligations to all such corporate constituencies, the only conventional corporate law remedy that can possibly be afforded to these corporate constituencies is the derivative action proceedings. This is because any breach of fiduciary obligations by directors results in the company, and only the company, being a beneficiary of the resultant remedies. It is for that reason that the only possible remedy is that of derivative proceedings. Although this eventuality may be disruptive to the conventional corporate law assumption, which associates derivative action proceedings with shareholders alone, to limit the other corporate constituency groups to this remedy alone is a step in the right direction, but more is needed, as such corporate constituencies would have no standing to challenge corporate actions that they claim have injured them and not the company.

## THEORIES SUPPORTING THE EXTENSION OF LEGAL STANDING FOR NON-SHAREHOLDER CORPORATE CONSTITUENCIES TO ACCESS CORPORATE LAW REMEDIES

In recent years, we have seen the emergence of approaches widely accepted as being relatively progressive. These approaches are known as the 'Entity Maximisation and Sustainability Model' and the 'Actionable Enlightened Shareholder Value Approach'.[148]

In an interesting article published in 2007, Professor Andrew Keay concludes that "while the Enlightened Shareholder Value Approach provided for by s 172(1) [of the UK Companies Act, 2006] is seen as providing a significant new development in UK law, the approach is in fact little different from the Shareholder Value Approach.[149] The same author argued later in 2010 that although a new theory known as the Entity Maximisation and Sustainability Model has recently been formulated, problems associated with its enforcement effectively means that one particular enforcement mechanism, namely; the derivative action procedure, can be the only effective way of enforcing the theory, effectively implying that unless the scope for bringing derivative action is broadened beyond the traditional company law enforcement scheme, even the introduction of this new theory will prove to be futile.[150]

Both these approaches are dealt with in detail in this chapter.

## Entity Maximisation and Sustainability Model (EMS)

According to Professor Andrew Keay, on the Entity Maximisation and Sustainability Model (EMS):

> [EMS] was devised because the two dominant theories for dealing with the issue of what the ultimate objective of public companies is – the shareholder primacy and stakeholder theories – have been subjected to extensive criticism (much of it warranted) and been found to be wanting.[151]

This theory is not necessarily new and finds its origin in the fundamental corporate law concept of the nature of a corporate entity as having a 'separate legal personality'.[152]

### *The Content of the Theory*

As is apparent from the name of this theory, it focuses on the company as an entity or enterprise; that is, the company as an institution in its own right. Consequently, all directorial obligations (including fiduciary duties) are owed to the company as an entity and not to any of the company's constituencies.

In essence:

> [The theory] involves the fostering of entity wealth, which will involve directors endeavouring to increase the overall long-run market value of the company. This will entail enhancing the value to the company as a whole, taking into account the investment made by various people and groups. An entity maximisation approach entails the directors making decisions that will maximise the general wealth of the company. In other words, directors should do that which value maximises the corporate entity, so that the net present value to the company as a whole is enhanced.[153]

In contrast with the shareholder primacy theory, which envisages the maximisation of the shareholders' profit within a company, the 'maximisation of the company's wealth [under EMS] is not always measured by how much profit has been made by the company in a given period'.[154] In addition to maximising the entity's wealth, directors have to ensure that the company survives by not falling into an insolvent position from which it cannot escape, thereby being able to stay afloat and pursue the development of the company's position.[155] This, therefore, means that the theory's ultimate purpose is two-pronged: maximising the entity's wealth and, at the same time, ensuring the entity's financial sustainability.

Under this theory, the fiduciary duties of the directors are owed exclusively to the company as an entity, that is, the entire corporate enterprise,[156] and not to the company's present and future shareholders[157] or both the company and its shareholders,[158] as has traditionally been the case.

### *The Primary Proponents of the Theory*

In its current form, this theory on corporate objectives was only formulated in 2008. However, since its origins can be traced to the corporate law concept of separate legal personality, there is case law within the commonwealth which supports the proposition that directors' fiduciary duties are owed to the company 'as a separate legal person and not any corporate constituency'.[159] Commenting in relation to the extension of the *locus standi* in relation to derivative claims when fiduciary duties are owed to the company as a separate legal entity, Janice Dean stated that: 'there seems to be no a priori reason why others [besides shareholders] should not enjoy similar access to the courts to protect the company from harm, under a regime of judicial supervision similar to that envisaged to "manage" shareholder actions'.[160]

With the exception of judicial pronouncements, the most direct assertion that fiduciary duties of directors are owed to the company as a legal entity was made in 2002 by South Africa's King Report on Corporate Governance, which observed that:

> The logic has been that shareowners are entitled to expect directors to run the company in their sole interests – the so-called shareowner dominant theory. This approach has been rejected by Courts in various jurisdictions, because on incorporation the company becomes a separate persona in law and no person whether natural or juristic can be owned. Courts have also held that shareowners have no direct interest in the property, business or assets owned by a company, their only rights being a right to vote and a right to dividends. Shareowners also change from time to time while as the owner, the company remains constant. Consequently, directors, in exercising their fiduciary duties, must act in the interest of the company as a separate person.[161]

### *Some of the Documented Justifications of the Theory*

With EMS, the emphasis is not on non-shareholder constituencies taking action to protect their own positions directly, as with the Stakeholder Theory, but to enforce any failure of the directors to comply with the objective of the company, which effectively prescribes that fiduciary obligations are owed to the company as a separate legal persona.

Professor Andrew Keay observes that:

> [U]nder any model of the corporate objective [including the EMS] there is the possibility of an economic enforcement mechanism that is able to be undertaken by several investors. First, investors might threaten to exit, engendering concern in the board that this threat, if put into action, might lead to a reduction in the company's share price. Such a threat might be seen as a bluff. All of this could lead to brinkmanship, which is unlikely to be good for the company. Secondly, some investors might be able to bring various forms of political pressure to bear on directors. There are a range of political pressure mechanisms that could be used, such as the formation of coalitions, public relations campaigns and the reference of matters to regulatory agencies. Some investors may be willing to take action that would see their concerns about the company become public and, therefore, would possibly be detrimental to the company's reputation. This might be prejudicial to the investor, but it might be reasoned that this damage would only be short term, but could be fruitful in the long term.[162]

Finally, it would appear that where the corporate objective is based on the EMS theory, there is no justifiable reason why the legal standing to institute derivative proceedings cannot be extended to non-shareholder constituencies as well.

### *The Shortcomings of the Theory*

Regardless of the possibility that, under the EMS theory, non-shareholder corporate constituencies could potentially enforce any failure of the directors to comply with the objective of the company through derivative proceedings, such enforcement is only possible in South Africa, the only commonwealth jurisdiction which has extended legal standing to bring derivative claims to non-shareholder constituencies within the company.[163] Moreover, as derivative proceedings constitute the only enforcement mechanism available under EMS theory for non-shareholder corporate constituencies,[164] the lack of other remedies to further benefit these constituent groups is unsatisfactory.[165]

Other possible extra-regulatory economic enforcement mechanisms such as (a) threatening to exit, (b) being able to bring various forms of political pressure to bear on directors, and (c) going public on their concerns against the company may be dismissed as mere bluff by the directors and may also be detrimental to the company's reputation and, consequently, prejudicial to non-shareholder constituencies themselves.

To sum up, even in the context of the Enlightened Shareholder Value Approach, which could easily have justified the adoption of the EMS theory, there is no justifiable reason why the legal standing to institute derivative proceedings cannot be extended to non-shareholder constituencies in

Anglo-American and commonwealth jurisdictions that share company law traditions with the United Kingdom and the United States.

### *Concluding Observations*

Even if the EMS theory may be seen as viable for the promotion of non-shareholder constituencies' interests, the main drawback is that the only enforcement mechanism that can potentially be extended to those non-shareholder constituencies is the derivative proceedings, which are effectively only beneficial to the company.

## THE ACTIONABLE ENLIGHTENED SHAREHOLDER VALUE APPROACH OR STRUCTURAL STAKEHOLDERISM

Professor Irene-Marié Esser correctly observed that '[t]he protection of stakeholders was also debated during the company law review process in South Africa'.[166] She continues to highlight that '[t]he drafting of the new Companies Act provided the ideal opportunity to resolve this issue, and to indicate which theory is preferred and how it should be applied practically'.[167] While I find myself in agreement with Professor Esser's observation that the drafters of the Act should ideally have [expressly] indicated which theory is preferred, a closer examination of certain specific provisions of the 2008 Companies Act reveals the clear practical application of the theory referred to in this book as the 'Actionable Enlightened Shareholder Value Approach' (AESVA). Although the AESVA is essentially a version of a Structural Stakeholderism described by Paine,[168] as it calls for the extension of voting or other powers to non-shareholder stakeholders in the governance process, it also has features of beneficial stakeholderism as it recognises that optimising returns for shareholders over the past four decades has led many companies to underinvest in their other constituencies and has, thus, led to 'a disproportionate share of gains to the owners of capital'.[169]

Although the Companies Act does not explicitly make reference to the AESVA, it nevertheless directly provides a clear framework for the empowerment of stakeholders and includes a number of specific remedies to enhance not only shareholder profits but also societal welfare.[170]

John F. Olson observes that in order '[t]o ensure that these purposes are fulfilled, the South African Government is provided greater power in governance decisions [in the Act] than is typically found in most other general corporate statutes'.[171]

This observation is hardly surprising because, after having accepted the undesirability of the continued application of the shareholder primacy theory, particularly in view of the constitutional imperatives, the company law review team made it clear in the Guidelines for Corporate Law Reform that

> a company should have as its objective the conduct of business activities with a view to enhancing the economic success of the corporation, taking into account, as appropriate, the legitimate interests of other stakeholder constituencies.[172]

While the above approach appears to resemble the Enlightened Shareholder Value Approach (ESVA), particularly if the term 'corporation' is interpreted to mean the members of the company as a whole, it is also capable of being categorised as the 'Entity Maximisation and Sustainability Model' (EMS) if the corporation refers to the entity as a separate legal person.

The assessment of the relevant provisions of the Act highlighting the practical application of the remedies clearly indicates the ultimate preference of neither ESVA nor the EMS.

## Actionable Enlightened Shareholder Value Approach

### *The Content of the Theory*

The AESVA model was formulated during the National Economic Development and Labour Council's (NEDLAC's) Corporate Law Reform Task Team's deliberations between June 2004 and February 2008, and it refers to the corporate governance approach which provides an expanded enforcement framework for the empowerment of all corporate constituent groups. By providing an inclusive actionable enforcement scheme, the approach recognises that companies operate to enhance not only shareholder profits but also societal welfare. This expanded corporate legal enforcement framework is, however, not accompanied by a clear normative statement of responsibilities towards the non-shareholder corporate constituent groups. It is conceded that this normative statement can, at best, only be inferred from reading the expanded enforcement framework within the context of the Companies Act, 2008, as a whole, particularly with regard to specific sections of the Act.[173]

Moreover, the lack of clear guidelines on how directors should overcome the dilemma of being accused of favouring one corporate constituent group at the expense of another is concerning. That said, however, the expanded corporate legal enforcement framework is clearly justified within the context of the South African corporate landscape.[174]

### *The Primary Proponents of the Theory*

Ever since the AESVA's first appearance in corporate governance circles following the promulgation of the Companies Act (Act No. 71 of 2008) by the then South African President, Mr Kgalema Motlanthe, on 8 April 2009, the only two major publications that commented extensively on the approach are John F. Olson's chapter within the *Modern Company Law for a Competitive South African Economy* in 2010,[175] and Carl Stein's publication entitled *The New Companies Act Unlocked – A Businessperson's Guide* in 2011.[176] John F. Olson observes that the new approach to 'enhance not only shareholder profits but also societal welfare' is signified primarily by 'the amount of power, including that of direct participation, bestowed on employee [and other stakeholder] groups to participate in [the] governance of enterprises and . . . the number of opportunities provided by the Companies Act for access to the courts'.[177]

### *Some of the Documented Justifications of the Theory*

As the AESVA approach is formally launched for the first time in these terms in this book, there has not been any documented justification thereof of which I am aware. Therefore, the justifications provided hereunder are presented for the first time with respect to the AESVA.

It is worth noting that the documentation of these justifications can only be properly accomplished if the fundamental elements of the approach, as reflected in different sections of the Act, are examined closely.[178] Those fundamental elements, arising from the wording of the AESVA approach, are as follows: (a) the empowerment of corporate constituencies beyond just shareholders, (b) the availability of a broad range of remedies, (c) the opportunity for corporate constituencies to apply for remedies in the public interest, with leave of the court, (d) the recognition that the protection of the company's legal interests can be undertaken by a broad range of corporate constituencies and, generally, with leave of the court, and (e) the ability to hold any person liable for loss or damage suffered as a result of the contravention of any provision of the Act by that person. These elements are discussed in turn.

## The Empowerment of Corporate Constituencies Beyond Just Shareholders

The notion of empowering non-shareholder corporate constituencies by means of access to remedies, primarily judicial ones, is at the heart of the AESVA approach. The specific remedies that are provided will, if widely accepted, differ from jurisdiction to jurisdiction, but the element of empowering stakeholders, rather than leaving them at the mercy of directors and shareholders as far as enforcement is concerned, will remain constant and invariable.

The range of stakeholders empowered with a right of action, other than shareholders, includes directors, prescribed officers, a trade union representing employees of the company or another representative of employees of the company, representatives of persons who, for some other reason, cannot act in their own names; and any person who may have suffered any loss or damage as a result of a contravention of any provision of the Act. The range of corporate constituent groups empowered by different sections of the Act clearly indicates an intentionally broad coverage of constituencies by the legislature. This is particularly interesting as this coverage appears to acknowledge or appreciate a broad role of remedies as the supervision of the use of corporate power to minimise or eradicate directorial self-serving misconduct, rather than the exclusive protection of shareholders.[179]

Lawrence E. Mitchell argues that since fiduciary obligations, for example, are designed to deal with a variety of different types of conflict of interest, and not only directors' self-dealing at the expense of shareholders, the indiscriminate blending of these different types of restraint, together with limited enforcement mechanisms, as reflected within the conventional corporate law structure, has unfortunately (and erroneously) produced the fiduciary formulation that focuses directors' duties on shareholders' interests.[180]

Consequently, if the role of corporate law is to be understood in this manner (that is, as intended, to restrain a variety of conflicts of interest in respect of which there is a potential for any of the corporate constituencies to be victims), then the apparent significance of directors' duties as a determining factor for designing a legal enforcement framework is terribly misplaced, particularly since most of the actions leading to the vindication of the interests of the company will invariably be a result of a breach of some fiduciary obligation by directors. This is notwithstanding that the current Companies Act appears to regulate derivative litigation proceedings independently of the fiduciary obligations.

As argued throughout this book, a variety of judicial and statutory corporate constituency mechanisms permitting the consideration of non-shareholder corporate constituencies' interests may well lead to increased public scrutiny, extra-legal constituent group responses, and possible external governmental regulation. This will overcome the limitation of having derivative action proceedings as the only enforcement mechanism that should be made available to non-shareholder corporate constituencies.

This recognition is reflected, for example, in the specific mechanics of stakeholder empowerment as they apply under the South African Companies Act of 2008. Unlike other corporate governance models under corporate laws of other jurisdictions, the AESVA approach proactively encourages and bestows powers of direct participation in the governance of enterprises upon shareholder and non-shareholder corporate constituent groups.

## The Availability of a Broad Range of Remedies

Unlike the EMS approach, which avails corporate constituencies only the opportunity to institute derivative proceedings, the AESVA goes further and avails a complete bouquet of corporate law remedies to corporate constituencies. From the relevant statutory provisions in the Act, remedies that can be instituted include (a) an application for an order to restrain the company from doing anything inconsistent with the Act,[181] (b) representative actions,[182] (c) legal proceedings to protect the legal interests of the company (i.e., derivative actions),[183] and (d) proceedings to claim any loss or damage suffered as a result of the contravention of any provision of the Act.[184] This makes the AESVA the only approach in corporate governance that affords a broad right of action to a variety of corporate constituencies, in addition to shareholders. However, the Act's silence on whether the interpretation of 'the best interests of the company' is broader than the conventional meaning accorded at common law renders unworkable the enforcement of derivative litigations by corporate constituent groups other than shareholders. This is particularly concerning as the language of s 76(3)(b) restates the exact wording of the directors' duty to promote the best interests of the company at common law without indicating whether a different meaning is intended under the Act.

## The Opportunity for Corporate Constituencies to Apply for Remedies in the Public Interest, with Leave of the Court

In addition to being broadly inclusive of a broad range of stakeholders and providing for an extensive range of remedies, the AESVA also permits the enforcement of corporate law remedies in the public interest, with leave of the court. The classic example of such public interest litigation is found in s 157(1)(d) of the Companies Act, 2008.[185] Although this is a standing provision, it nevertheless provides no cause of action as a basis for the standing. But, it is extremely important as it covers all causes of action that are provided for or recognised under the Act. Taking into account the broad remedies that are provided for in the Act, this sub-section basically means that one can apply, in the public interest, for an order to restrain the company from doing anything inconsistent with the Act or commence proceedings to protect the legal interests of the company in the public interest. It appears that claims for loss or damage suffered as a result of contraventions of provisions of the Act may also be brought in the public interest pursuant to the provisions of this section.

The Constitutional Court confirmed the far-reaching implications of the legal standing that is exercised in the public interest.[186] In the case of *Ferreira v Levin*,[187] O'Reagan J observed that:

> [T]he possibility that applicants may be granted standing on the grounds that they are acting in the public interest is a new departure in our law. Even the old *actiones populares* of Roman Law afforded a right to act in the public interest only in narrowly circumscribed causes of action. [This] is the provision in which the expansion of the ordinary rules of standing is most obvious and it needs to be interpreted in the light of the special role that the courts now play in our constitutional democracy.[188]

Given the similarities between the section of the Interim Constitution which was being applied and s 157(1)(d) of the Companies Act, the views of the Court in the case of *Ferreira v Levin*[189] are equally applicable in determining the breadth of the AESVA approach in the exercise of legal standing in the public interest.

It must, however, be appreciated that the exercise of legal standing in the public interest is subject to leave of the court. The case of *Ferreira v Levin*[190] still offers guidance as to how courts should approach the granting of legal standing in the public interest. In that case, O'Reagan J continued to say

> [The court] will be circumspect in affording applicants standing . . . and will require an applicant to show that he or she is genuinely acting in the public interest. Factors relevant to determining whether a person is genuinely acting in the public interest will include considerations such as: whether there is another reasonable and effective manner in which the challenge can be brought; the nature of the relief sought, and the extent to which it is of general and prospective application; and the range of persons or groups who may be directly or indirectly affected by any order made by the court and the opportunity that those persons or groups have had to present evidence and argument to the court. These factors will need to be considered in the light of the facts and circumstances of each case.[191]

This legal standing can be extremely useful in the context of attempts by members of the public to take measures to put an end to illicit financial flows perpetrated within groups of companies, for example.[192]

The recognition that the protection of the company's legal interests can be undertaken by a broad range of corporate constituencies and, generally, with leave of the court, is one of the contributions of AESVA is the appreciation that the protection of the company's legal interests is not the exclusive domain of the shareholders, as it was previously taken for granted. The conventional belief that the company's legal interest could only be protected by the company alone and, exceptionally, by the shareholders, was admittedly based on a belief that the fiduciary obligations of directors solely serve the purpose of exclusively protecting the interests of the company and its shareholders.[193] The AESVA departs from this conventional approach by recognising that the company's legal interests can be protected by other corporate constituencies, as the overarching purpose of fiduciary obligations is not the exclusive protection of the shareholders, but the supervision of the use of corporate power in order to minimise or eradicate directorial self-serving misconduct. In the South African context, this realisation is reflected in the wording of s 165(2), which provides for extended standing to commence proceedings to protect the legal interests of companies (i.e., derivative actions).

The ability to hold any person liable for loss or damage suffered as a result of the contravention of any provision of the Act by that person.

The seemingly far-reaching element of the AESVA is reflected in s 218(2) of the South African Companies Act, which purports to impose liability upon any person for any loss or damage that could be suffered by any other person as a result of the first person's contravention of any provision of the Act. The language of the subsection, although seemingly overly broad, is circumscribed by the commonly accepted corporate law conventions which are either reflected in the Act or have not been constitutionally challenged as being outdated and unnecessary.

Firstly, liability for loss or damage does not automatically accrue without there having been a cause of action, which is followed by legal proceedings. This is acknowledged by the Companies Act itself when it makes it clear that any application or action under the Act may be exercised either directly, indirectly pursuant to some representative action, or in the public interest.[194] Therefore, the first hurdle that a person seeking to hold another liable has to clear is that such liability has to be determined by the court following formal legal proceedings which are based on a legally recognisable cause of action. Absent these, one cannot attach liability to any other person merely on the basis of a contravention of the Act.

Secondly, if the liability asserted in terms of s 218(2) relates to the breach of the corporate constitution, then the party seeking compensation for loss or damage has to prove that he is a party to the corporate constitution. Section 15(6) of the South African Companies Act entrenches a universally accepted rule that:

> [A] company's Memorandum of Incorporation, and any rules of the company, are binding – (a) between the company and each shareholder; (b) between or among the shareholders of the company; and (c) between the company and – (i) each director or prescribed officer of the company; or (ii) any other person serving the company as a member of a committee of the board – in the exercise of their respective functions within the company.[195]

This provision endorses a longstanding legal principle that 'a third party cannot interfere in the terms and conditions contained in an agreement between [two] other parties'.[196] In the cases of *Letseng Diamonds Ltd v JCI Ltd and Others; Trinity Asset Management (Pty) Ltd and Others v Investec Bank Ltd*,[197] the court decided that 'the terms of the agreement only operate between [contracting parties] and no one else. . . . This rule preventing strangers from interfering in contracts is fundamental to any rational system of jurisprudence'.

The above limitations on the application of s 218(2) clearly show that the last element of the AESVA, as reflected therein, does not unguardedly open up instances of liability for the contravention of the Act. What this element, and by implication subsection 218(2), does is to provide the statutory basis for aggrieved parties to claim for loss or damage suffered as a result of the contravention of the Act without compromising the requirement for a cause of action and for privity of contract, as it relates to the company's Memorandum of Incorporation.

## *The Shortcomings of the Theory*

The lack of standard, universal mechanisms for the empowerment of stakeholders in accordance with the core elements of the AESVA approach is concerning. The standardisation of stakeholder empowerment mechanisms could be pivotal, as the proliferation of dissimilar mechanisms will invariably affect the practical application and utility of the AESVA approach at a universal level.

It also appears that the extended standing to institute derivative proceedings under the AESVA approach is without any substantive normative foundation as the meaning of what constitutes 'the best interests of the company' in terms of s 76(3)(b) has not been clarified in the statute. This is the primary reasoning that the proponents of the shareholder primacy theory use when they insist that any other model which may subject the interests of shareholders to any other corporate constituent group under any circumstance is effectively nonsensical, as it could lead to multiplicity of litigation (the so-called 'floodgates' argument).

The AESVA theory's non-expressive response to the question of whether 'the best interests of the company' extend to all corporate constituent groups is arguably capable of being justified by the apparent legislature's preparedness, as demonstrated in the extended standing for derivative actions under s 165(2), to accept that the ability to vindicate the breach of the company's legal interests should be grounded on the need to supervise the use of corporate power rather than the exclusive protection of shareholder interests, as it was previously the case.

The main shortcoming of the AESVA approach is alleged to lie in its potential to encourage floodgates of litigation in commercial law. Carl Stein argues that a generous enforcement scheme to which a plethora of stakeholders may avail themselves could '[u]nfortunately . . . lead to increased litigation and a fair amount of "remedy shopping"'.[198]

In dismissing a similar objection to class actions in terms of section 38 of the Constitution on the basis that the courts would be engulfed by interfering busy-bodies rushing to court for spurious reasons, Froneman J responded by vehemently stating that:

> But I also think that the possibility of unjustified litigation can be curtailed by making it a procedural requirement that leave must be sought from the High Court to proceed on a representative basis prior to actually embarking on that road.[199]

The main argument in this case of *Ngxuza and Others v Permanent Secretary, Department of Welfare, Eastern Cape*[200] was that because of the limited standing provisions in common law, this Constitutional provision needed to be accorded restricted interpretation. The Judge was at pains to point out that there was no cogent reason for a restrictive interpretation of the provisions of a similarly worded section 38 because of the narrow content given to standing under the common law, particularly not in relation to so-called public law litigation.[201] Quoting *Maluleke v MEC, Health and Welfare, Northern Province*,[202] the judge clarified that the many practical difficulties that may arise 'cannot justify the denial of such action when the Constitution makes specific provision for it'.[203]

While it is commendable that the remedies for non-shareholder constituencies under the AESVA approach are not limited to the derivative action proceedings, the threat that any of the relevant corporate constituency groups could institute legal proceedings against companies at a whim is, as shown in the above case, more imaginary than real. Therefore, the threat that corporate directors will not be free to take business decisions without the fear of being second-guessed is not backed up by practical reality.

### *Concluding Observations*

Despite its shortcomings, the AESVA approach appears to be the better approach for balancing the interests of both shareholder and the non-shareholder corporate constituencies in corporate law enforcement. In an environment where the different normative statements on the protection of non-shareholder constituencies, as contained in different statutory corporate constituency mechanisms, lack a clear enforcement scheme and are thus rendered nugatory, the AESVA approach presents a relatively consistent and effective scheme of enforcement.

## ANALYSIS OF THE CRITIQUE AGAINST THEORIES SUPPORTING THE EXTENSION OF LEGAL STANDING FOR NON-SHAREHOLDER CORPORATE CONSTITUENCIES

This part of the chapter is dedicated to the full consideration of the main critique against the theories supporting the possible extension of legal standing for non-shareholder corporate constituencies to access corporate law remedies. Much has been written on the shareholder primacy norm and the Stakeholder Theory, and the analysis of the critique of those theories is outside the scope of this research.

The core objection to any broadly inclusive approach to corporate law enforcement is that such an approach will invariably require directors to engage in an almost impossible task of balancing the interests of various constituencies.[204]

## IS BALANCING THE INTERESTS OF VARIOUS CONSTITUENCIES IMPOSSIBLE?

Writing in connection with corporate constituency statutes in the United States, the Committee on Corporate Laws of the Business Law Section of the American Bar Association commented that:

> [T]o require directors to balance the interests of various constituencies without according primacy to shareholder interests, would be profoundly troubling. . . . If directors are required to consider other interests as well, the decision-making process will become a balancing act or search for compromise. When directors must not only decide what their duty of loyalty mandates, but also to whom their duty of loyalty runs (and in what proportions) poorer decisions can be expected.[205]

Many years later, Henry Hansmann and Reinier Kraakman insisted that a move towards a single model of corporate law in the world was unavoidable as, in their words, 'all [alternative models to the shareholder primacy norm] have lost much of their normative appeal'.[206]

It is quite clear from the above sentiments that the core of the critique against broadly inclusive normative and enforcement approaches is, firstly, the potential impossibility or difficulty posed to directors in balancing competing interests of various constituencies; and, secondly, the lack of consistent normative basis for the justification of the balancing results arrived at by directors. The discussion below shows that balancing competing interests is neither impossible nor unduly difficult, as any suggestion that the conflicts of shareholders and those of non-shareholder constituencies are direct is not only fallacious,[207] but that there is, within Anglo-American jurisdictions, a normative justification for balancing conflicting interests of corporate constituencies. In this regard, I will show the relevance of the directors' duty to promote the best interests of the company as a means of empowering directors to balance competing interests, as a matter of law. Then the book will show that the business judgment rule provides a normative basis for justifying the balancing act by the directors.

## THE DUTY TO PROMOTE THE BEST INTERESTS OF THE COMPANY AND THE BALANCING OF COMPETING INTERESTS

In response to the above core critique, the close analysis of universal corporate law tools, which have been in use for a number of decades, points out that it is neither impossible nor extremely difficult to balance the competing interests of various corporate constituencies.

It is universally accepted within common law jurisdictions that directors owe the duty to promote the 'best interests of the company'. While the 'the best interests of the company' are required to be determined objectively by interpreting that concept as it is understood in the law, it is indisputable that the test for determining whether the duty is complied with by the director is subjective as to means (what is to be done in order to promote the company's interests), but objective as to ends (the interests to be promoted, i.e., the interests of the company). In so far as the subjective element of the test is concerned, directors are required to act *bona fide* in what they consider – not what the courts consider – to be in the interests of the company. This means that the directors must proceed upon what, in their honest opinion, is for the benefit of the company as a whole. Herein lies the opportunity for the directors to be able to balance competing interests of various corporate constituencies. In fact, and particularly in relation to large public companies, there exists an important strain of normative thought that recognises the virtues of granting substantial discretion to directors in corporate decision-making, which is known as 'the Manager-oriented Model'.[208]

The essence of the above model is underpinned by the belief that professional corporate managers are capable of serving as disinterested technocratic fiduciaries who can guide business corporations to perform in ways that would serve the general public interest.[209] In other words, as disinterested fiduciaries, directors can, using this approach, subjugate, if necessary, the narrow interests of shareholders to the broader interests of the general public and that can be justified as being in accordance with the subjective test of the duty to promote the interests of the company as a whole.

This discretion is bolstered by the reality that, even in jurisdictions with no formal business judgment rule, the law will not question the wisdom of the director's decision as to the means to serve the company's interests.

## THE BUSINESS JUDGMENT RULE

The business judgment rule, which, in its simplest form, is a rule that enjoins the courts to defer to the board of directors' judgment absent highly unusual exceptions, is arguably a potent normative justification for balancing conflicting interests of corporate constituencies. This is because the rule does not apply as a defence only to the allegation of a director's breach of the duty of care. The rule has always been regarded as a defence to the allegation of a director's breach of the duty to promote the best interests of the company as well.

In the jurisdiction of the rule's origin – Delaware – the Supreme Court in *McMullin v Beran*,[210] confirmed that the business judgment rule 'operates as both a procedural guide for litigants and a substantive rule of law [and applies to] any one of [the board's] triad of fiduciary duties, loyalty, good faith or due care'.[211] In the South African context, s 76 (4) provides, in material terms, that:

> [A] particular director of a company will have satisfied the obligations of subsection (3)(b) [relating to the duty to exercise the powers and perform the functions of director in the best interests of the company] and (c) [relating to the duty of care, skill & diligence] if (i) the director has taken reasonably diligent steps to become informed about the matter; (ii) either (aa) the director had no material personal financial interest in the subject matter of the decision, and had no reasonable basis to know that any related person had a personal financial interest in the matter; or (bb) the director complied with the requirements of section 75 with respect to any interest . . . and (iii) the director made a decision, or supported the decision of a committee or the board, with regard to that matter, and the director had a rational basis for believing, and did believe, that the decision was in the best interests of the company.[212]

The application of the business judgment rule effectively presupposes that a director will satisfy the duty to promote the best interests of the company if he or she (i) took reasonably diligent steps to be informed about the matter, (ii) had no conflicting personal financial interest, and (iii) had a rational basis for believing, and did believe, that the decision was in the best interests of the company. It is the last requirement that shows that in order to comply with the duty, the director's subjective judgment as to whether the decision was in the best interests of the company will suffice. This test elevates the director's discretion in the balancing of competing interests of various corporate constituencies to a similar status as that reflected within the manager-oriented model discussed above.

As correctly observed by Stephen Bainbridge, 'the reference to a "rational business purpose," properly understood, does not contemplate substantive review of the decision's merits'.[213] Michael Dooley confirms this and maintains that '[the word] "rational" is to be equated with conceivable or imaginable and means only that the court will not even look at the board's judgment if there is any possibility that it was actuated by a legitimate business reason'.[214] He concludes that '[i]t clearly does not mean, and cannot legitimately be cited for the proposition, that individual directors must have, and be prepared to put forth, proof of rational basis for their decisions'.[215]

The legal position in determining compliance with the duty to promote the best interests of the company points to the existence of wide directorial discretion, mainly due to the application of the subjective test and the existence of the Manager-oriented Model of governance as an alternative to the shareholder primacy norm. Moreover, the subjection of the duty to promote the best interests of the company to business judgment – with its lower standard of rationality – evidently can easily erode into a prerequisite of reasonableness. This makes the balancing of competing constituencies' interests possible and justifiable as a matter of law. Even if the objective test for determining the best interests of the company can still be insisted upon in jurisdictions that have not formally adopted the business judgment rule, just like the United Kingdom, recent corporate law developments institutionalising the Enlightened Shareholder Value Approach (just like under s 172(1) of the UK Companies Act, 2006) may effectively imply the extension of what constitutes 'the best interests of the company' by including non-shareholder corporate constituencies.

## CONCLUSION AND CHAPTER SYNOPSIS

The intention in this chapter has been to outline the theoretical foundation for recommending the appropriate enforcement legal enforcement framework to be made accessible to non-shareholder corporate constituencies. The chapter opened with a consideration of the theories which are supportive of the traditional corporate law view linking corporate law enforcement to the promotion of shareholder interests. The primary example of these theories was identified as the shareholder primacy theory, in respect of which the main argument is that the single corporate objective of shareholder wealth maximisation is more easily monitored than a disparate, vaguely defined goal of accommodating all affected interests. The theory insists that the shareholders are better suited to guide and discipline directors in carrying out their duties rather than a large group of stakeholders, possibly with irreconcilably divergent views.

It is also at the heart of the shareholder primacy theory that the need for the protection of the shareholder interests, to the exclusion of all others, is necessitated by the fact that non-shareholder corporate constituencies are, unlike shareholders, allegedly able to protect themselves by the terms of the contracts they conclude with the companies. The theory assumes, therefore, that the continued application of the traditional company law enforcement scheme, in terms of which shareholders, directors and liquidators are the primary possible litigants with legal standing, is the only viable legal enforcement framework. This view presupposes that this legal enforcement framework is also capable of being used by shareholder corporate constituencies to benefit non-shareholder corporate constituencies. On the contrary, shareholders and directors lack the incentive to use available avenues of enforcement to benefit non-shareholder corporate constituencies. As for the liquidators, the natural and sensible agenda to be pursued is that of only one non-shareholder constituency group, that is, the creditors.

The second theory discussed under the category of theories supportive of the traditional corporate law view was referred to as the Enlightened Shareholder Value theory (ESVA). Under the ESVA, it has been argued that the essence of the theory is to refrain from burdening directors with the responsibility of owing fiduciary obligations to all affected stakeholders, but at the same time, to allow those directors to promote the interests of non-shareholder constituencies without the fear of being in breach of their fiduciary responsibilities.

While it appears that this may be beneficial to non-shareholder constituencies, the difficulty is that the ability to enforce compliance with or to remedy the breach of such seemingly expanded directors' responsibilities continues to be at the initiative of and exclusively available to shareholders and directors primarily through derivative action proceedings, which, incidentally, consider the right of recovery to be exclusively for the companies.

Addressing the alternative theory to those that perpetuate the continued marriage to traditional corporate law enforcement, the chapter discussed the Stakeholder/Pluralist Theory. It has been seen that the main argument of this theory is that corporate law rules should refrain from constraining directors to an excessively narrow interpretation of their fiduciary responsibilities, which could actually work against the company's interests and require the extension of fiduciary obligation, as a matter of law, to all relevant stakeholders within the company. It has been seen that the same argument is made in respect of the statutory corporate constituency mechanisms, which are in effect in a majority of the states of the United States. It has been pointed out that while the extension of fiduciary duties of directors to all affected corporate constituencies may not be disputable under this theory, one major drawback of the theory concerns the lack of complementary extension of legal standing to all corporate constituencies to institute corporate law remedies.

It was shown that the possible extension of fiduciary obligations to all corporate constituent groups, without a clear enforcement scheme for the benefit of such constituencies, is of no practical utility. This is so because, regardless of being the potential beneficiaries of fiduciary responsibilities, non-shareholder corporate constituencies continue to be at the mercy of shareholders and directors for the enforcement of any breach of such fiduciary responsibilities to them. Moreover, the extension of fiduciary obligations to corporate constituencies, with no further legal mandate, simply implies that the only corporate law remedy which can possibly be considered is that of derivative action proceedings, as any remedy for breach of fiduciary duties should, according to the traditional corporate law view, only benefit the company.

The two theories supporting the possible extension of legal standing to non-shareholder corporate constituent groups were considered in this chapter, as well. These were identified as the Entity Maximisation and the Sustainability Model (EMS) and the Actionable Enlightened Shareholder Value theory (AESVA). Regarding the EMS, it has been argued that the acceptance of the fact that fiduciary obligations are owed to the company as a separate legal person effectively militates against the argument that certain constituencies, particularly the shareholders, are entitled to be given preeminence in the exercise of directors' fiduciary obligations.

As the fiduciary obligations are owed exclusively to the company as an enterprise and not to any of the corporate constituencies, including shareholders, it was argued that there is a potential for all corporate constituencies to bring derivative action proceedings on behalf of the company in an attempt to redress any breach of fiduciary obligations by the directors. While such a potential exists, the reality is that no jurisdiction, except South Africa, has to date extended legal standing for non-shareholder corporate constituencies to bring such derivative action proceedings for the benefit of their companies.

Finally, the chapter considered the introduction to the corporate governance scene of the Actionable Enlightened Shareholder Value Approach (AESVA) following the enactment of the South African Companies Act in 2008. The chapter highlighted that although the specific enforcement mechanisms for stakeholder empowerment under the AESVA may differ from jurisdiction to jurisdiction, what should be common across all jurisdictions that may adopt the AESVA are the fundamental elements concerning (a) the empowerment of corporate constituencies beyond just shareholders, (b) the availability of a broad range of remedies, (c) the opportunity for corporate constituencies to apply for remedies in the public interest, with leave of the court, (d) the recognition that the protection of the company's legal interests can be undertaken by a broad range of corporate constituencies and, generally, with leave of the court, and (e) the ability to hold any person liable for loss or damage suffered as a result of the contravention of any provision of the Act by that person.

It was pointed out that even though the AESVA has its own potential drawbacks, this model is objectively preferable in the quest to find a clear and reasonably enforceable scheme for the benefit of non-shareholder corporate constituencies. That said, the reality is that none of the statutory corporate constituency mechanisms adopted in the Anglo-American jurisdictions of the United Kingdom and the United States, as discussed in detail in chapter 2, expressly incorporate the fundamental elements of this theory in their legal enforcement frameworks, regardless of the theory's utility. Finally, it was shown that the core criticism of inclusive enforcement approaches on the basis of the alleged impossibility or difficulty of balancing competing interests of corporate constituencies is exaggerated.

These theories are illustrated in the following diagram, which serves as a point of reference for the discussion in this book:

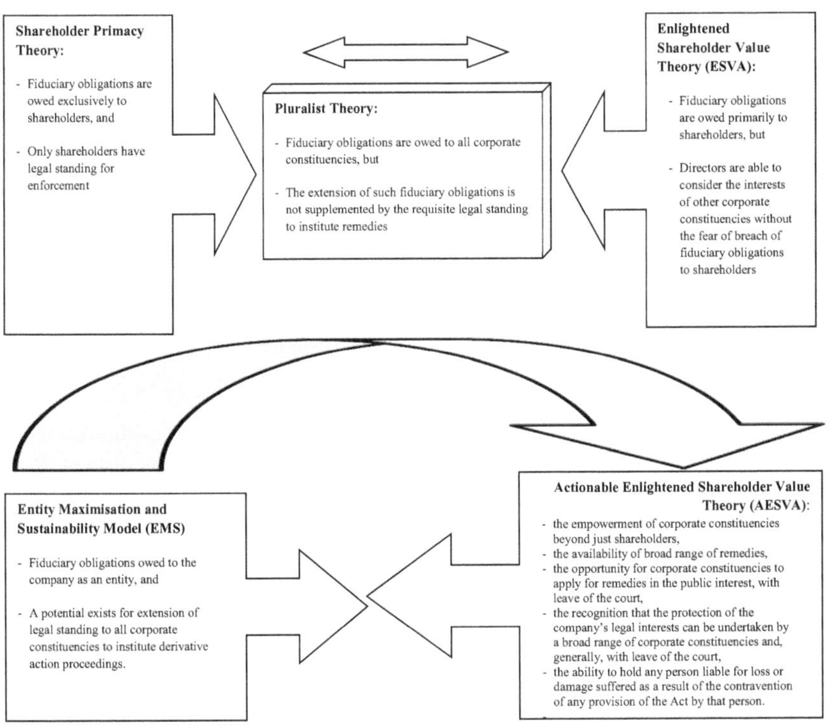


**Figure 1.1 The Rigidity and the Progression of Shareholder Theories.** *Source*: Chapter 2 Mongalo, Tshepo Herbert, 'Corporate Actions and the Empowerment of Non-Shareholder Constituencies' (2015). PhD Thesis submitted at the University of Cape Town.

## NOTES

1. Of late, the debate is being spearheaded by the British Academy, particularly through its publication of a detailed report on 'Purposeful Business' entitled *Policy & Practice for Purposeful Business: The Final Report of the Future of the Corporation Programme* (2021). See also Keay A, 'Tackling the Issue of Corporate Objective: An Analysis of the United Kingdom's Enlightened Shareholder Value Approach' (2007) 29 *Sydney Law Review* 577 (hereafter Keay 'Tackling the Issue of Corporate Objective'). See also Dodd 'For Whom Are Corporate Managers Trustees?' op cit note 3; Berle 'For Whom Corporate Managers Are Trustees', op cit note 4. In Hanks Jr. JJ, 'Non-Stockholder Constituency Statutes: An Idea Whose Time Should Never Have Come' (1989) 3 (12) *INSIGHTS* 20 (hereafter Hanks 'An Idea Whose Time Should Never Have Come'). See also Stephen Bainbridge, 'In Defense of the Shareholder Wealth Maximization Norm: A Reply to Professor Green' (1993) 50 *Washington and Lee Law Review* 1423; The Company Law Review Steering Group, UK Department of Trade and Industry, *Modern Company Law for a Competitive Economy: The Strategic Framework* (1999) at 37, available at http://www.berr.gov.uk/files/file23279.pdf; Roe M, 'The Shareholder Wealth Maximization Norm and Industrial Organization' (2001) 149 *University of Pennsylvania Law Review* 2063; Bainbridge S, 'Director Primacy: The Means and Ends of Corporate Governance' (2003) 97 *Northwestern University Law Review* 547 at 549, 552, 563.

2. Salacuse JW, 'Corporate Governance in the New Century' (2004) 25 (3) *The Company Lawyer* 69, at 74. Today, legal sources such as Connecticut's mandatory Corporate Constituency statute and the British Academy's Recommendations in its Final Report of the Future of the Corporation Programme ('British Academy's *Policy & Practice for Purposeful Business'*) unequivocally demonstrate the existence of fiduciary duties for directors towards non-shareholder interests within companies. In particular, the 'British Academy's *Policy & Practice on Purposeful Business*' recommendation that the legal position in many common law jurisdictions that directors must promote the interests of shareholders ('shareholder primacy') and those of other stakeholders only to the extent that they enhance long-term shareholder value ('enlightened shareholder value'), is unsatisfactory as it subordinates the interests of most stakeholders to those of shareholders, even in the long term. The Academy maintains that directors should, rather, be required to promote the interests of other stakeholders in their own right. (Op cit note 48, at 22).

3. Arguing that the Enlightened Shareholder Value Approach (ESVA) does not take the consideration of non-shareholder constituencies' interests very far, Andrew Keay argues that ESVA only seeks to provide a broader context for directors to fulfil their fiduciary duty only to the shareholders generally. In this manner, the ESVA can be classified as a 'shareholders first interpretation'. This point is confirmed by the British Academy's *Policy & Practice on Purposeful Business* (op cit note 49). See also Corporations and Markets Advisory Committee, *The Social Responsibility of Corporations* (2006) at 103–107, available at http://www.camac.gov.au/camac/camac.nsf/byHeadline/PDFFinal+Reports+ 2006/$file/CSR_Report.pdf, accessed on 4 January 2013; This view is also reflected in the Parliamentary Joint Committee

on Corporations and Financial Services, Commonwealth of Australia, *Corporate Responsibility: Managing Risk and Creating Value* (2006), available at www.aph.gov.au/Senate/committee/corporations_ctte/corporate_responsibility/report/report.pdf at 51, accessed on 4 May 2023.

4. Op cit note 49, at 578. See also a passionate argument strongly motivating why the shareholder primacy theory is the only appropriate one in business corporations in Stephen M Bainbridge, *The Profit Motive: Defending Shareholder Value Maximization* (Cambridge University Press, 2023) and Anita Indira Anand, *Shareholder-driven Corporate Governance* (Oxford University Press, 2020). This argument is further enhanced by James J. Hanks Jr. in 'Playing with Fire', op cit note 7, at 109–118. However, some management and ethics scholars have argued forcefully that stakeholder theory is so pervasive that shareholder primacy is in fact extinct. See, for example, Freeman RE, 'The Politics of Stakeholder Theory: Some Future Directions' (1994) 4 *Business Ethics Quarterly* 409 at 413.

5. Keay, 'Tackling the Issue of Corporate Objective' op cit note 48, at 578.

6. As shown fully in this chapter and chapter 3, this belief is regarded as being problematic because there are forceful authorities who have argued that the primary role of the fiduciary obligations of directors is to restrain directorial or managerial self-dealing, the impact of which is not only detrimental to shareholders but also to other corporate constituencies whose financial well-being is tied to the success of the corporation. See, among others, Mitchell, 'A Theoretical and Practical Framework', op cit note 6.

7. Company Law Review Steering Group, UK Department of Trade and Industry, *Modern Company Law for a Competitive Economy: The Strategic Framework* (1999), op cit note 41, at 34–35. This view is in clear contrast with the view of the British Academy on 'purposeful company' and the view that the primary role of fiduciary duties is to prevent self-interested conduct or managerial misconduct by directors, rather than solely protecting shareholders. (See, infra, para. 4.2).

8. Ibid., at 37.

9. The Hampel Committee, *Report on Corporate Governance (Final Committee Report)* (1998), Para 1.17.

10. Sheehy B, 'Scrooge – The Reluctant Stakeholder: Theoretical Problems in the Shareholder-Stakeholder Debate' (2005) 14 *University of Miami Business Law Review* 193, at 208.

11. Tshepo Mongalo, 'Corporate Governance and the Constitution: A Case for Broadening the Stakeholders' in S. Pete and M. du Plessis (eds.), *Constitutional Democracy in South Africa 1994–2004* (2004) 169, at 172.

12. R. Clark, *Corporate Law* (1986), 17–19. See also the encapsulation of the Shareholder Primacy Theory in the American Law Institute's *Principles of Corporate Governance* (op cit note 43).

13. Op cit note 48, at 580.

14. Berle, 'For Whom Corporate Managers Are Trustees', op cit note 4, at 1049.

15. Milton Friedman & Rose Friedman, *Capitalism and Freedom* (40th Anniversary ed. 2002), 133.

16. Playing with Fire, op cit note 7.

17. Macey JR, 'An Economic Analysis of the Various Rationales for Making Shareholders the Exclusive Beneficiaries of Corporate Fiduciary Duties' (1991) 21 *Stetson Law Review* 23.

18. Bainbridge, 'In Defense of the Shareholder Wealth Maximization Norm', op cit note 48.

19. Black B & Kraakman R, 'A Self-Enforcing Model of Corporate Law' (1996) 109 *Harvard Law Review* 1911.

20. Smith DG, 'The Shareholder Primacy Norm' (1998) 23 *Journal of Corporate Law* 277. As it is argued in para 4.2 below, this view is in clear contrast with the view that the primary role of fiduciary duties is to primarily prevent self-interested conduct or managerial misconduct by directors, rather than the sole protection of shareholders.

21. Hansmann H & Kraakman R, 'Toward a Single Model of Corporate Law?' in JA McCahery, P Moerland, T Raaijmakers, and L Renneboog (eds.), *Corporate Governance Regimes: Convergence and Diversity* (2003), 56–82.

22. This view is in clear contrast with the view that the primary role of fiduciary duties is to primarily prevent self-interested conduct or managerial misconduct by directors, rather than the sole protection of shareholders. (See, infra, para. 4.2).

23. Op cit note 48.

24. Op cit note 1.

25. Op cit notes 7 and 48.

26. Ibid. However, as argued elsewhere (para 4.2 below), this view is in clear contrast with the view that the primary role of fiduciary duties is to primarily prevent self-interested conduct or managerial misconduct by directors, rather than the sole protection of shareholders.

27. Hanks, 'An Idea Whose Time Should Never Have Come', op cit note 48.

28. R. Clark, op cit note 533, at 679–680. This view is in clear contrast with the view that the primary role of fiduciary duties is to primarily prevent self-interested conduct or managerial misconduct by directors, rather than the sole protection of shareholders. (See, infra, para. 4.2).

29. Tackling the Issue of Corporate Objective, at 583–584.

30. Jensen M & Meckling W, 'Theory of the Firm: Managerial Behaviour, Agency Costs, and Ownership Structure' (1976) 3 *Journal of Financial Economics* 305.

31. See also Van der Weide ME, 'Against Fiduciary Duties to Corporate Stakeholders' (1996) 21 *Delaware Journal of Corporate Law* 27 at 56–57.

32. The Committee on Corporate Law, 'Other Constituency Statutes: Potential for Confusion' (1990) 45 *The Business Lawyer* 2253 at 2269.

33. Van der Weide, 'Against Fiduciary Duties to Corporate Stakeholders', op cit note 78, at 68.

34. Ibid., at 69. This view is in clear contrast with the view that the primary role of fiduciary duties is to primarily prevent self-interested conduct or managerial misconduct by directors rather than the sole protection of shareholders. (See infra, para. 4.2).

35. An Idea Whose Time Should Never Have Come, op cit note 48, at 22.

36. 'To the extent that stakeholder contracts are imperfect or incomplete, stakeholders may retain a residual interest as well as a fixed claim'. See Fisch J, 'Measuring Efficiency in Corporate Law: The Role of Shareholder Primacy' (2005) *Fordham Law Legal Studies Research Paper No. 105*, at 30. See http://papers.ssrn.com/sol3/papers.cfm?abstract_id=878391, accessed on 14 January 2013.

37. Playing with Fire, op cit note 7, at 115.

38. As Professor Fisch has observed: '[T]hey [the shareholders] will bear the costs of misdeeds or self-dealing by other stakeholders even if they exit'. Op cit note 83, at 26.

39. Hansmann and Kraakman, 'A Single Model of Corporate Law', op cit note 68, at 58.

40. Ibid.

41. Ibid.

42. Ibid.

43. Ibid.

44. See, for example, Millon D, 'Communitarianism in Corporate Law: Foundations and Law Reform Strategies' in Lawrence E. Mitchell (ed.), *Progressive Corporate Law: New Perspectives on Law, Culture, and Society* (1995), at 5.

45. Ibid.

46. Ibid., at 6.

47. Ibid.

48. See, for example, Playing with Fire, op cit note 7, at 117, where it is acknowledged that 'the corporation is not the only form of business organisation in which the residual owners benefit from goods and services furnished by others'.

49. Op cit note 6, at 592.

50. See, for example, Melvin A. Eisenberg, *The Structure of the Corporation: A Legal Analysis* (1976), at 3–4, pointing out that many fundamental corporate changes do not require shareholder approval.

51. Mitchell, 'A Theoretical and Practical Framework', op cit note 6, at 592.

52. R. Clark, *Corporate Law* (1986), at 678.

53. Since directorial duties, particularly fiduciary obligations, have been found to be more about the supervision of the use of corporate power for the primary purpose of minimising or eradicating self-serving misconduct on the part of the directors, using corporate law remedies to ensure exclusive protection of shareholders is fundamentally mistaken. This is discussed in detail in chapter 3.

54. See the full exposition of this conundrum in chapter 3.

55. Mitchell, 'A Theoretical and Practical Framework', op cit note 6, at 641.

56. See Millon D, 'Theories of the Corporation' (1990) *Duke Law Journal* 201, at 201.

57. See, for example, *Blasius Indus. v Atlas Corp.*, 564 A.2d 651, 663 (Del. Ch. 1988), describing directors as stockholders' agents.

58. Of course, legal doctrine traditionally has held that directors possess original and undelegated power and are not agents of the stockholders.

59. [1906] 2 Ch 35.

60. Ibid., at 42. See also *R v Mall* 1959 (4) SA 607, at 623.

61. *Ngxuza and Others v Permanent Secretary, Department of Welfare, Eastern Cape & another,* op cit note 246, 624D-E.

62. Millon, 'Theories of the Corporation', op cit note 103, at 224.

63. Mitchell, 'A Theoretical and Practical Framework', op cit note 6, at 585.

64. Ibid., at 34. See also Keay, 'Tackling the Issue of the Corporate Objective', op cit note 48, at 589. Ho 'Director's Duty to Promote the Success of the Company', op cit note 17, at 19.

65. Although this theory is not expressly adopted by the South African Companies Act, 2008, Mongalo and Scott note that the theory is encapsulated in the King Report on Corporate Governance for South Africa (2016) (King IV), which recognises the need for the governing body to adopt a stakeholder-inclusive approach that balances the needs, interests and expectations of material stakeholders in the best interests of the organisation over time. (King IV, 2016, at 71) (See Mongalo TH & Scott T, *Corporate Law and Corporate Governance: An Overview of Business Undertakings in South Africa,* 2ed (2022), at 252).

66. This possible impact of the Pluralist Approach was acknowledged by the CLRSG as early as 1999 in the Company Law Review Steering Group, Modern Company Law for a Competitive Economy: The Strategic Framework, op cit note 41, at 33–36.

67. Ibid., at 37–38. The CLRSG effectively acknowledged that the Pluralist theory would require the law:

> [Being] modified to include other objectives [besides maximising shareholder value] so that a company is required to serve a wider range of interests, not subordinate to, or as a means of achieving shareholder value (as envisaged in the enlightened shareholder value view), but as valid in their own right. (Ibid.)

See also Ho, 'Director's Duty to Promote the Success of the Company', op cit note 17, at 17, who argues that '[a] careful examination of section 172 of the [UK] Companies Act, 2006 shows that it simply reflects existing law and modern business practices [and] does no more than reinstate the practical reality'. (Ibid.)

68. Op cit note 39, at 111–112.

69. Ibid., at 111.

70. Armour J, Deakin S & Konzelmann S, 'Shareholder Primacy and the Trajectory of UK Corporate Governance' (2003) 41 *British Journal of Industrial Relations* 531 at 537.

71. The Company Law Review Steering Group, *Modern Company Law for a Competitive Economy: Developing the Framework* (1999), at 35. Available at http://www.berr.gov.uk/bbf/co-act-2006/clr-review/page25086.html.

72. See s 172(1) of the UK's Companies Act, 2006.

73. Non-Stockholder Constituency Statutes are also referred to as 'Non-Shareholder Constituency Statutes', 'Constituency Statutes', or 'Stakeholder Statutes'.

74. For a list of States with the Non-Stockholder Constituency Statutes, see Anthony Bisconti, 'The Double Bottom Line: Can Constituency Statutes Protect Socially Responsible Corporations Stuck in *Revlon* Land' (2009) 42 *Loyola of Los Angeles Law Review* 765, at 768. Bisconti stated that at the time of writing [the

note] (in 2009), the following states had enacted constituency statutes: Arizona, Connecticut, Florida, Georgia, Hawaii, Idaho, Illinois, Indiana, Iowa, Kentucky, Louisiana, Maine, Maryland, Massachusetts, Minnesota, Missouri, Nebraska, Nevada, New Jersey, New Mexico, New York, North Dakota, Ohio, Oregon, Pennsylvania, Rhode Island, South Dakota, Tennessee, Vermont, Virginia, Wisconsin and Wyoming.

75. See Oswald LJ, 'Evaluating Corporate Constituency Statutes Under the Takings Clause' (1998) *The Journal of Corporation Law* 1, at 4; Bainbridge SM, 'Interpreting Nonshareholder Constituency Statutes' (1992) 19 *Pepperdine Law Review* 971, at 973; Anderson JA, 'Maine's Non-Shareholder Constituency Statute' (1993) 45 *Maine Law Review* 153, at 153–154; Alexander JC, Spivey MF & Marr MW, 'Nonshareholder Constituency Statutes and Shareholder Wealth' (1997) 21 *Journal of Banking and Finance* 417–432, at 418; McDonnell BH, 'Corporate Constituency Statutes and Employee Governance' (2004) 30 (4) *William Mitchell Law Review* 1227, at 1228; Macey JR & Miller GP, 'Corporate Stakeholders: A Contractual Perspective' (1993) 43 *University of Toronto Law Journal* 401, at 402; Hale, 'Corporate Law and Stakeholders', op cit note 32, at 827.

76. See, for example, Hale, 'Corporate Law and Stakeholders', op cit note 32.

77. See also Ho, 'Director's Duty to Promote the Success of the Company', op cit note 17.

78. CLRSG, 'Modern Company Law for a Competitive Economy: Developing the Framework' (URN 00/656), para 3.51.

79. J. Clarke, 'Introduction' in *Theories of Corporate Governance* (2004), at 13–14.

80. Keay, 'Tackling the Issue of Corporate Objective', op cit note 47, at 602.

81. Hansmann H & Kraakman R, 'The End of History for Corporate Law' (2001) 89 *Georgetown Law Journal* 439, at 439.

82. Michael Jensen M, 'Value Maximisation, Stakeholder Theory and the Corporate Objective Function' (2001) 7 (3) *European Financial Management* 297, at 309.

83. Parliamentary Joint Committee on Corporations and Financial Services, Commonwealth of Australia, *Corporate Responsibility: Managing Risk and Creating Value* (2006), at 59. Available at www.aph.gov.au/Senate/committee/corporations _ctte/corporate_responsibility/report/report. pdf.

84. Ho VH, '"Enlightened Shareholder Value": Corporate Governance Beyond the Shareholder-Stakeholder Divide' (2010) *SelectedWorks* (From the SelectedWorks of Virginia E Ho). Available at http://works.bepress.com/virginia_ho/3, accessed on 11 May 2012.

85. Ibid., at 3.

86. Ibid., 20–21.

87. Ibid.

88. Ibid., at 21. See also Williams CA & Conley JM, 'An Emerging Third Way? The Erosion of the Anglo-American Shareholder Value Construct' (2005) 38 *Cornell International Law Journal* 493, at 500.

89. 116. Dodd, 'For Whom Are Corporate Managers Trustees?' (1932) op cit note 3, at 1161.

90. See, for example, Norwitz TS, 'The Metaphysics of Time: A Radical Corporate Vision' (1991) 46 *Business Law* 377, at 378; Gavis AC, 'A Framework For Satisfying Corporate Directors' Responsibilities Under State Nonshareholder Constituency Statutes: The Use Of Explicit Contracts' (1990) 138 *University of Pennsylvania Law Review* 1451, at 1466, wherein the author emphasises that non-shareholder constituencies' ability to contract with corporation is an inadequate protection, if at all. See also Johnson L & Millon D, 'Missing the Point About State Take-over Statutes', (1989) 87 *Michigan Law Review* 846, at 848.

91. For example, shareholders can protect themselves through diversification, selling their shares, etc.

92. Writing in 1997, Kathleen Hale observed that 'Nearly all states have enacted laws known as Stakeholder Statutes that allow corporate directors and executives to consider stakeholders' interests without breaching fiduciary obligations to shareholders' (Hale, 'Corporate Law and Stakeholders', op cit note 32). The CLRSG also eschewed the Pluralist Theory in favour of the ESVA, as the former would have necessitated extensive reforms in the area of directors' duties by requiring the directors to owe fiduciary duties to non-shareholder constituencies. On the other hand, the ESVA does not extend directors' fiduciary duties to non-shareholder constituencies, but it allows the directors to consider the interests of these constituencies without breaching their fiduciary obligations to shareholders.

93. Hart RM & Degener CM, 'Non-Stockholder Constituency Statutes' (1990) 203 *New York Law Journal* 1, at 4.

94. See Greene EF, 'Regulatory and Legislative Responses to Takeover Activity in the 1980s: The United States and Europe' (1991) 69 *Texas Law Review* 1539, at 1564; see also Hanks, 'An Idea Whose Time Should Never Have Come', op cit note 48, at 20.

95. Arguing in relation to Non-Stockholder Constituency Statutes, Garcia FJ, 'Protecting Nonshareholder Interests In The Market For Corporate Control: A Role for State Takeover Statutes' (1990) 23 *University of Michigan Journal of Law Reform* 507, at 518, maintained that the board is *required* to consider the effects on the corporation, including other constituencies.

96. Writing in 1997, Kathleen Hale observed that 'Nearly all states have enacted laws known as Stakeholder Statutes that allow corporate directors and executives to consider stakeholders' interests without breaching fiduciary obligations to shareholders'. Op cit note 125. The CLRSG also eschewed the Pluralist Theory in favour of the ESVA as the former would have necessitated extensive reforms in the area of directors' duties by requiring the directors to owe fiduciary duties to non-shareholder constituencies. On the other hand, the ESVA does not extend directors' fiduciary duties to non-shareholder constituencies, but it allows the directors to consider the interests of these constituencies without breaching their fiduciary obligations to shareholders.

97. See Keay, 'Tackling the Issue of Corporate Objective', op. cit. note 48, at 600.

98. Hart & Degener, 'Non-Stockholder Constituency Statutes', op cit note 135, at 4.

99. 23 Ch D 654.

100. Ibid., at 672.

101. Ibid., at 673.

102. See, for example, *Fulham Football Club Ltd v Cabra Estates plc* [1992] BCC 863 at 876 (Lord Justice Neill).

103. See Greene, 'Regulatory and Legislative Responses to Takeover Activity in the 1980s', op cit note 136, at 1564; see also 'An Idea Whose Time Should Never Have Come' op cit note 41, at 20.

104. The language of s 172(1) of the UK Companies Act, 2006 makes it clear that over and above having regard to non-shareholder constituency considerations, '[a] director of a company must act in the way he considers . . . would be most likely to promote the success of the company *for the benefit of its members as a whole*'. [Emphasis added].

105. Arguing in relation to Non-Stockholder Constituency Statutes, Frank J. Garcia (Garcia, 'Protecting Nonshareholder Interests in the Market for Corporate Control', op cit note 137, at 518) maintained that the board is *required* to consider the effects on the corporation, including other constituencies.

106. See A Global Picture of Business, op cit note 30, at 210. See also Company Law Review Steering Group, UK Department of Trade and Industry, *Modern Company Law for a Competitive Economy: The Strategic Framework* (1999), op cit note 41, Chapter 5.1.

107. See Keay, 'Tackling the Issue of Corporate Objective', op cit note 47, at 578.

108. Ibid. See also R. Edward Freeman, 'A Stakeholder Theory of the Modern Corporation' in Tom L. Beauchamp & Norman E. Bowie (eds.), *Ethical Theory and Business* (5th ed., 1997) at 69.

109. Ibid. Salacuse (Salacuse, 'Corporate Governance in the New Century', op cit note 48, at 75) states that 'in Europe, both law and policy recognise to varying degrees that corporations also have the objective of advancing the interests of other persons and groups beyond the narrow category of shareholders'. He goes on to assert that 'Germany, with its system of codetermination granting employees a formal role in corporate governance, is often cited as the prime example of the stakeholder model'. (Ibid.)

110. See Karmel RS, 'Implications of the Stakeholder Model' (1993) 61 *George Washington Law Review* 1156 at 1171. By acknowledging that the corporation is not the only form of business organisation in which the residual owners benefit from goods and services furnished by others, James J. Hanks appears to concede that these stakeholders, in fact, contribute to company capital.

111. See Page A, 'Has Corporate Law Failed? Addressing Proposals for Reform' (2009) 107 *Michigan Law Review* 979, at 980.

112. Op cit note 39, at 112. Paine maintains that this form of stakeholderism distinguishes between stakeholders whose interests are protected by some form of ethical or legal norm and those whose interests are a matter of wishes or desires. It is the former, argues Paine, that should receive protection under this theory, but not the latter.

113. Keay A, 'The Ultimate Objective of the Company and the Enforcement of the Entity Maximisation and Sustainability Model' (2010) 10 *Journal of Corporate Law Studies* 35 (hereafter 'Enforcement of the EMS Model'), at 36. See also McDaniel M, 'Bondholders and Stockholders' (1988) 13 *Journal of Corporation Law* 205, at 309, where it is stated that 'a right without a remedy is worthless'.

114. See Irene-Marié Esser, *Recognition of Various Stakeholder Interests in Company Management*, an LLD thesis submitted at the University of South Africa (UNISA) (2008) (hereafter 'Stakeholder Interests in Management'), 33–34.

115. Ibid., at 34.

116. Ibid.

117. Enforcement of the EMS Model, at 36.

118. In two of his oft-quoted scholarly writings, R. Edward Freeman has gone to the extent of boldly proclaiming that stakeholder theory is generally so pre-eminent that shareholder primacy is in fact dead: see Freeman, 'The Politics of Stakeholder Theory', op cit note 50, at 413. See also R. Edward Freeman, 'A Stakeholder Theory of the Modern Corporation' in Tom L. Beauchamp & Norman E. Bowie (eds.), *Ethical Theory and Business* (5th ed., 1997) at 69.

119. See Dodd, 'For Whom Are Corporate Managers Trustees?' op cit note 3. See also White JB, 'How Should We Talk About Corporations? The Languages of Economics and of Citizenship' (1985) 94 *Yale Law Journal* 1416.

120. Fisch, 'Measuring Efficiency in Corporate Law', op cit note 81.

121. Greenfield K, 'New Principles for Corporate Law' (2005) 1 *Hastings Business Law Journal* 89 at 89.

122. Blair M & Stout L, 'A Team Production Theory to Corporate Law' (1999) 85 *Virginia Law Review* 247.

123. Kent Greenfield, *The Failure of Corporate Law: Fundamental Flaws and Progressive Possibilities* (2007).

124. Ibid., at 242.

125. Ibid.

126. Ibid., at 131.

127. Op cit note 131.

128. Adams ES & Matheson JH, 'A Statutory Model for Corporate Constituency Concerns' (2000) 49 *Emory Law Journal* 1085.

129. Karmel, 'Implications of the Stakeholder Model', op cit note 152, at 1171. While James J. Hanks Jr. emphatically argues in favour of the shareholder primacy theory, he nevertheless appears to concede that shareholders (or residual owners) within a corporation benefit from goods and services furnished by other stakeholders, although he quickly reminds the audience that corporations are not the only form of business organisations in which residual owners benefit in that manner: See Hanks, 'Playing with Fire', op cit note 7, at 117. This view is in clear contrast with the view that the primary role of fiduciary duties is to primarily prevent self-interested conduct or managerial misconduct by directors rather than the sole protection of shareholders. (See, infra, para 4.2).

130. UK Department of Trade and Industry, Company Law Reform: Modern Company Law for a Competitive Economy (March 1998), at 10.

131. See Adams & Matheson, 'A Statutory Model for Corporate Constituency Concerns', op cit note 175, at 1101.

132. See, for example, Wallman SMH, 'The Proper Interpretation of Corporate Constituency Statutes and Formulation of Director Duties' (1991) 21 *Stetson Law Review* 163, at 169.

133. Ibid., at 168–169.

134. See Matheson JH & Olson BA, 'Corporate Cooperation, Relationship Management, and the Trialogical Imperative for Corporate Law' (1994) 78 *Minnesota Law Review* 1443.

135. As argued by Professor E. Merrick Dodd in Dodd, 'For Whom Are Corporate Managers Trustees?' op cit, note 3, at 1161.

136. Keay, 'The Enforcement of the Entity Maximisation and Sustainability (EMS) Model', op cit note 160, at 43.

137. Ibid.

138. Ibid.

139. Dodd, 'For Whom Are Corporate Managers Trustees?' op cit note 3, at 1161.

140. Adams & Matheson, 'A Statutory Model for Corporate Constituency Concerns', op cit note 175.

141. See Roberta S Karmel, 'Implications of the Stakeholder Model' (1993) 61 *George Washington Law Review* 1156 at 1171. See also, Playing with Fire, op cit note 7, at 117.

142. UK Department of Trade and Industry, *Company Law Reform: Modern Company Law for a Competitive Economy* (March 1998), op cit note 102, at 10.

143. Adams & Matheson, 'A Statutory Model for Corporate Constituency Concerns', op cit note 175, at 1101.

144. See Matheson & Olson, 'The Trialogical Imperative for Corporate Law', op cit note 181.

145. Hart O, 'An Economist's View of Fiduciary Duty' (1993) 43 *University of Toronto Law Journal* 299, 303.

146. Ibid.

147. Company Law Review, *Modern Company Law for a Competitive Economy: The Strategic Framework* (1999), op cit note 48, at 40.

148. This theory is largely reflected in the different enforcement provisions under South Africa's 2008 Companies Act, which, among other things, extend legal standing for all corporate constituencies to access corporate law remedies, make derivative action proceedings available to all corporate constituencies rather than just to shareholders, and permit all corporate constituencies to restrain the company from doing anything inconsistent with the Companies Act.

149. See Keay, 'Tackling the Issue of Corporate Objective', op cit note 48, at 611.

150. See Keay, 'The Enforcement of the Entity Maximisation and Sustainability (EMS) Model', op cit note 160, at 70–71.

151. Keay, 'The Enforcement of the Entity Maximisation and Sustainability (EMS) Model', op cit note 160, at 38.

152. Although this theory in its current caption was formulated in Keay A, 'Ascertaining the Corporate Objective: An Entity Maximisation and Sustainability Model'

(2008) 71 *Modern Law Review* 663, at 679–685, its origins can be traced to the well-known classic cases which popularised the concept of 'separate legal personality', which include *Salomon v A. Salomon & Co* [1897] 2 AC 22 (per Lord Halsbury LC, at 30–31 and Lord MacNaughten, at 51); and *Lee v Lee Air Farming* [1961] AC 12 (per Lord Morris of Borth-y-Gest, at 25–26). This view is in line with the view that the primary role of fiduciary duties is to primarily prevent self-interested conduct or managerial misconduct by directors rather than the sole protection of shareholders. (See, infra, para. 4.2).

153. Keay, 'Ascertaining the Corporate Objective', op cit note 199, at 685.

154. Keay, 'The Enforcement of the Entity Maximisation and Sustainability (EMS) Model', op cit note 160, at 38.

155. Keay, 'Ascertaining the Corporate Objective', op cit note 199, at 691.

156. As it was held in the following cases, for example: *Lonrho Ltd v Shell Petroleum Co Ltd* [1980] 1 WLR 627; *Fulham Football Club Ltd v Cabra Estates plc* [1994] 1 BCLC 363; *Nicholson v Permakraft (NZ) Ltd* (1985) 3 ACLC 453; *Brunninghausen v Glavanics* [1999] NSWCA 199, (1999) 17 ACLC 1247; *Peoples' Department Stores v Wise* [2004] SCC 68, (2004) 244 DLR (4th) 564.

157. As it was famously held in the cases of *Greenhalgh v Arderne Cinemas* [1951] Ch 286; *Parke v Daily News Ltd* [1962] Ch 927; *Brady v Brady* (1987) 3 BCC 535.

158. *Darvall v North Sydney Brick and Tile Co Ltd* (1987) 12 ACLR 537, 554 (1988) 6 ACLC 154, 176. In the famous classic American case of *Dodge v Ford Motor Co.* (1919) 170 NW 668, the court accepted that the duty is owed to the corporation, which must be interpreted as the shareholders. Indeed, in the absence of a 'non-shareholder constituency' statute, the general rule in US jurisdictions would be that other stakeholder interests can only be taken into account through the lens of shareholder interests (See Norwitz, 'The Metaphysics of Time', op cit note 132, at 377–378.

159. Op cit note 161.

160. Dean J, Directing Public Companies (2001), at 155.

161. Institute of Directors in Southern Africa (IODSA), 'King Committee's Report on Corporate Governance' (2002), para 17.3 at 10.

162. Enforcement of the EMS Model, op cit note 44, at 47–48.

163. Section 165(2) of the South African Companies Act, 2008 (Act No. 71 of 2008) explicitly provides that:

> [A] person may serve a demand upon a company to commence or continue legal proceedings, or take related steps, to protect the legal interests of the company if the person – is a shareholder or a person entitled to be registered as a shareholder, of the company or of a related company; is a director or prescribed officer of the company or of a related company; is a registered trade union that represents employees of the company, or another representative of employees of the company; or has been granted leave of the court to do so, which may be granted only if the court is satisfied that it is necessary or expedient to do so to protect a legal right of that other person'.

This view is aligned with the view that the primary role of fiduciary duties is to primarily prevent self-interested conduct or managerial misconduct by directors rather than the sole protection of shareholders. This is said to be a jurisprudential basis, if one was needed, to justify an inclusive corporate law enforcement framework. (See, infra, para. 4.2).

164. After considering issues relating to the enforcement of shareholder primacy and stakeholder theories, Andrew Keay identified and then examined the difficulties that existed with the enforcement of EMS. He concluded that one particular mechanism, namely the derivative action procedure, can potentially be utilised by non-shareholder constituencies to enforce the breach by directors of their fiduciary obligations to the company.

165. Contrast this with s 218(2) of the South African Companies Act, 2008, which provides that 'Any person who contravenes any provision of this Act is liable to any other person for any loss or damage suffered by that person as a result of that contravention. This is supplemented by the provisions of s 157, which provides for the extended standing to apply for remedies'.

166. Stakeholder Interests in Management, at 23.

167. Ibid.

168. Op cit note 39, at 118.

169. Paine, op cit note 39, at 118 & 115.

170. This observation is made by, among others, John F. Olson, 'South Africa Moves to a Global Model of Corporate Governance but with Important National Variations' in Tshepo H. Mongalo (ed.), *Modern Company Law for a Competitive South African Economy* (2010), at 220.

171. Ibid.

172. The Department of Trade and Industry, *South Africa: South African Company Law Reform for the 21st Century: Guidelines for Corporate Law Reform* (May 2004).

173. For example, the existence of s 5(2) authorising courts to consider the application of foreign company law in the interpretation of the Act may justify the importation of substantive normative statements on the responsibilities towards non-shareholder corporate constituent groups, such as the one enacted in terms of s 172(1) of the UK Companies Act, 2006. Furthermore, such a normative statement can also possibly be inferred from the purpose clause in s 7 of the Act, which, inter alia, propagates the promotion of compliance with the Bill of Rights and the consideration of the significant role of enterprises within the social and economic life of the nation as some of the purposes of the Act (See, in particular, s 7(a) and (b)(iii)).

174. This approach was documented for the first time by John F. Olson, 'South Africa Moves to a Global Model of Corporate Governance but with Important National Variations' (2010), op cit note 178, at 219–227.

175. See John F. Olson's chapter entitled 'South Africa Moves to a Global Model of Corporate Governance but with Important National Variations' in Tshepo H. Mongalo (ed.), *Modern Company Law for a Competitive South African Economy* (2010), op cit note 178, at 219–247.

176. In Chapter 2 of Carl Stein's (assisted by Geoff Everingham) *The New Companies Act Unlocked – A Businessperson's Guide* (2011), the author observes that

'The Act also gives significantly greater rights and remedies to stakeholders, including minority shareholders, and thus encourages stakeholder activism'. The author continues to assert that:

> [T]wo of the most striking – even alarming, in some instances – aspects of the Act are . . . the number of remedies it provides, in particular the number of remedies it provides to minority shareholders, employees and directors; and . . . the number of methods by which its remedies may be enforced.

The author concludes that [i]n both these respects, the Act generally goes further than the companies legislation of other Western countries, including the United States and the United Kingdom. He concludes by observing that '[u]nfortunately this could lead to increased litigation and a fair amount of "remedy shopping"'. Available at http://www.siberink.co.za/siber-ink-blog/two-essential-keys-to-unlocking-the-new-companies-act-carl-stein, accessed on 13 June 2012.

177. John F. Olson, 'South Africa Moves to a Global Model of Corporate Governance but with Important National Variations' (2010), at 225 and 226. This approach is in alignment with the view that the primary role of fiduciary duties is to primarily prevent self-interested conduct or managerial misconduct by directors rather than the sole protection of shareholders, justifying the need for an inclusive corporate law approach. (See, infra, para. 4.2). See also a detailed description of beneficial stakeholderism and Structural Stakeholderism by Prof Lynn S. Paine in the *Harvard Business Review*, op cit note 39, at 115–119.

178. The sections which are considered for the purposes of the examination of the fundamental elements of the AESVA are the following: ss 20(4), 157(1), 165(2), and 218(2).

179. See Mitchell, 'A Theoretical and Practical Framework', op cit note 6, at 584.

180. Ibid., at 590.

181. Section 20(4) of the Companies Act, 2008.

182. Section 157(1)(b) and (c) of the Companies Act, 2008.

183. Section 165 of the Companies Act, 2008.

184. Section 218(2) of the Companies Act, 2008.

185. Section 157(1)(d) provides, in material terms, that:

> When, in terms of this Act, an application can be made to, or a matter be brought before, a court, the Companies Tribunal, the Panel or the Commission, the right to make the application or to bring the matter may be exercised by a person . . . acting in the public interest, with leave of the court.

186. See *Ferreira v Levin NO and Others; Vryenhoek and Others v Powell NO and Others* 1996 (2) SA 621 (CC) (Hereafter referred to as *Ferreira v Levin*).

187. Ibid., at Para 233.h

188. Ibid.

189. Ibid

190. Ibid.

191. Ibid., at para 234. The idea of an inclusive corporate law enforcement regime is aligned with the view that the primary role of fiduciary duties is to primarily

prevent self-interested conduct or managerial misconduct by directors rather than the sole protection of shareholders. (See infra, para. 4.2).

192. In this regard, see Mongalo TH, 'Possible Contribution of Corporate Law Remedies to Curbing Illicit Outflow of Capital from Africa' (2015) 1 (1) *Journal of Corporate and Commercial Law & Practice*, 1–29.

193. Since the violation of the company's legal interests is almost invariably occasioned by the directors as a result of their breach of fiduciary obligations, the argument is that any vindication of those legal interests can be undertaken by the company itself, through directors or by the shareholders. This is reflected in the corporate objective set out by corporate statutes in Anglo-American jurisdictions, where the duties of directors are expressly owed to the company and its shareholders.

194. Section 157(1) of the Companies Act, 2008, provides that:

> [W]hen, in terms of this Act, an application can be made to, or a matter can be brought before, a court . . . the right to make the application or bring the matter may be exercised by a person (a) directly contemplated in the particular provision of this Act; (b) acting on behalf of a person contemplated in paragraph (a), who cannot act in their own name; (c) acting as a member of, or in the interest of, a group or class of affected persons, or an association acting in the interest of its members; or (c) acting in the public interest, with leave of court.

195. Section 15(6) of the Companies Act, 2008.

196. See, for example, *Letseng Diamonds Ltd v JCI Ltd and Others; Trinity Asset Management (Pty) Ltd and Others v Investec Bank Ltd* 2007 (5) SA 564 (W) para 19.

197. 2007 (5) SA 564 (W).

198. Carl Stein's (assisted by Geoff Everingham) *The New Companies Act Unlocked – A Businessperson's Guide* (2011), op cit note 180.

199. *Ngxuza and Others v Permanent Secretary Department of Welfare, Eastern Cape* 2001 (2) SA 609 (ECD), at 624D–E.

200. 2001 (2) SA 609 (ECD).

201. Ibid., at 619A–D.

202. 1999 (4) SA 367 (T).

203. Ibid., at 623C.

204. See, among others, The Committee on Corporate Laws, 'Other Constituencies Statutes: Potential for Confusion' (1990) 45 *Business Lawyer* 2253.

205. The Committee on Corporate Laws, 'Other Constituencies Statutes: Potential for Confusion' (1990) 45 *Business Lawyer* 2253, at 2269; Hansmann H & Kraakman R, 'Toward a Single Model of Corporate Law?' in JA McCahery, P Moerland, T Raaijmakers, & L Renneboog (eds.), *Corporate Governance Regimes: Convergence and Diversity* (2003), 56. Although he does not believe that there can ever be a direct conflict between the interests of shareholders, on the one hand, and those of non-shareholder corporate constituencies, on the other, Lawrence E. Mitchell nevertheless acknowledges that such a concern exists in corporate law circles (Mitchell, 'A Theoretical and Practical Framework', op cit note 6, at 592).

206. Hansmann & Kraakman, 'Toward a Single Model of Corporate Law?' op cit note 67, at 60.

207. See discussions on this aspect in para 2.2.1.4 above.

208. According to Hansmann and Kraakman, (Hansmann & Kraakman, 'Toward a Single Model of Corporate Law', op cit note 67, at 60), this model was predominant in the 1930s through the 1960s and prominent scholars who are associated with this model include Merrick Dodd, John Kenneth Galbraith and, later, Adolph Berle.

209. Ibid., at 60.

210. *McMulin v Beran*, 765 A.2d 910, at 916–917 (Del. 2000). See also *Emerald Partners v Berlin*, 726 A.2d 1215, at 1221 (Del. 1999).

211. Ibid., at 916–917.

212. See s 76(4)(a) of the Companies Act, 2008.

213. Bainbridge SM, *Corporation Law and Economics* (2002), at 274.

214. Dooley MP, 'Two Models of Corporate Governance' (1992) 47 *Business Law* 461, at 478–479.

215. Ibid., at 479.

*Chapter 2*

# Comparative Analysis

## GENERAL INTRODUCTION

In this chapter, a comparative analysis of primary statutory corporate constituency mechanisms in the United Kingdom and the United States is undertaken, with a view primarily to exposing their consistent lack of a legal enforcement framework favourable to non-shareholder corporate constituencies. The chapter also attempts to highlight that not all of these statutory corporate constituency mechanisms propagate the corporate law assumption that the law focuses directorial duties on – and limits enforcement powers to – shareholders. It is further shown that, notwithstanding the existence of statutory corporate constituency mechanisms which do not reinforce the corporate balance of power, the lack of legal standing for non-shareholder corporate constituent groups to pursue corporate law remedies is nevertheless pervasive across all statutory corporate constituency mechanisms.

Statutory corporate constituency mechanisms in the Anglo-American jurisdictions of the United Kingdom and the United States, in particular, were conceived with the primary purpose of developing a scheme of responsibilities by corporate controllers to corporate constituencies beyond just the shareholder constituency group. A little over fifty years after the Berle-Dodd debate led to the proposal of a scheme of responsibilities to parties other than shareholders – a scheme which was expected to be clearly and reasonably enforceable – corporate law developments in these two jurisdictions took a trajectory which endeavoured to address at least the first part of the proposal which emanated from that debate. Curiously, however, these statutory corporate constituency mechanisms largely stopped short of fulfilling their ultimate goal of ensuring that the scheme of responsibilities, so designed, was capable of being clearly and reasonably enforceable in the instance of the identified corporate constituencies.

The aim of this chapter is to demonstrate that these corporate constituency mechanisms generally fall short of this ultimate goal. At the same time, it is also envisaged that a cogent argument can be advanced that while some of these statutory corporate constituency mechanisms are clearly unfavourable to the possible incorporation of a legal enforcement framework for the benefit of all corporate constituencies, some of these statutory mechanisms are less hostile. The hostility towards the incorporation of such a legal enforcement framework is demonstrated in a number of ways, as exhibited in some of these mechanisms by the express disclaimer of any duty of the board to the very corporate constituencies they recognise. While almost all of these statutory mechanisms are permissive in the sense of imposing no requirement that the board should consider identified corporate constituencies' interests, even that which imposes such a requirement (i.e. the Connecticut corporate constituency statute) fails to explicitly grant legal standing to recognised corporate constituency groups to enforce consideration of their interests, thus effectively making the statute of questionable utility.

The main indication of the disclaimer of any enforceable duty of the board to the identified corporate constituencies lies in the articulation of the board's fiduciary obligations as being owed primarily to the corporation's shareholders. If, indeed, the board continues to be primarily indebted to shareholders with regard to its fiduciary obligation to act in the best interests of the corporation, how can it also be obligated to consider the conflicting interests of a variety of other corporate constituency groups?

As argued elsewhere, to even suggest that fiduciary obligations are owed only to shareholders in a typically large public company is disingenuous, as the central corporate law focus on the problems engendered by the separation of ownership and control in such companies has led to the drive toward restraining managerial self-dealing as the clear objective of both statutory and common law rules of the duty of loyalty.[1] This is the main reason for this chapter's assessment of the significance of, and the viability of imposing, the all-inclusive legal enforcement framework in respect of each of the statutory corporate constituency mechanisms.

The chapter starts off by tracing the origins of these legislative and judicial measures within the United Kingdom, highlighting a few judicial pronouncements and *obiter dicta* which set in motion considerations for a proposed shift in corporate objectives. This is followed by the analysis of the earliest legislative attempt in that country to incorporate non-shareholder constituencies' considerations in corporate decision-making in the form of s 309 of the Companies Act, 1985. Although the non-shareholder corporate constituencies mentioned in that statute are limited to just one category, the initiative prepared the groundwork for the extension of non-shareholder corporate constituencies, as is reflected in the subsequent legislative initiative, in the form of s 172 of the Companies Act, 2006.

Subsequent to that, the chapter unpacks the transatlantic statutory corporate constituency initiatives in the form of the corporate constituency, flexible purpose and benefit corporation statutes applicable in most jurisdictions of the United States of America.[2] The analysis of corporate statutory mechanisms within the United Kingdom is consistently set out by considering six specific aspects compared across the two statutory corporate mechanisms respectively historically adopted in that country. These specific aspects cover (a) the content of the statutory mechanism in question; (b) its relation to the traditional corporate law proposition on corporate objectives; (c) the similarities to other corporate constituency mechanisms; (d) the main differences from other corporate constituency mechanisms; (e) the significance of the corporate constituency mechanism in justifying the all-inclusive enforcement framework, if any; and (f) a conclusion addressing the viability of imposing the all-inclusive enforcement framework under the corporate constituency mechanism concerned.

With regard to corporate constituency statutes' relation to the traditional corporate law proposition on corporate objective, the chapter shows that the widespread application of the Model Business Corporation Act makes the determination of the primary corporate objective applicable in each of the states of the United States relatively easy.[3] The discussion of so many statutory corporate constituency mechanisms applicable within the United States is justified on the basis that the statutory sources of these mechanisms are largely worded differently and, in the absence of authoritative judicial pronouncements in many of those jurisdictions, the conclusions reached herein in respect of each such statutory corporate constituency mechanism should prove helpful for predicting any future possible judicial interpretation.

Subsequent to the analysis of specific provisions of the Non-Stockholder Constituency Statutes, flexible purpose and benefit corporation statutes, the chapter draws conclusions around the effectiveness (or lack thereof) of these statutes as enforcement mechanisms for the benefit of all corporate constituency groups.

## UK COMPANY LAW DEVELOPMENTS

### Introduction

A somewhat confusing picture is presented by UK law developments regarding the primary corporate objective pursued for public companies under UK jurisprudence. Notable judicial pronouncements made in the middle of the twentieth century indicate the dominance of the shareholder primacy or the Shareholder Value Approach. This was confirmed by the Company Law Review Steering Group (CLRSG), established in 1998 by the UK Department of Trade and Industry in order to review UK corporate law between 1998 and 2006. This overwhelming evidence of the application of the Shareholder Value Approach notwithstanding, the celebrated classic judgment made during the late nineteenth century and the dicta emitted by the UK courts in the late twentieth century presented a picture which suggested the application of a broader approach even prior to the institutionalisation of the Enlightened Shareholder Value Approach, pursuant to the provisions of the Companies Act, 2006. This state of affairs is further elaborated upon hereunder.

Following the launch of the Corporate Law Reform process in the United Kingdom in 1998, the CLRSG observed in 1999 that UK law reflected the position that companies are managed for the benefit of the shareholders and that the law confers on them the ultimate control of the undertaking, with the result that '[t]he directors are required to manage the business on their behalf'.[4] The CLRSG concluded that the ultimate objective of companies is to generate maximum wealth for shareholders.[5]

Again, one of the committees appointed to make recommendations for the consolidation of corporate governance principles in the United Kingdom, under the chairmanship of Sir Ronald Hampel, observed that the single overriding concern under the UK law was 'the preservation and the greatest practicable enhancement over time of . . . shareholders' investment'.[6]

The prevalence of this legal position, prior to the institutionalisation of the Enlightened Shareholder Value Approach, is epitomized in a celebrated mid-twentieth century decision in the case of *Greenhalgh v Arderne Cinemas*[7] in which the court, per Evershed, MR, said:

> I think it is now plain that 'bona fide for the benefit of the company as a whole' means not two things but one thing. It means that the [director] must proceed upon what, in his honest opinion, is for the benefit of the company as a whole. The second thing is that the phrase, 'the company as a whole', does not (at any rate in such a case as the present) mean the company as a commercial entity, distinct from the corporators: it means the corporators as a general body.[8]

Eleven years later, this decision was reiterated in the case of *Parke v Daily News Ltd.*[9] in which the board of directors of a media company decided to sell the copyright of the newspapers, together with the newspapers' plant and premises, in order to prevent any further possible loss of assets following losses incurred in the two previous years in the newspaper trade. It was found that the company intended to distribute the balance of the purchase money, after meeting the inevitable costs of the transaction, by giving compensation to the staff. This was an *ex gratia* payment to be made by the company since it was in addition to payments (made to employees) in lieu of notice, in respect of holiday money and in respect of accrued pension rights. The shareholders of the company sued the directors on the basis that they were not acting in the best interest of the company.

The court held that:

> [The directors were] prompted by motives which, however laudable, and however enlightened from the point of view of industrial relations, were such as the law does not recognise as a sufficient justification. Stripped of all its side issues, the essence of the matter is this, that the directors of the defendant company are proposing that a very large part of its funds should be given to its former employees in order to benefit those employees rather than the company, and that is an application of the company's funds which the law . . . will not allow.[10]

Later judicial pronouncements confirmed this traditional common law position that 'the interest of the company' is the same thing as the interests of the shareholders[11] *qua* shareholders,[12] as a general body.[13]

Under this legal position, directors ought to treat the company as a going concern, taking into consideration the interests of both its present and future shareholders.[14] They may not exercise their powers for the benefit of the company as a legal or commercial entity as distinct from the shareholders, although this position is argued by the proponents of the Entity Maximisation and the Sustainability Model (EMS) as discussed above in chapter 1.[15] Under this duty to promote the interests of the company, directors are also prohibited from exercising their powers to favour one group of shareholders over another.[16] In the same vein, a director appointed by a class of shareholders may not identify the interests of the company with the interests of that class.

The identification of the interests of the company with the interests of the shareholders has been criticised on the ground that it ignores the existence of the company as a legal *persona* separate from its members.[17] However, the jurisprudential significance of the separate legal personality of a company has not managed to affect the principle that the members collectively make up, or are, the company. Regardless of the separateness of the corporate entity, the economic advantage of the shareholders alone was, and still is, regarded as the measure of 'the interests of the company' in which directors must act under UK law. This is so even in the aftermath of the Enlightened Shareholder Value Approach (ESVA) as, according to Professor Andrew Keay's pertinent observation, '[i]t is difficult to find the benefits that the ESVA approach brings to UK corporate law'.[18] Notwithstanding the judicial acceptance and the dominance of the equation of the interests of the company with those of the shareholders, some commentators have argued that, as a matter of law, the interests of the shareholders are not the interests of the company, and that the assertion that they are is misleading – the directors owe their fiduciary duties to the company and not to its shareholders.[19]

It is apparent that the principle that the interests of the company are the interests of its shareholders is not based on the idea that the company is actually nothing other than its members. It is rather based on the economic reality that links shareholders' interests to the prosperity of the company as a business concern. It is, therefore, obvious that what the UK courts were fully convinced of was that a mere legal entity can have no interests of its own. This is underscored by Nourse LJ's statement in *Brady v Brady*[20] when he said '[t]he interests of a company, an artificial person, cannot be distinguished from the interests of the persons who are interested in it'.[21] Indeed, Professor Len Sealy emphatically stated that 'the economic advantage of the shareholders alone is still regarded as the measure of 'the interests of the company' in which directors must act'[22]

### *Notable Judicial Pronouncements on Consideration of Non-Shareholder Constituencies*

The earliest indication that an approach broader than that of the Shareholder Value Approach was applicable under the UK law was the 1883 decision in the case of *Hutton v West Cork Railway*,[23] where the court stated that: '[T]he law does not say that there are to be no cakes and ale, but there are to be no cakes and ale except such as are required for the benefit of the company'.[24] Although the phrase 'the benefit of the company' was accepted as meaning the interests of the shareholders as a whole, the reference to the existence of 'the cakes and ale' was to the benefits of other corporate constituent groups, such as the employees. The language of the court's decision clearly indicates, however, that the interests of these non-shareholder corporate constituencies are only to be considered through the 'prism' of the shareholders – i.e. 'except such as are required for the benefit of the company'.

Ever since the intimation that the interests of non-shareholder constituencies, particularly the employees, may be considered under the English law as a result of the *Hutton v West Cork Railway*[25] case, the next major indication that such considerations may be taken into account was under the UK Companies Act of 1985, which, essentially, provided that '[t]he matters to which the directors of a company are to have regard in the performance of their functions include the interests of the company's employees in general, as well as the interests of its members'.[26] The provision did not, however, give any indication as to what the directors were required to do where the interests of the employees actually conflicted with those of the shareholders or members. Furthermore, the section provided no enforcement mechanisms for the benefit of the employees as it clearly indicated that 'the duty . . . is enforceable in the same way as any fiduciary duty owed to a company by its directors'.[27]

While the question of whether the law ought to require directors to hold regard for interests other than their company's shareholders received considerable attention in many commonwealth countries and the United States,[28] the only judicial pronouncements came in the form of the dicta emitted by the UK courts in the late twentieth century.[29]

## Section 309(1) of the Companies Act, 1985

Long before the institutionalisation of the Enlightened Shareholder Value Approach in terms of s 172 of the Companies Act, 2006, UK law had a statutory provision which permitted directors to have regard for the interests of employees. This statutory provision was introduced upon the consolidation of the Companies Act in 1985 and was enacted as s 309.

### *The Content*

Section 309 of the Companies Act, 1985, entitled '[d]irectors to have regard to interests of employees' and consisted of three sub-sections. The first sub-section specifically included the interests of the company's employees in general as some of the matters to which directors were permitted to have regard. The use of the term 'include' in this sub-section presupposed that 'the interests of the employees' were not the only ones to which directors were permitted to have regard, although the heading of the section only made mention of 'interests of employees', and no other non-shareholder corporate constituency was specifically mentioned.

The second sub-section is important for two particular reasons. Firstly, it identified the constituency to whom the duty is owed, and, secondly, it explained the manner in which the duty was to be enforced. As regards the first aspect of the second sub-section, it categorically stated that the duty imposed in that section was owed by the directors to the company, and the company alone. The language of this sub-section clearly indicates that the intention of the legislature was to incorporate the common law definition of the term 'company' within the context of 'the interests of the company', which, as shown above, was interpreted to mean the interests of the shareholders *qua* shareholders, as a general body.

The second part of the sub-section poignantly acknowledged enforcement mechanisms which could be resorted to by qualifying constituencies in enforcing compliance with or addressing any breach of fiduciary duties. This was also a clear incorporation of the common law rules relating to enforcement of fiduciary duties, which recognise the company (interpreted as shareholders) as the only beneficiary of directors' fiduciary duties. In keeping with the recognition of the shareholders as the only beneficiaries, the common law accords them the legal standing of the only constituency able to enforce fiduciary duties.

In order to understand who has legal standing to enforce compliance with or remedy the breach of fiduciary duties, one has to bear in mind that as the duties are owed to the company, it is only the company that is able to enforce compliance therewith, in line with the 'proper plaintiff principle'[30] established in the case of *Foss v Harbottle*,[31] which is the cornerstone for the common law principles governing the enforcement of rights or remedies vested in a company as a matter of substantive law.[32] As a result, given the fact that compliance with fiduciary duties can be enforced derivatively on behalf of the company, it is only the shareholders who have the legal standing to bring derivative claims at common law.[33] It, therefore, means that irrespective of s 309's permission for directors to have regard to the interests of employers, it had limited significance as the employees were not able to enforce compliance with the fiduciary duties owed by the directors.

The section is worded as follows:

> 309 Directors to have regard to interests of employees
>
> The matters to which the directors of a company are to have regard in the performance of their functions include the interests of the company's employees in general, as well as the interests of its members.
>
> Accordingly, the duty imposed by this section on the directors is owed by them to the company (and the company alone) and is enforceable in the same way as any other fiduciary duty owed to a company by its directors.
>
> This section applies to shadow directors as it does to directors.
>
> The Section's Relation to the Traditional Corporate Law Proposition.

In this regard, one has to question whether the section proposes a shift from the traditional corporate law proposition which links corporate law enforcement exclusively or primarily with shareholder oriented corporate law remedies. As mentioned above, the language of sub-section (2) of section 309 specifically envisages an enforcement model which considers directors as fiduciaries on behalf of the company, which has traditionally been interpreted to be tantamount to the shareholders. Phrasing the enforcement model in this manner effectively demonstrates the marriage of the section to the traditional corporate law proposition. The language of the sub-section was, therefore, a clear incorporation of the common law rules relating to the enforcement of fiduciary duties exclusively by shareholders. This is because in keeping with the recognition of the shareholders as the only beneficiaries, the common law accords them legal standing as the only constituency group to enforce fiduciary duties.

## Similarities to Other Corporate Constituency Mechanisms

While the first and the clearly legitimate comparison of this section should be with other UK corporate constituency mechanisms, the similarity of the role played by the US corporate constituency mechanisms also necessitates the consideration of some aspects of those mechanisms.

The main and most striking similarity between this section and other UK and US statutory corporate constituency mechanisms (consisting primarily of s 172 of the UK Companies Act, 2006 and the US Non-Stockholder Constituency Statutes) is its identification of employees as a corporate constituency group, which directors may have regard to in addition to shareholders in corporate decision-making. Another similarity with other statutory corporate constituency mechanisms relates to the section's enforcement. In this regard, the similarity is to those statutory corporate mechanisms, such as s 172 of the UK Companies Act, 2006,[34] which subject the interests of employees to those of the shareholders.[35] By doing so, these mechanisms all perpetuate the continued enforcement of corporate law remedies solely by shareholders and allow the consideration of the interests of specified non-shareholder corporate constituencies only through the 'prism' of the shareholders' interests.

## Main Differences from Other Corporate Constituency Mechanisms

The main difference between this section and other corporate constituency mechanisms is in relation to the variety of non-shareholder corporate constituencies to which directors may have regard. While the section specifies employees as the only non-shareholder corporate constituency group to which directors are allowed to have regard, other statutory corporate constituency mechanisms, like s 172(1), are not so limited.[36]

On the other hand, a typical Non-Stockholder Constituency Statute requires a director to consider the interests of the corporation's shareholders and, at his discretion, to consider (a) the interests of the corporation's employees, suppliers, creditors, and customers; (b) the economy of the state and nation; (c) the impact of any action upon the communities in or near which the corporation's facilities or operations are located; (d) the long-term interests of the corporation and its shareholders, including the possibility that those interests may best be served by the continued independence of the corporation; and (e) any other factors relevant to promoting and preserving public or community interests.[37]

## The Significance of the Corporate Constituency Mechanism in Justifying the All-Inclusive Enforcement Framework

Here, the question in relation to section 309 of the UK Companies Act, 1985 is 'Did Section 309 of the UK Companies Act grant standing to identified corporate stakeholders?' In other words, was there a possibility that the extension of legal standing to identified non-shareholder corporate constituencies could be achieved under the section? It does not seem that such a possibility existed, as the section explicitly states that the duty to employees 'is enforceable in the same way as any other fiduciary duty owed to a company by its directors', effectively reinforcing the continued application of the shareholder-initiated corporate law remedies.

## Conclusion on the Viability of Imposing the All-Inclusive Enforcement Framework Under the Current Corporate Constituency Mechanism

The usefulness of s 309 of the UK Companies Act, 1985 as a tool for allowing the consideration of employee interests by companies in corporate decision-making is questionable, as no cases involving any breach of the provision exist, leading to the conclusion that it is 'a "lame duck" provision'.[38]

While the consideration of employee interests is something that is regularly done in continental Europe, one of the primary problems with s 309 is that the employees of companies had no right to bring any action to enforce a breach of the provision.[39]

The upshot is that just like s 172 of the Companies Act, 2006, s 309 of the Companies Act, 1985 did not significantly move the United Kingdom away from the shareholder value paradigm, as it does not appear that this seemingly enlightened approach requires directors to have a different role to play compared to the role they played in the past. This is so notwithstanding the fact that on occasions, UK courts have produced dicta that suggest a broader approach.[40]

This weakness is particularly signified by the inability of the non-shareholder constituencies referred to in s 309 to address any failure by the directors to have regard to the interests of those constituencies. In other words, the problem is: what happens if directors pay lip service to the matters referred to in s 309? If 'A', a member of one of those constituents that are referred to in s 309(1), is of the view that directors have breached the provision, in that the directors failed to have regard to the interests of A's constituency, is A able to take any legal action against the directors? The plain answer appears to be 'no'.[41] It is, therefore, clear that the 'have regard to' language used in s 309 does not expand directors' duties but merely provides some guidance for them in the exercise of their powers, effectively meaning that the statutory provision has not extended the law beyond its state prior to its enactment.

It is thus indisputable that regardless of the fact that 'this section requires directors to consider the interests of employees in determining what is in the best interests of the company', it has been next to useless, particularly as the provision has hardly been used and there is very little case law on it. In the words of Morey McDaniel, 'a right without a remedy is worthless'.[42]

## THE APPROACH UNDER THE 2006 COMPANIES ACT (S172 OF THE COMPANIES ACT, 2006, AND THE INSTITUTIONALISATION OF THE ENLIGHTENED SHAREHOLDER VALUE APPROACH)

After just one year in power, the Labour Party Government under Tony Blair's administration in the United Kingdom commenced a process to comprehensively reform company law in that country by setting up the Company Law Review Steering Group (CLRSG) in 1998 with a view to devising a framework of company law that 'provides straightforward, cost-effective and fair regulation which balances the interests of business with those of shareholders, creditors and others'[43] With the intention of giving effect to this objective, the CLRSG assisted the UK government in enacting the Companies Act, 2006, which became fully operative in October 2009 after a decade of consultation.

The Companies Act, 2006 repeals s 309 of the Companies Act, 1985 and, seemingly, as consideration for this, includes employees as one of the groups for whose interests the directors are allowed to have regard.[44] The 2006 Act includes the first ever statement in the statute of directors' duties in respect of the environmental and social impacts of their companies' business. According to David Chivers QC, '[t]he new law explicitly enables directors to take into regard these issues, highlighting the important link between responsible business behaviour and business success'.[45]

### The Content

The language previously used (by the court) to describe that the obligations of a director were to act 'bona fide in the interests of the company' is, in essence, repeated in the Act, as the obligation of 'good faith' remains and it is the company's interests, defined as the benefit of its members as a whole, that must be advanced.

According to David Chivers QC, '[w]hat has changed is that the Act now prescribes not only the basic duty of the director, but how the director must go about discharging that duty [and] must now have regard to the specific matters set out in section 172(1)(a)-(f)'. While the inclusion of other non-shareholder corporate constituencies could have been presumed from the use of the term 'include' in s 309(1) of the Companies Act, 1985, s 172(1) specifies such constituencies. Regardless of the extension of the constituencies for whose interests the directors need to have regard beyond the employees, s 172 continues with the fallacy of not providing rights or remedies to those constituencies to enforce any breach of the provision.[46]

## The Section's Relation to the Traditional Corporate Law Proposition

Just like s 309 of the previous Act, no cases involving any breach of the provision have to date been decided in the UK courts. That said, David Chivers QC observes that '[b]efore the Act was passed, concern was expressed that setting out a list of matters to which directors were to have regard would lead to all decisions of directors being made only after a formal 'box ticking' exercise had been conducted'.[47] He states that '[i]t was feared that this would lead to an increased administration burden but no substantive change in directors' behaviour'.[48]

This fear has, arguably, been allayed by the Ministerial statements made by the UK government's Department of Trade and Industry as follows:

> The words 'have regard to' mean 'think about'; they are absolutely not about just ticking boxes. If 'thinking about' leads to the conclusion, as we believe it will in many cases, that the proper course is to act positively to achieve the objectives in the clause, that will be what the director's duty is. In other words 'have regard to' means 'give proper consideration to'.[49]

While the ability of the specified non-shareholder corporate constituencies to enforce any remedies related to a breach of the provision is in doubt and, as such, the section may thus lead to the perpetuation of the status quo, it is accepted by one practitioner that:

> [A] director who gives proper consideration to the statutory matters will not be in breach of the duty to have regard to them [whereas] a director who pays lip service to the list of matters, but gives no proper consideration to them will be in breach of duty'.[50]

The practitioner observes that '[f]or the competent director, this imposes no additional burden [but] will assist in:

Justifying (as well as requiring) the proper consideration of these matters;

Ensuring that all directors are, prior to making any decision, provided with adequate information about the consequences of that decision; and Protecting directors from shareholder pressure to achieve short term gain at the expense of long term progress'.[51]

Even if the practitioner's view that a director who pays lip service to the list of matters enumerated in s 172(1) without giving proper consideration to such matters will be in breach of duty, the question of whether such breach is capable of being addressed by corporate constituencies so enumerated or representing the matters so enumerated remains. It appears as if any possible remedy is still linked to the conventional corporate law proposition, which associates the institution of possible corporate law remedies exclusively with shareholders. This leads to the unavoidable conclusion that regardless of the expansion in the matters that the directors need to have regard to, section 172(1) is still inextricably intertwined with the traditional corporate law proposition which reserves corporate law remedies for shareholders.

## Similarities with Other Corporate Constituency Mechanisms

The language of section 172(1) is strikingly similar to the language employed with respect to Non-Stockholder Constituency Statutes. This similarity is particularly noticeable in the peremptory language used with regard to the consideration of the factors relevant to the company's shareholders, as contrasted with the clearly discretionary nature of the language used with respect to considerations pertaining to non-shareholder corporate constituencies. While the Non-Stockholder Constituency Statutes generally use the peremptory 'must' in relation to shareholder considerations, they adopt the discretionary 'may, in their discretion' language when describing the duty with regard to non-shareholder corporate constituencies. With respect to s 172(1) of the UK Companies Act, 2006, the use of the peremptory word 'must' in relation to shareholder considerations is not expressly complemented by the discretionary language of 'may, in their discretion' in relation to non-shareholder corporate constituency considerations. That notwithstanding, the silence of the section on whether the consideration of non-shareholder corporate constituencies' interests is mandatory creates a strong presumption that the intention of the legislature could only have been to make such considerations of a discretionary nature, particularly as the consideration of the interests of the shareholder corporate constituencies is expressly made peremptory or mandatory by the use of the term 'must'. This conclusion is further bolstered by the clear lack of enforcement remedies on the part of these non-shareholder corporate constituencies in both the Non-Stockholder Constituency Statutes and section 172(1) of the UK Companies Act, 2006.

## Main Differences from Other Corporate Constituency Mechanisms

What is clearly pervasive across Non-Stockholder Constituency Statutes but which is lacking under s172(1) of the UK Companies Act, 2006, is the embellishment of the consideration of 'the long-term interests of the corporation and its shareholders' by 'the possibility that those interests may be best served by the continued independence of the corporation'. While this seems to reinforce the generally accepted corporate law proposition that the continued independence of the company is primarily pursued by the consideration of the long-term interests of the shareholders in corporate decision-making, its wide usage in US statutory corporate constituency mechanisms has been largely ignored in the UK statutory measures. The reason is probably because, besides re-instating the traditional corporate law proposition, this embellishment adds nothing further to the debate in the absence of an interpretation contrary to that which is commonly accepted.

## The Significance of the Corporate Constituency Mechanism in Justifying the All-Inclusive Enforcement Framework

Because of the expressly stated duty of the directors as being to promote the success of the company for the benefit of the members [shareholders] as a whole, it clearly appears that any duty to have regard to the interests of the non-shareholder corporate constituencies is secondary to the duty to the shareholder corporate constituent group. The result is that the available corporate law remedies to enforce the duty are limited to usage solely by the shareholder corporate constituent group. Indeed, this eventuality is confirmed by a number of commentators, who have lamented the limited impact of the Enlightened Shareholder Value Approach in moving the corporate law trajectory in UK corporate law beyond the traditional 'shareholder primacy norm'.[52]

## Conclusion on the Viability of Imposing the All-Inclusive Enforcement Framework under the Current Corporate Constituency Mechanism

The description of the approach embodied in s 172 appears to suggest that it is more enlightened than that which preceded it, particularly as directors are required to take into account interests other than those of the shareholders. It is, however, questionable whether the new approach can ever transcend the Shareholder Value Approach, as the directors continue to owe their fiduciary duties primarily to the shareholders. There are no enforcement mechanisms which can be resorted to by or for the benefit of the specified non-shareholder corporate constituencies in the event of a breach of the provision[53]. The inability of the Enlightened Shareholder Value Approach model to break away completely from the Shareholder Value Approach effectively means that the application of the all-inclusive enforcement framework remains far out of sight.

Speaking at the expert meeting on Corporate Law and Human Rights, held in support of the Corporate Law Tools Project of the UNSRSG on Business and Human Rights (Professor John Ruggie), David Chivers QC commented that 'although the duty of directors under s 172 of the Companies Act, 2006 is phrased in mandatory terms, it is in fact permissive'.[54] He continued to observe that 'under the duty, there is no obligation on directors to act in a particular way rather the duty merely states what the director needs to have regard to when making the decision'.[55] He concludes that 'the major weakness of the duty lies in enforcement because as the duty is owed to the company, it is only the shareholders who can enforce it'.[56]

This weakness is epitomized by the fact that:

> [T]he Act does not require a director to compromise the interests of the company to achieve any particular social and environmental object [even though] it recognizes that companies whose directors have regard to the relevant social and environmental objects are likely, in the long term to perform better than those whose directors do not.[57]

Professor Andrew Keay insists that '[i]t must be noted that directors cannot pursue a course of action that might be good for all material interests, unless it ultimately benefits the members [or the shareholders]'.[58]

He further observes that because 'the employees of companies have no right to bring any action to enforce a breach of the provision'[59] and that even if there were, it would be extremely difficult to prove a breach [given that no duty is owed to the employees]; s 172 of the Companies Act, 2006 'is likely to be as (in)effective as'[60] s 309 of the Companies Act, 1985'.

In the final analysis, the overall effect of s 172(1) is that the approach adopted therein can be classified as a 'shareholders first interpretation'. This interpretation is explained as follows:

> The basic legal position is quite straightforward: the duty of directors to act in good faith and in the best interests of the company . . . requires directors to treat *shareholders'* interests as paramount. The interests of employees, or other

> stakeholders, can be considered in performing these duties – but only where this would be in the company's (i.e. the shareholders') interests.[61] (Emphasis in original).

As with the Non-Stockholder Constituency Statutes, which are considered hereunder, s 172 has only managed to address the main concern of directors by clarifying that they were permitted (but not obliged) to have regard for non-shareholder corporate constituent groups when making decisions. It can, therefore, only be hoped that s 172, just like the Non-Stockholder Constituency Statutes, will, in the future, point 'the way towards a change in corporate law that will account actively for [stakeholder] interests'.[62]

That said, however, the peremptory language of the ESVA in s 172(1) of the UK Companies Act, 2006, coupled with the broad nature of the corporate constituencies specifically stated therein, possibly justifies a broader enforcement framework. This is mainly justified on the basis that directors' consideration of non-shareholder constituencies' interests, even at the expense of those of shareholders, is unlikely to sustain a claim of a breach of fiduciary duties against those directors. The adoption of this position is similar to that used in the justification for the possible extension of derivative litigation remedy to non-shareholder corporate constituencies under the Stakeholder/Pluralist Theory. The latter theory recognises that the extension of fiduciary remedies to all corporate constituencies inevitably implies that the derivative litigation remedy should be available to those stakeholders as the availability of the remedy effectively signifies some breach of a fiduciary obligation by a director, which obligation is widely owed to all corporate constituencies. The difficulty of applying this reasoning under the ESVA, however, will be that not breaching a fiduciary duty to shareholders because you took the interests of non-shareholder constituencies into consideration is not the same as owing a fiduciary obligation to those constituencies.

## UNITED STATES CORPORATE LAW DEVELOPMENTS

## LEGAL DEVELOPMENTS CONCERNING CORPORATE CONSTITUENCY STATUTES, FLEXIBLE STATUTES, FLEXIBLE PURPOSE, AND BENEFIT CORPORATION STATUTES

### Corporate Constituency Statutes

In an attempt to stem the tide of the obsession with short-termism in corporate decision-making, brought about primarily by the dominant and all-pervasive shareholder-oriented corporate objective approach, perpetuated by corporate statutes in the United States, particularly during the heydays of hostile takeovers in the 1980s and 1990s in that country, a number of states adopted what came to be known as Corporate Constituency Statutes (otherwise known as Non-Stockholder Constituency Statutes). It is commonly accepted that the primary aim of these corporate constituency statutes is to alter the primary corporate objective for public corporations in the states in which those statutes are enacted.[63] These statutes were initially limited to authorising board consideration of non-shareholder interests in takeovers, effectively giving boards a broader basis for 'just saying no' to hostile takeovers.[64] While the American Bar Association's Committee on Corporate Laws has remained resolute on its conclusion that corporate constituency statutes were a bad idea to begin with and has, as a result, refused to adopt non-shareholder constituency provisions into the Model Business Corporation Act, corporate constituency statutes remain in the statute books of no less than 30 states of the US, regardless of their dismissal by the Committee. This is a powerful vote against the policy wisdom of such statutes.

The unmistakably broad corporate objective of corporations propagated by corporate constituency statutes is in clear contrast to the very private corporate objective of corporations as preferred by most corporation statutes of the individual states of the United States, which have, because of their adoption of the Model Business Corporation Act ('the Model Act') in recent times, largely been universal in that country. While the Model Act is designed as a free-standing general corporation statute that can be enacted substantially in its entirety by a state legislature, as of 2020, thirty states had adopted all or substantially all of the Model Act as their general corporation statute,[65] and three other jurisdictions had statutes based on the 1969 version of the Act.[66] Many other states have adopted selected provisions of the Model Act.[67]

What is clear is that in all states which have adopted the Model Act, corporate governance has historically been grounded on shareholder primacy.[68] It is, therefore, hardly surprising that of all thirty states that have adopted all or substantially all of the Model Act as their general corporation statute, only 10 of them do not have corporate constituency statutes.[69]

Even if the Model Act was not of such wide application in the United States, what seems clear is that Delaware corporate law has been widely recognised as 'national corporate law' in the United States.[70] For a long time, it has been established that under Delaware law, a board of directors has a 'broad mandate [that] includes a conferred authority to set a corporate course of action . . . designed to enhance corporate profitability'.[71] It is noteworthy that this position has been greatly enhanced by the reluctance of Delaware to enact a corporate constituency statute.[72]

The Pennsylvania legislature passed the first corporate constituency statute in 1983.[73] Kathleen Hale observes that corporate constituency statutes were developed in an attempt to address the dilemma of corporate leaders not being able to legally consider the interests of non-shareholder constituencies. Even though it was clear that the massive wave of hostile takeovers during the 1980s had deleterious outcomes, which were usually borne by these stakeholders, the phenomenon continued and was exacerbated by the unwavering obligation of these corporate leaders to maximise shareholder wealth at all costs.[74] Notwithstanding that Pennsylvania is not a Model Act state, the literature and case law available point to the fact that, just like all the other states with corporate constituency statutes, the law applicable in that state imposed a legal obligation upon corporation directors to maximise shareholder wealth as part of their duty to promote the interests of the corporation.[75] In other words, just like in many states of the United States, directors and officers of a Pennsylvania corporation are under an obligation to 'exercise their powers and discharge their duties in good faith *with a view to the interests* of the corporation and of the shareholders'.[76] In fact, it is well-known that corporate constituency statutes were not originally conceptualized as non-shareholder corporate constituency empowerment tools generally, but, according to one of the principal originators of these statutes, Martin Lipton, the idea was that these statutes, many of which are limited to board consideration of non-shareholder interests in takeovers, would give boards a broader basis for 'just saying no' to hostile takeovers.[77] As it has turned out in the past 20 to 25 years, they have not been of any use even in that limited role, mainly because of the success of other takeover defence measures, such as the poison pill.[78] According to one authority, the total number of states with corporate constituency statutes amounted to no less than 32 by 2009.[79] However, Alissa Mickels observed that a total of 29 states had some variation of a corporate constituency statute.[80] Interestingly, even other states which are not Model Act states have adopted some form of corporate constituency statutes. The total number of non-Model Act states with corporate constituency statutes is ten.[81] Confirmation of the fact that the overriding concern in all of the states which have adopted these statutes is the maximisation of shareholder wealth within corporations is offered by professor Andrew Keay, who observes, arguably correctly, that '[t]hese kinds of statutes have been introduced so as to ensure that the harshest application of the shareholder value principle does not prevail, certainly to the point of promoting short-termism'.[82] It has also been contended that prior to Stakeholder Statutes, corporate leaders could only be certain that they were 'legally required to manage a corporation for the exclusive benefit of its shareholders'.[83]

This is known within corporate law as the 'shareholder primacy norm',[84] and it refers to management's responsibility and also to corporate law's commitment to shareholder welfare as the primary objective of corporate activity.[85]

## Overview of the Statutes

As has been pointed out in the earlier chapters, the primary reason for Adolf A. Berle's objection to a communitarian approach to corporate law was that this approach would not be workable until 'a reasonably clear and enforceable scheme of responsibilities' to someone else (i.e. non-shareholder corporate constituencies) has been established. The analysis of corporate constituency statutes enacted in the United States since the late 1980s reveals that this objection by Adolf A. Berle is only partially addressed. While most of these statutory corporate constituency measures clearly reveal the identities of corporate constituencies that are to be included in the scheme, the enforceability of the scheme remains unaddressed. Upon analysis of the corporate constituency statutes, it remains clear that there are a number of factors presented by these statutes which militate against the possible imposition of a reasonably and clearly enforceable framework favourable to those corporate constituency groups, as envisaged by Adolf A. Berle.

Before the close analysis of these statutes, in accordance with these factors, it is desirable to outline the many kinds of variation in the statutes, which, for a long time, provided the framework for analysing them as a group.

What could be considered to be the main variation relates to whether consideration of non-shareholder corporate constituencies is mandatory or permissive, with all but one statute giving directors (and officers if applicable) the discretion to consider the interests of, or the impact of their decisions on, non-shareholder corporate constituencies in corporate decision-making. Connecticut is the only state that requires, rather than allows, directors and executives, to consider the interests of enumerated corporate constituencies in corporate decision-making.[86]

The second variation concerns whether it is the directors alone or the directors and the officers who are permitted or required to have regard to the interests of non-shareholder corporate constituencies. Most of the statutes apply only to decisions made by directors of corporations, while a small minority extend to the decisions of directors and officers.[87]

The third difference between the statutes concerns whether reference is made to the 'best interests of the corporation' or 'the best interests of the shareholders'. Most states allow non-shareholder corporate constituencies to be taken into account only when considering the best interests of the corporation. Only a few states add the best interests of the shareholder into this consideration.[88]

The fourth variation relates to whether it is the interests of the non-shareholder corporate constituencies or the effect of corporate decisions on them which may be taken into account. Some statutes allow consideration of the interests of non-shareholder corporate constituencies when making corporate decisions, while others limit consideration to the effects such actions would have on them.[89]

The fifth variation among Non-Stockholder Constituency Statutes relates to whether consideration of non-shareholder corporate constituencies applies to any corporate decision or exists in respect of a particular situation. Most states allow consideration of non-shareholder corporate constituencies during any corporate decision, while a few states limit consideration to only change of control transactions or merger-type situations.[90]

Another important variation relates to the consideration of 'the continued independence of the corporation', with a few statutes specifically stating that the interests of these other corporate constituencies may be best served by the continued independence of the corporation.[91]

The seventh variation concerns the creation of presumptions of validity in statutes. A few states have included sections that create presumptions of validity regarding determinations concerning non-shareholder corporate constituencies.[92]

The eighth variation speaks to the identification of specific non-shareholder corporate constituencies. All of the statutes give examples of the constituencies intended to be considered. Some statutes limit their application to those specified, while others are not limited.[93]

The last noteworthy variation relates to whether statutes apply only when permitted by the articles of incorporation and not automatically. Maryland's statute, for example, does not automatically apply to corporations but allows corporations to include provisions for non-shareholder corporate constituencies in the articles of incorporation.

## The Inclusion of the Statutory Measures Within Core Corporate Law Statutes and Not in Specific Statutory Instruments

In all the states which have adopted these statutory corporate constituency measures,[94] they are incorporated within their primary corporate law statutes, thereby making it difficult to argue convincingly for the adoption of corporate objectives which are diametrically opposed to the traditional corporate law objectives ordinarily espoused by the state concerned. Such existing directives are usually in line with the Model Act. Moreover, these corporate constituency statutes are, almost invariably, always adopted within the context of the provisions dealing with directors' duties. For example, in the context of Florida, which offers a perfect example of incorporating the corporate constituency statute within the context of directors' duties,[95] the obligations of a director to discharge his or her duties '(a) [i] n good faith, (b) [w]ith the care an ordinarily prudent person . . . would exercise under similar circumstances . . . and (c) [i]n a manner he or she reasonably believes to be in the best interests of the corporation' are contained within the first sub-section of the section in which the corporate constituency statute is enacted. Then, in the third sub-section, the statute deals with the content of the corporate constituency statute, expressly making it part of the discharge of the director's duties.[96]

Although the creation of a different corporate objective which enables the adoption of an all-inclusive enforcement framework will invariably fit poorly with the pre-existing one which characterizes the core duties of directors, it is nevertheless necessary, if not inevitable, for the corporate enforcement framework to be reformulated to accommodate clearly altered corporate objectives within the context of statutory corporate constituency mechanisms. This is because the core duties of directors in the United States are, without exception, subject to the shareholder-oriented corporate objective, which effectively militates against the adoption of an all-inclusive legal enforcement framework.[97]

Mainly because most of the states which have adopted corporate constituency statutes are the Model Act states, it is not surprising that under their corporate laws, 'the interests of the corporation' mean the interests of the company, and the 'shareholders' wealth maximisation' or the 'shareholder primacy norm' is every board of directors' primary preoccupation in corporate decision-making.

## The Creation of Priority of Interests in the Statutes, with Shareholder Interests Assuming Pre-eminence

Another important factor regarding corporate constituency statutes, which vividly highlights the fact that the adoption of an all-inclusive legal enforcement framework in the United States remains less an accomplished fact (even in the context of the adoption of these statutes) than an academic inspiration, is the pervasive prioritisation of shareholders' and/or corporations' interests in the language of the statutes.

The close analysis of all corporate constituency statutes reveals that the common denominator of these statutes, with a few notable exceptions, is the creation of an obligation upon the directors to consider the interests of the corporation and/or shareholders, in the first instance, and the complimentary discretion to consider the interests of all other non-shareholder corporate constituent groups, in the second instance.

Although the wording used is not consistent in the prioritisation the *modus operandi* remains the same, nonetheless. The common features of this *modus operandi* consist, in the first place, of the common usage of peremptory terms such as 'must', 'shall' and 'required' when referring to the duties of the directors towards the corporation and/or its shareholders.[98] In the second instance, this prioritisation is shown by the clear indication that the consideration of the interests of non-shareholder corporate constituencies is additional to the interests of the corporation's shareholders.[99] In the third instance, the clear indication that the consideration of the interests of non-shareholder corporate constituent groups is subservient to those of the corporation and/or its shareholders is typified by the clear statements that this is secondary to the discharge, consideration or determination of duties by directors.[100]

The indication that the consideration of non-shareholder corporate constituencies' interests is merely discretionary and thus secondary to the primary obligation to the corporation and/or its shareholders is exemplified by the consistent use of discretionary terms such as 'may', 'allow', and 'in their discretion, consider'.[101]

The use of the 'may' language within the statutes establishes, in the strongest possible terms, that these statutes have 'left consideration of stakeholder groups entirely to corporate directors' and executives' discretion'.[102]

The most ambivalent example is provided by the state of New York, whose corporate constituency statute provides that:

> [I]n taking action, including, without limitation, *action which may involve or relate to a change or potential change in the control of the corporation*, a director *shall* be entitled to consider, *without limitation*, (1) both the long-term and the short-term *interests* of the corporation and its shareholders and (2) *the effects* that the corporation's actions may have in the short-term or in the long-term upon any of the following: (i) the prospects for potential growth, development, productivity and profitability of the corporation; (ii) the corporation's current employees; (iii) the corporation's retired employees and other beneficiaries receiving or entitled to receive retirement, welfare or similar benefits from or pursuant to any plan sponsored, or agreement entered into, by the corporation; (iv) the corporation's customers and creditors; and (v) the ability of the corporation to provide, as a going concern, goods, services, employment opportunities and employment benefits and otherwise to contribute to the communities in which it does business.[103] [Emphasis added].

As though to mitigate the possible far-reaching ramifications of the provision above, the statute provides further that '[n]othing in this paragraph shall create any duties owed by any director to any person or entity *to consider or afford any particular weight* to any of the foregoing *or abrogate any duty of the directors, either statutory or recognized by common law or court decisions'.*[104] [Emphasis added].

Regardless of the fact that New York has not adopted the Model Act as its general corporation statute, its Business Corporation Law clearly subscribes to the notion of 'the interests of the corporation' as the interests of the shareholder body,[105] although this has arguably been weakened by the corporate constituency statute, particularly in the situation of 'a change or potential change in the control of the corporation'.[106]

At first, New York's corporate constituency statute appears to be treating both shareholder and non-shareholder corporate constituencies equally, particularly because of the use of the phrase 'without limitation' when prescribing a duty upon directors to 'consider'. However, the use of the mandatory 'shall' is diluted by the term 'entitled' which follows almost immediately. Furthermore, the term 'interests' is used with regard to shareholders, while only 'the effects [of] the corporation's actions' upon other non-shareholder corporate constituencies may be considered. Consideration of 'interests' may imply the need for proactive measures on behalf of the corporation, while the 'effects' may necessitate reactive measures.

Commenting on the legislation, then Commissioner Joseph Grundfest of the United States Securities and Exchange Commission remarked:

> The grant of authority without accountability raises the real and present danger that boards will use [the statute]as a figleaf. Specifically, [the statute] may allow boards to rationalize decisions that they would not otherwise support in the name of *constituencies who are powerless to monitor or challenge the actions that are purportedly taken in their interest.*[107] [Emphasis added].

This comment confirms the conclusion reached in this book that the single most fundamental weakness of the statutory corporate constituency mechanisms is the lack of legal enforcement framework which empowers non-shareholder corporate constituencies to monitor or challenge actions that are purportedly taken in their interests as explicitly identified corporate constituencies.

It turns out that the creation of this prioritisation of shareholders over other non-shareholder constituencies is, understandably, the most common feature of corporate constituency statutes categorised as permissive, rather than mandatory. Given that all but one of these statutes are permissive, a typically common and comprehensive corporate constituency statute provides that:

> [I]n determining what he reasonably believes to be in or not opposed to the best interests of the corporation, [a director] *shall* consider the interests of the corporation's shareholders and, *in his discretion, may* consider any of the following:

> (1) the interests of the corporation's employees, suppliers, creditors and customers; (2) the economy of the state and nation; (3) the impact of any action upon the communities in or near which the corporation's facilities or operations are located; and (4) the long-term interests of the corporation and its shareholders, including the possibility that those interests may be best served by the continued independence of the corporation.[108] [Emphasis added].

In Connecticut, the only state with a corporate constituency statute characterised as mandatory:

> [A director of a corporation] shall consider, in determining what he reasonably believes to be in the best interests of the corporation, (1) the long-term as well as the short-term interests of the corporation, (2) the interests of the shareholders, long-term as well as short-term, including the possibility that those interests may be best served by the continued independence of the corporation, (3) the interests of the corporation's employees, customers, creditors and suppliers, and (4) community and societal considerations including those of any community in which any office or other facility of the corporation is located.[109]

Furthermore, in Connecticut:

> [A] director may also in his discretion consider any other factors he reasonably considers appropriate in determining what he reasonably believes to be in the best interests of the corporation.[110]

The Connecticut statute is characterised as being mandatory because, unlike other corporate constituency statutes, it employs the peremptory 'shall' to cover the interests of all corporate constituencies, including those of shareholders. The discretion is given to the directors only in respect of any other factors the director reasonably believes to be in the interests of the corporation. These any other factors are in addition to the interests of enumerated shareholder and non-shareholder corporate constituent groups.

Notwithstanding the mandatory nature of Connecticut's corporate constituency statute, the state remains a Model Act state, and it is unsurprising that its corporate statute appears to deal with the content of the duty to promote the best interests of the corporation similarly to § 8.30 of the Model Act, as it provides that '[a] director shall discharge his duties as a director, including his duties as a member of a committee: (1) [i]n good faith; (2) with the care an ordinarily prudent person in a like position would exercise under similar circumstances; and (3) in a manner he reasonably believes to be in the best interests of the corporation'.[111]

Even though Connecticut's statute requires, rather than permits, directors to consider other constituencies, the lack of any decided cases on this mandatory statute makes it almost impossible to determine the practical impact of the statute, particularly in light of the generally stated duty of a director to act in good faith in a manner he reasonably believes to be in the best interests of the corporation. The mandatory language of the statute appears to be of very limited purpose as the statute itself does nothing further in facilitating or enabling the enforcement of the rights, which appear to be created in favour of the non-shareholder corporate constituencies. By not providing the non-shareholder corporate constituencies with legal standing to enforce this statute, Connecticut may have missed the opportunity to supplement the mandatory nature of its statute with a meaningful enforcement mechanism. As Stephen Bainbridge said, in relation to permissive statutes, '[b]ecause *these statutes do not mandate* that directors consider non-shareholder constituents, these [stakeholder] groups probably do not have standing to enforce these statutes' [emphasis added].[112] As the same argument stands even in relation to the single instance of a mandatory corporate constituency statute (i.e. Connecticut), Bainbridge is arguably correct in his analysis.

While the Connecticut statute appears to be advantageous in that it is mandatory, its effect does not seem to be any different from that of permissive statutes, as the legal enforcement framework is clearly not inclusive of all corporate constituent groups. This is the defect equally suffered by all permissive corporate constituency statutes.

At the same time, some corporate constituency statutes categorised as permissive, curiously, either as a result of judicial interpretation or the specific wording employed in the relevant statute, have elements which appear to go beyond the prioritisation of shareholder interests and the perpetuation of the traditional corporate law objective typified by the 'shareholder primacy norm'. The existence of these seemingly transcendental elements notwithstanding, the consistent lack of a legal enforcement framework espousing meaningfully extended legal standing within all the corporate constituency statutes effectively means that these seemingly non-shareholder-centric elements are of limited or no utility in litigiously empowering non-shareholder corporate constituent groups to enforce any failure by the directors to consider their interests.

Notwithstanding that these elements are suggestive of the possible introduction of extended legal standing provisions inclusive of non-shareholder corporate constituent groups, the reality is that in all the states with these elements in their corporate constituency statutes, no such extended legal standing provisions are in existence. The extravagant language used in some of these corporate constituency statutes creates the impression that they are more effective in protecting the interests of non-shareholder corporate constituencies.

However, the reality is that because of the perpetuation of the traditional legal enforcement framework in those statutes, the language only functions as decorative linguistic ornamentation in many states' statute books, while masquerading as potential weapons which non-shareholder corporate constituent groups might be able to employ in launching offensive and defensive suits in protecting their interests. This is because of the lack of express extension of legal standing to the very non-shareholder corporate constituencies targeted by these statutes. In some instances, the expressed denial of the existence of legal standing to enforce the observance of the corporate constituencies' interests possibly militates against an interpretation which suggests the extension of such legal standing to those non-shareholder corporate constituencies.

A detailed analysis of the situation in most of the states having seemingly non-shareholder-centric elements within their corporate constituency statutes is undertaken hereunder. However, the analysis does not include every state with a permissive corporate constituency statute.

### Consideration of the Possibility That the Long-Term and Short-Term Interests of the Corporation and Its Shareholders May Be Best Served by the Continued Independence of the Corporation

The immediate impression created by the consideration of 'the continued independence of the corporation' is that no particular interests, including those of shareholders, should be paramount but should yield to the importance of the continued independence of the corporation. However, a closer analysis of the statutes espousing this phrase clearly shows that 'the continued independence of the corporation' is not an end in itself.[113] On the contrary, it is inextricably linked to the quest for the determination of the long-term and short-term interests of the corporation and its shareholders. It is this qualification which points to the reality that 'the independence of the corporation' is merely the 'prism' through which the long-term and short-term interests of the corporation and its shareholders are given pre-eminence.

As to what is meant by the phrase 'the continued independence of the corporation', Robert M. Hart and Carol M. Degener[114] maintain that it refers to the proposition that 'the directors may consider the possibility that the best interests of the *corporation and its stockholders* may be best served by remaining independent'.[115] [Emphasis added].

However, John A. Anderson insists that the authors may be incorrect in this interpretation.[116] Regardless of the fact that Anderson does not state the reason for his conclusion regarding the incorrectness of this interpretation, it appears that he is opposed to the idea that 'the interests of the corporation' may be served independently of the interests of the shareholder body, something which appears to be in line with the literal reading of the statutes incorporating the phrase. To the extent that the language of the statutes incorporating this phrase does not lend itself to the interpretation suggested by Hart and Degener, Anderson's conclusion seems to be correct. The consideration of all other interests by directors appears, from the language of the statute, to continue to be subject to the interests of shareholders, thus leading to those corporate constituency statutes having no impact on the interpretation of the duty to promote the interests of the corporation. Notwithstanding the aforegoing, James J. Hanks Jr. insists that in takeover situations, the pursuit of the interests of the corporation by maintaining the continued independence of the corporation may effectively lead to a likelihood that non-shareholder corporate constituent groups will identify their best interests with the continued independence of the corporation, while stockholders may view a sale as in their best interests.[117]

Examples of states which have this wording within their corporate constituency statutes include Arizona, which requires directors of publicly held corporations, in discharging their duties and '*in considering the best interests of the corporation*', to '*consider the long-term as well as the short-term interests of the corporation and its shareholders including the possibility that these interests may be best served by the continued independence of the corporation*'.[118] [Emphasis added].

The Hawaiian statute provides that:

> (b) In determining the best interests of the corporation, a director, in addition to considering the interests of the corporation's shareholders, *may consider*, in the director's discretion . . . (4) *[t]he long-term as well as short-term interests of the corporation and its shareholders, including, without limitation, the possibility that these interests may be best served by the continued independence of the corporation.*[119] [Emphasis added].

Another example of a corporate constituency statute making reference to the 'continued independence of the corporation' is that of Idaho, which provides thus:

> In discharging the duties of the position of director of an issuing public corporation, a director, in considering the best interests of the corporation, *shall consider the long-term as well as the short-term interests of the corporation and its shareholders including the possibility that these interests may be best served by the continued independence of the corporation.* In addition, a director may

consider the interests of Idaho employees, suppliers, customers and communities in discharging his duties.[120] [Emphasis added].

Unlike other corporate constituency statutes, which provide for the consideration of 'the continued independence of the corporation' as part of the discretionary power, which includes the consideration of other non-shareholder corporate constituent groups, the Idaho statute has clearly elevated this element to within the ambit of the mandatory duties of the directors. Whether this has the intended impact of supporting the possible bolstering of the legal enforcement framework is questionable.

At most, the message conveyed by this statute is that as it is invariable that the continued independence of the corporation is intertwined with the long-term as well as the short-term interests of the corporation and its shareholders, these interests are of paramount importance. In contrast with the corporation and the shareholders' long-term and short-term interests, and apparently considered as if an after-thought, the interests of non-shareholder corporate constituencies appear to be secondary and not necessarily reliant upon the continued independence of the corporation.

Although of limited application, the Iowa statute also offers another example of a corporate constituency statute giving consideration to the 'continued independence of the corporation'. The statute expressly permits a director, 'in determining what is in the best interest of the corporation when considering a tender offer or proposal of acquisition', to consider the 'effects' of the action on the corporation's employees, suppliers, creditors, and customers, and on communities in which the corporation operates as well as the '*long-term [and] short-term interests of the corporation and its shareholders, including the possibility that these interests may be best served by the continued independence of the corporation*'.[121] [Emphasis added].

Other states incorporating this phrase include Massachusetts, Minnesota, Nevada,[122] Idaho, Kentucky,[123] New Jersey,[124] New Mexico,[125] Ohio,[126] Wisconsin[127] and Wyoming.[128]

## The Existence of Limited Instances of Optional Adoption of the Measures Through Corporate Charters

At least two states in the United States allow the consideration of non-shareholder corporate constituencies' interests by companies only if those companies' articles of incorporation authorize them to do so. This is yet another example of the reluctance by legislatures in the United States to effect any changes to the existing legal enforcement framework, which frowns upon the possible incorporation of extended standing provisions pursuant to the law of general application.

One such state is Georgia, whose corporate constituency statute provides that:

> (b) The articles of incorporation may set forth: . . .
> (5) A provision that, in discharging the duties of their respective positions and in determining what is believed to be in the best interests of the corporation, the board of directors, committees of the board of directors, and individual directors, *in addition to considering the effects of any action on the corporation or its shareholders, may consider the interests of the employees, customers, suppliers, and creditors of the corporation and its subsidiaries, the communities in which offices or other establishments of the corporation and its subsidiaries are located, and all other factors such directors consider pertinent; provided, however, that any such provision shall be deemed solely to grant discretionary authority to the directors and shall not be deemed to provide to any constituency any right to be considered.*[129] [Emphasis added].

While corporations are given the latitude to incorporate corporate constituency statutes only in their articles of incorporation in Georgia, that latitude is extremely limited. A provision authorising the adoption of the permission to consider the interests of non-shareholder corporate constituencies is qualified in at least two important respects. In the first respect, such a provision should clearly clarify that the consideration of non-shareholder corporate constituencies' interests is, in addition to being merely discretionary (because of the use of the discretionary 'may'), it should only be in addition to considering the effects of any action on the corporation or its shareholders. Further, the authorization does not envisage the adoption of a provision which puts the interests of non-shareholder corporate constituencies at par with those of the corporation or its shareholders.

The second state with a corporate constituency statute whose operation is subject to the adoption by corporations through their Articles of Incorporation is Maryland.

Maryland General Corporation Law § 2–104(b)(9) provides that:

> [T]he articles of incorporation may include: . . . [a] *provision that allows* the board of directors, in considering a potential acquisition of control of the corporation, to consider the effect of the potential acquisition of control on . . .; (i) Stockholders, employees, suppliers, customers, and creditors of the corporation; and (ii) Communities in which offices or other establishments of the corporation are located.[130]

The section concludes by stating that:

> [T]he inclusion or omission of a provision in the charter that allows the board of directors to consider the effect of a potential acquisition of control on persons specified in sub-section (b)(9) of this section *does not create an inference concerning factors that may be considered by the board of directors* regarding a potential acquisition of control.[131] [Emphasis added].

Clearly, this unusual Maryland provision is of very limited application in two important respects. First, the statute is optional and can only be invoked by means of the corporation's articles of incorporation. Second, the statute allows consideration of non-shareholder corporate constituencies by the board of directors only in considering a potential acquisition of control of the corporation and not in any circumstance of corporate decision-making as many of the permissive Non-Stockholder Constituency Statutes do.

It is, therefore, indisputable that this statute has no effect on the directors' duty to promote the interests of the corporation under the Maryland General Corporation Law. Even if the statute's adoption by a particular corporation in its articles of incorporation results in fiduciary obligations owed to specified non-shareholder corporate constituencies, its practical efficacy is questionable in the absence of extended standing provisions favourable to non-shareholder corporate constituencies.

## The Lack of Clarity on the Significance of the Provision That 'The Effects of a Proposed Corporate Action on Any Particular Corporate Constituent Group or Interest Should Not Be Considered as a Dominant or Controlling Factor' in Some Statutes

In addition to permitting directors to consider the interests of non-shareholder corporate constituencies in promoting the interests of their corporation, some statutes, like that of Indiana, provide that 'directors are not required to consider the effects of a proposed corporate action on any particular corporate constituent group or interest as a dominant or controlling factor'.[132]

Springer argues that the statute of Indiana, together with the similarly worded one of Pennsylvania, may be seen to defeat the shareholder primacy norm.[133] While the requirement not to 'consider the effects of a proposed corporate action on any particular corporate constituent group or interest as a dominant or controlling factor' may be interpreted to mean that non-shareholder corporate constituent interests may not trump shareholder interests, context suggests that it means that no interest (including shareholder interests) necessarily dominates over any other interest (including non-shareholder corporate constituent interests). This interpretation is supported by the official comment regarding the enumeration of corporate constituents in the Indiana statute, which notes: '[t]he subsection makes clear that a director is not required to view presently quantifiable profit maximization as the sole or necessarily controlling determinant of the corporation's "best interests"'.[134]

Statutes like that of Indiana are different from most of the other corporate constituency statutes in one important respect. It appears from the language of the statute that the effects of any corporate decision on shareholders are not considered differently or as more important than the effects of corporate decisions on other non-shareholder corporate constituencies. Indeed, Professor Andrew Keay acknowledges that '[t]he statutes enacted in Indiana and Pennsylvania[135] expressly provided in their respective Codes that directors are not required to give dominant effect to any constituency, thereby ruling out mandatory adherence to the Shareholder Value Approach'.[136] He further provides endorsement of this conclusion by the Committee on Corporate Laws of the Section of Business Law of the American Bar Association.[137] While it may seem as if Indiana is among those few states which are 'ahead of the pack' in 'ruling out mandatory adherence to the Shareholder Value Approach', this may not be enough to ensure that the non-shareholder corporate constituencies are vested with enforcement powers, as they do not have explicit legal standing powers to enforce their rights in court. Like all other corporate constituency statutes, this substantially reduces the effects of any gains resulting from the alteration of the common law 'shareholder-oriented' Shareholder Value Approach.[138]

The state of Iowa also takes an approach similar to that of Indiana, particularly in relation to takeovers.[139] If the board determines, 'on the basis of the community interest factors', that a takeover 'is not in the best interests of the corporation, it may reject the proposal or offer'.[140] In that case, the board 'has no obligation to facilitate, to remove any barriers to, or to refrain from impeding, the proposal or offer'.[141] Interestingly, the statute further provides that:

> [C]onsideration of any or all of the community interest factors is not a violation of the business judgment rule or of any duty of the director to the shareholders, or a group of shareholders, *even if the director reasonably determines that a community interest factor or factors outweigh the financial or other benefits to the corporation or a shareholder or group of shareholders.* [142] [Emphasis added].

Because of the wording of Iowa's corporate constituency statute, it is clear that directors may consider the interests of other corporate constituencies equally with shareholders' interests.[143] The statute specifically contemplates the possibility of the interests of non-shareholder corporate constituencies being equated to the interests of the corporation, even when directors reasonably determine that such non-shareholder corporate constituencies' interests outweigh the financial or other benefits to a shareholder or group of shareholders. While this development has the potential to revolutionise the interpretation of 'the interests of the corporation', its major weakness lies in the fact that it is only limited to change of control situations (particularly, tender offers) and is not supplemented by enforcement powers for the benefit of those non-shareholder constituencies or extended legal standing provisions benefitting those constituencies.

With regard to directors' duty of care, the Pennsylvania statute also specifies that consideration of non-shareholder constituencies' interests is in accordance with directors' duty of care, that takeover defences do not implicate a higher standard of judicial scrutiny, and that this duty does not require directors to consider only share price in a takeover attempt. This statute explicitly rejects *Unocal*[144] and the *Revlon*[145] duty to auction in a change of control transactions.

Another interesting example of the statute worded in these terms is found in the state of Nevada, whose statute also explicitly states that '[d]irectors and officers are not required to consider the effect of a proposed corporate action upon any particular group having an interest in the corporation as a dominant factor'.[146]

Interestingly, however, the statute further states that '[t]he provisions of sub-sections 4 and 5 do not create or authorize any causes of action against the corporation or its directors or officers'.[147]

Even though Nevada is not a Model Act state, it is, nevertheless, still subject to the 'shareholder primacy norm' as is evidenced by the relevant provision of the state's corporate statute, which provides that '[d]irectors and officers shall exercise their powers in good faith and with a view to the interests of the corporation'.[148]

While it appears, at first glance, that the Nevada statute is not unlike the other permissive corporate constituency statutes, what stands out is the unusual provision which effectively states that no effect of a proposed corporate action upon the interest of any particular group, in respect of which directors and officers are expected to consider, should be considered as a dominant factor. This is clearly an attempt to indicate that even the interests of the shareholders are not to be regarded as being dominant within Nevada corporations. It remains to be seen how this particular provision will be interpreted by Nevada courts. Before any authoritative confirmation of the fact that shareholder interests are not dominant and should thus be considered equally with those of the other non-shareholder corporate constituencies, the prevailing interpretation of the interests of the corporation as the interests of the shareholder body remains applicable.

The statute concludes by confirming that the permission granted to the directors and officers to consider both shareholder and non-shareholder constituencies' interests does not necessarily authorize any cause of action against the corporation or its directors or officers, thus discounting the possible existence of any legal standing to bring an action against the corporation, its directors or officers to enforce the consideration of the relevant interests referred to in the statute. What if the affected corporate constituent group can adduce evidence that their interests, as referred to in the relevant statute, have been violated? Should that not be enough to sustain an action by or on behalf of that constituent group? Of course, proof of violation of a person's interests is very likely to point to the existence of a cause of action, such as the commission of a delict or a breach of some contractual commitments.

## The (In)Significance of the Existence of Limited Case Law Which Represents a Significant Departure from the Established and Accepted Conventional Fiduciary Law

Although the state of Maine, in addition to being a Model Act state, has a corporate constituency statute which appears to echo the 'shareholder primacy' norm,[149] some limited case law emanating from that state, suggests otherwise.

The shareholder-oriented nature of Maine's corporate laws did not appear to have been altered by the amendment to that state's corporate constituency statute in 1987 when the Maine legislature added the following new section to the statute:

> [A] director shall not be held personally liable for monetary damages for failure to discharge any duty as a director unless the director is found not to have acted honestly or in the reasonable belief that the action was in or not opposed to the best interests of the corporation *or* its shareholders.[150] [Emphasis added].

That said, however, the judiciary appeared to have viewed things differently in the state's controversial case of *Georgia-Pacific Corp. v Great Northern Nekoosa Corp.*[151] concerning the interpretation of the statute. In that case, the court in the US District Court for the District of Maine concluded that:

> Maine law suggests that the Directors of a corporation, in considering the best interests of the shareholders and corporation, *should* also consider the *interests* of the company's employees, its customers and suppliers, and communities in which offices of the corporation are located.[152] [Emphasis added].

It has been observed that as 'the Maine Legislature or the Maine Supreme Judicial Court have refuted the *Georgia-Pacific* interpretation, which comes close to creating a duty on directors to consider non-shareholder constituencies, this represents a significant departure from Maine fiduciary duty law'.[153]

John A. Anderson argues that '[w]hen reading the literal words of the statute in conjunction with the *Georgia-Pacific* court's interpretation . . . it is harder to argue that no duties flow to other constituencies'.[154]

However, James B. Zimpritch argues that:

> [O]ther than this one isolated and unique case, there is no Maine case law that supports making 'other constituencies' beneficiaries of [directors' fiduciary] duties, and [the corporate constituency statute] literally allows directors and officers to consider other constituencies only while adhering to their duties to the shareholders and the corporation.

He concludes that the words of the statute do not impose upon the directors and officers the obligation to consider these other constituencies.[155] Even if this isolated judicial interpretation of the corporate constituency statute of Maine (which is similar to all the other permissive corporate constituency statutes) were to be supported, the lack of complementary expanded legal standing, which includes non-shareholder corporate constituent groups, significantly reduces the utility of that interpretation, particularly in the light of the 1987 amendment referred to above.

This narrow interpretation of the statute, with a view to ensuring the preservation of the 'shareholder-oriented approach', is supported by the Official Comment to § 8.30 of the Model Act, which authoritatively states as follows:

> The phrase 'best interests of the corporation' is key to an explication of a director's duties. The term 'corporation' is a surrogate for the business enterprise as well as a frame of reference encompassing the shareholder body. In determining the corporation's 'best interests', the director has wide discretion in deciding how to weigh near-term opportunities versus long-term benefits as well as in making judgments where the interests of various groups within the shareholder body or having other cognizable interests in the enterprise may differ.[156]

Another relevant judicial interpretation of the meaning of the corporate constituency statute emanates from the state of Pennsylvania, which, similarly to other states with permissive corporate constituency statutes, only affords directors discretion (i.e. because of the use of the language '*may*' in relation to non-shareholder corporate constituencies) to pay attention to non-shareholder considerations. As if the discretionary language were not enough, the statute also permits directors to consider solely the effects of any action on non-shareholder corporate constituencies and not the interests of such constituencies. Regardless of the explicit language of the statute, the court in the case of *Baron v Strawbridge & Clothier*[157]found that, because of the statute, the 'interests of corporate constituent groups' statute constituted one component to consider in determining whether the directors had satisfied their duties. The court said this without clearly showing the significance of the difference between the consideration of 'the effects of corporations' actions upon non-shareholder constituencies' and the consideration of 'the interests of' those constituencies. Nevertheless, by signifying the differences between the two, state legislatures appear to recognise the importance of the distinction.

While the corporate constituency statute of Wisconsin clearly states that 'the consideration of the effects of corporate actions on non-shareholder corporate constituencies by directors is secondary or subservient to the consideration of corporate actions on the corporation's shareholders',[158] in the case of *Amanda Acquisitions Corp. v Universal Foods Corp.*,[159] the court placed the considerations of the other constituencies on a par with those of the shareholders, despite the limited scope of the statute. In this case, the court found that '[t]he board has the *responsibility* to exercise its business judgment in accord with the best *interests* of the shareholders, the company, and the other constituencies'.[160] [Emphasis added]. This was said by the court regardless of the fact that Wisconsin's statute at that time stated that directors *could* consider the *effects* of actions on constituencies.[161] As correctly observed by John A. Anderson,[162] '[i]n *Amanda,* the court expanded the scope of the statute in much the same way that the literal meaning of Maine's statute was expanded in *Georgia-Pacific*'.[163]

The *Amanda* case was appealed to the Seventh Circuit,[164] which although not focusing on the lower court's discussion of non-shareholder corporate constituencies, appeared to agree with the lower court's conclusion, effectively reading a discretionary statute to create a requirement for directors to consider the interests of other constituencies.[165] In the final analysis, the creation of the requirement through judicial interpretation, contrary to the expressed language of the statute, is of questionable utility unless and until confirmed by the Supreme Court of Wisconsin.

In conclusion, the apparent significance attached to non-shareholder corporate constituencies by the courts in Maine, Pennsylvania and Wisconsin notwithstanding, the lack of explicit extended standing provisions under any of the concerned statutes is evidence of the continued application of the conventional shareholder-oriented legal enforcement regime, particularly as the relevant cases discussed do not recognise much less create, means for non-shareholder corporate constituencies to enforce rights under the statutes.

## The Lack of Uniformity in the Categories of Corporate Constituencies to Be Taken into Account by the Directors

In the analysis of the statutes, one cannot help but wonder what the significance of the stark differences in the categories of corporate constituencies permitted to be taken into account by directors is. While the majority of the states (in fact, all but one) with corporate constituency statutes contain the explicit enumeration of a number of corporate constituent groups that directors are permitted to take into account in addition to the corporation and/or its shareholders, one state is silent on the specific categories of those corporate constituent groups, stating merely that directors are permitted to consider 'the possibility that the [long-term as well as the short-term] interests of the corporation and its shareholders may be best served by the continued independence of the corporation'.[166]

Except for Arizona, all states with corporate constituency statutes incorporate specific categories of non-shareholder corporate constituent groups which directors are permitted to take into account in considering the interests of the corporation and/or its shareholders. As discerned from the cross-section of the statutes discussed in this chapter, the most commonly mentioned categories of corporate constituent groups are 'the corporation's employees', 'suppliers', 'creditors', 'customers', 'the economy of the state' and 'the community' (in which the business of the corporation is undertaken).

The state of Wisconsin's statute is slightly expansive and authorizes the directors

> '[i]n determining what the director reasonably believes to be in the best interests of the corporation, to consider, *in addition*, the interests of the corporation's employees, suppliers, creditors and customers, the economy of the state, region and nation, community and societal considerations, including those of any community in which any offices or facilities of the corporation are located, and any other factors the director *in his or her discretion reasonably considers appropriate in determining what he or she reasonably believes to be in the best interests of the corporation*, and the long-term and short-term interests of the corporation and its stockholders, and including the possibility that these interests may best be served by the continued independence of the corporation.' [Emphasis added].

Another comprehensive statute is that of Wyoming, which provides thus:

> [A] director, in determining what he reasonably believes to be in or not opposed to the best interests of the corporation, *shall consider the interests of the corporation's shareholders* and, *in his discretion, may consider* any of the following: (i) the interests of the corporation's employees, suppliers, creditors and customers; (ii) the economy of the state and nation; (iii) the impact of any action upon the communities in or near which the corporation's facilities or operations are located; (iv) the long-term interests of the corporation and its shareholders, including the possibility that those interests may be best served by the continued independence of the corporation; and (v) any other factors relevant to promoting or preserving public or community interests.[167] [Emphasis added].

Prior to the amendment of the Wyoming Non-Stockholder Constituency Statute, the state had what was known as the 'bondholder protection statute', which permitted certain publicly traded Wyoming corporations to provide by charter for bondholder approval of a merger or acquisition, replacement of more than 24 per cent of directors, sale or disposition of specified percentages of assets or the acquisition of debt above certain percentages of assets and/or net worth.

It appears from the in-depth analysis of all the corporate constituency statutes that the limited or expansive nature of the categories of corporate constituent groups has no bearing on the impact of the statute in fostering the overall effectiveness of the consideration of the interests of non-shareholder corporate constituencies in the states concerned. As corporate law standards of directors proceed from the premise that '[e]ach member of the board of directors when discharging the duties of a director, shall act '(i) [i]n good faith and (ii) [i]n a manner he reasonably believes to be in or at least not opposed to the best interests of the corporation',[168] this effectively confirms the continued application of the traditional corporate law proposition, anchored on the 'shareholder primacy norm'.

In analysing the scope of Stakeholder Statutes across jurisdictions, Edward S. Adams & John H. Matheson argue that the Wyoming statute covers the major elements of all Stakeholder Statutes.[169] This commendation notwithstanding, the statute appears to be lacking in making inroads into the prevailing jurisprudence in the state, which regulates the determination of the primary corporate objective to be in line with the 'shareholder primacy norm'. This appears from the language of the statute itself, which (like the rest) mandates (i.e.'*shall* consider the interests of the corporation's shareholders') the consideration of the interests of the corporation's shareholders but only permits (i.e. '*in his discretion, may* consider') the consideration of the interests of non-shareholder corporate constituencies, the economy of the state and nation, the impact of any action upon the communities in or near which the corporation's facilities or operations are located, and the long-term interests of the corporation and its shareholders. Again, as with all statutory corporate constituency mechanisms addressed in this chapter, the extension of legal standing for non-shareholder corporate constituencies, as clearly mandated by the decades-old call for a clear and reasonably enforceable scheme for non-shareholder corporate constituency groups, remains largely unheeded.

## Preliminary Observations on Corporate Constituency Statutes

As observed in the above assessment, the majority of corporate constituency statutes are permissive in nature. In other words, directors are not obliged but are permitted, to have regard to the interests of non-shareholder corporate constituencies in their corporate decision-making or to consider the effects of their decisions on the relevant non-shareholder corporate constituencies.

As most of the states with corporate constituency statutes have adopted the Model Act in its entirety as their general corporation statute,[170] the single overriding concern in corporate governance in those states is, to use the words of Sir Ronald Hampel, 'the preservation and the greatest practicable enhancement over time of . . . shareholders' investment'.[171] In other words, shareholder wealth maximisation is the primary corporate objective under the corporate law of most of the statutes with non-shareholder corporate constituency statutes, thus rendering the extension of the legal standing provisions beyond shareholders to be out of the question.

Furthermore, corporate constituency statutes that apply only in limited instances, such as in change of control transactions such as takeovers, are clearly limited in their impact as compared to open-ended statutes of other states with permissive corporate constituency statutes. According to Kathleen Hale, '[a]lthough stakeholder interests are certainly at risk in a change of control situation, this view is less inclusive than state statutes recognizing that stakeholder interests are implicated by almost all corporate decisions.[172] It is forcefully maintained by James J Hanks Jr., however, that the situation may be different in takeover situations, as 'non-shareholder groups are likely to identify their best interests with the continued independence of the corporation, while stockholders may view a sale as in their best interests'.[173] In this regard, he maintains that non-shareholder constituency statutes introduce an almost unlimited number of potential new competitors for the residual assets of the corporation and, therefore, for the directors' attention.[174]

The permissive nature of most corporate constituency statutes, however, equally affects the usefulness of these statutes, whether they are of limited application or expansive. Permissive statutes are only beneficial to the extent that corporate controllers are now legally permitted, but not obliged, to have regard to non-shareholder corporate constituencies without breaching their fiduciary duties.[175] However, as there is no change in the fiduciary duties of corporate controllers, permissive corporate constituency statutes effectively have no impact on the corporate objective of shareholder wealth maximisation.[176]

Some corporate constituency statutes, such as that of Georgia, expressly discount any possible interpretation implying the existence of an enforceable legal scheme available to anyone other than shareholders. For example, sub-section (5) of Ga. Code Ann. § 14–2–202(b) effectively dashes any possibility of the existence of a legitimate expectation or a right in favour of the relevant non-shareholder corporate constituent groups to have their interests or the effects of the directors' decisions on them considered, as it expressly provides that any non-shareholder constituency provision incorporated in the corporation's Articles of Incorporation 'shall be deemed solely to grant discretionary authority to the directors and shall *not* be deemed to provide to any constituency any right to be considered'.[177] By making it clear that a company which has this provision in its articles of incorporation does not create a right for non-shareholder corporate constituent groups to be considered by the decision-makers in corporate decision-making, the statute clearly precludes any possibility of the inclusion of an all-inclusive legal enforcement framework.

Notwithstanding the many states that have adopted some form of corporate constituency statute, very few of these statutes have since been the subject of judicial interpretation. In one of the few reported cases, *Baron v Strawbridge & Clothier*,[178] which interpreted Pennsylvania's statute, the court found that the directors' consideration of the effects of a tender offer on non-shareholder corporate constituencies did not breach the duty owed to shareholders. It was held that 'it was proper for the company to consider the effects the . . . tender offer would have, if successful, on the Company's employees, customers and community'.[179]

That said, however, the fact that corporate constituency statutes do not breach the duty owed to shareholders does not mean that the statutes have the effect of altering that duty owed to the shareholder body. Neither does it mean that those non-shareholder corporate constituent groups have automatic legal standing to enforce the right or expectation created by the statute, particularly in the absence of any judicial pronouncement to that effect.

With many of the states that have corporate constituency statutes being Model Act states, the perpetuation of the current legal enforcement framework, characterised by the exclusive directorial accountability to, and legal enforceability by, the shareholders is almost invariably inevitable, with the term 'corporation' being 'a surrogate for the business enterprise as well as a frame of reference encompassing the shareholder body'.[180]

This means that the fact that any particular corporate constituency statute is as comprehensive as possible does not mean much because its possible impact on the duty to promote the interests of the corporation or shareholders is virtually non-existent, as the consideration of the interests of non-shareholder corporate constituencies appears, in almost all cases, to be required to be undertaken through the prism of the 'corporation', which is tantamount to the interests of shareholders. This approach is, at best, intended to protect directors rather than the enumerated corporate constituencies.

Regardless of the fact that some states with corporate constituency statutes have not adopted the Model Act and are, as such, not subject to the provisions of § 8.30 of the Model Act reinforcing the shareholder primacy norm such as Louisiana, this does not mean that they do not subscribe to 'the shareholder primacy norm'. On the contrary, reference to 'the best interest of the corporation and its shareholders', even in the corporate constituency statutes of states which are not Model Act states,[181] clearly signifies the application of the 'shareholder primacy norm'.

Moreover, the analysis of corporate constituency statutes by the American Bar Association Committee on Corporate Laws suggests that [all these statutes] 'may radically *alter some of the basic premises upon which corporation law has been constructed in this country* without sufficient attention having been given to all of the economic, social, and legal ramifications of *such a change in the law* . . .',[182] thereby suggesting that the generally applicable legal position in the whole of the United States with regard to the duty to promote the interests of the corporation is based on the primary consideration of the interests of the 'shareholders'. [Emphasis added].

During the late 1990s, the effectiveness, or otherwise, of the corporate constituency statutes was a topic of contention between their proponents and their critics, notable of whom were Lawrence E. Mitchell[183] and Jonathan D. Springer.[184]

For his part, Mitchell remained adamant that these statutes implicitly question the underlying precept that directors *ought* to be accountable exclusively to shareholders and that the statutes are also capable of being enforced by the very non-shareholder corporate constituencies identified in them.[185] He insists that the statutes challenge corporate law assumptions that the corporate balance of power is anchored on the supremacy of the shareholders as the only beneficiaries of directorial fiduciary duties and corporate law remedies.[186]

Lamenting the failure of the statutes to live up to expectations, Springer concluded that constituency statutes realised neither the hopes they initially inspired nor the fears they initially instilled.[187] He argued that the hopes instilled on the basis that the introduction of these statutes would protect the otherwise unprotected interests of corporate constituencies, notably employees, who might be adversely affected by corporate actions, never came to pass.[188] At the same time, the fears that these statutes would enable corporate constituent groups or unaccountable managers to wrest the reins of control from their rightful owners – corporate shareholders – never materialized either.[189]

Regardless of what the proponents and the critics of these statutes say, what remains indisputable is that the pervasive weakness of the statutes lies in their general lack of a clear and reasonably enforceable legal framework, which should ideally consist of the extension of legal standing to non-shareholder corporate constituencies to be able to bring corporate law remedies. Furthermore, as has been shown, the overall utility of these statutory measures is not greatly affected by whether the application of the relevant statutory measures is limited to a change of control transactions (such as takeovers, mergers and amalgamations, or proposals to dispose of all or greater parts of the corporation's undertaking) or whether the measures apply beyond those transactions.

## BENEFIT CORPORATION STATUTES AND THE FLEXIBLE PURPOSE CORPORATION STATUTE

### Introduction

The benefit corporation legislation was first introduced in the United States in 2010, and since then, other countries like Colombia, Ecuador, France and Italy have also passed similar laws (Benefit Corporation 2021). Currently, thirty-five states and Washington, D.C., have passed legislation allowing for the creation of benefit corporations. On 17 July 2013, Delaware became the eighteenth state to enact the benefit corporation statute. The following states have, to date, adopted the benefit corporation legislation: in alphabetical order, Arizona, Arkansas, California, Colorado, Delaware, Florida, Hawaii, Idaho, Indiana, Illinois, Louisiana, Kansas, Kentucky, Maryland, Massachusetts, Minnesota, Montana, Nebraska, Nevada, New Hampshire, New Jersey, New Mexico, New York, Oregon, Pennsylvania, Rhode Island, South Carolina, Tennessee, Texas, Utah, Vermont, Virginia, Washington, D.C., West Virginia and Wisconsin. When California became the seventh state to adopt the benefit corporation legislation, it also became the only state to enact the flexible purpose corporation statute.[190]

A typical flexible purpose corporation statute will provide for the establishment of a flexible purpose corporation in much the same way as a traditional for-profit corporation, with shareholders and a board of directors, but with its articles of incorporation and share certificates being required to state that the corporation is organized as a flexible purpose corporation, with its articles identifying a 'special purpose' from the following list:

(1) One or more charitable or public purpose activities that a non-profit public benefit corporation is authorized to carry out; or (2) the purpose of

promoting positive short-term or long-term effects of, or minimising adverse short-term or long-term effects of, the flexible purpose corporation's activities upon any of the following: (a) the flexible purpose corporation's employees, suppliers, customers, and creditors; (b) the community and society; or (c) the environment.

Both the flexible purpose corporation and the benefit corporation statutes are similar in the sense that, unlike the traditional corporate statute, which is subject to the corporate law dispensation which elevates the (financial) return to shareholders as the primary or the sole objective of the corporation, a flexible purpose corporation and a benefit corporation are intended to allow entrepreneurs and investors the choice of organizing companies that can pursue both economic and social objectives.

As the number of states with benefit corporation statutes has increased rapidly to thirty-five since the first statute was adopted in Maryland in 2010, this summary will not attempt to deal with the individual statutes of each of the states that have adopted the legislation. Instead, the summary will provide a global analysis of the statutes. A noteworthy point is that both Delaware and Maryland have benefit corporation statutes. The reason for mentioning these states specifically is that the two states are, respectively, the most popular and the second most popular states for incorporation of New York Stock Exchange-listed corporations.

Moreover, given Delaware's special position of having codified 'the national corporate law of the US', particularly for determining the applicable corporate objective within public corporations in that country, the adoption of the benefit corporation legislation in that state reportedly 'signals a seismic shift in corporate law for the United States'.

The benefit corporation statutes introduce the possibility of organizing companies that can pursue both economic and social objectives. In essence, each of the statutes permits a corporation to elect to pursue, for a corporate purpose, the providing of certain public benefits without subjecting the corporation or its directors to liability or derivative suits, except for specified reasons. These corporations are commonly known as benefit corporations or 'sustainable business corporations'.

After analysing California's flexible purpose corporation statute hereunder, the summary will turn to the global analysis of benefit corporation statutes in the states with such statutes.

## Flexible Purpose Corporation Statute in California

As in many US states, existing law in California allows for the incorporation of business (or 'for-profit') corporations that operate within a paradigm that places the interests of shareholders, and specifically return to shareholders, as the primary, if not sole, objective of the corporation.

The essence of the Flexible Purpose Corporation Statute in California:

> The flexible purpose corporation statute authorizes and regulates the formation and operation of a new form of corporate entity known as a flexible purpose corporation.
>
> According to the Act, '[o]ne or more natural persons, partnerships, associations, flexible purpose corporations, or corporations, domestic or foreign, may form a flexible purpose corporation . . . by executing and filing articles of incorporation'.

In the main, the articles of incorporation of a flexible purpose corporation must set out the following:

(a) The name of the flexible purpose corporation that shall contain the words flexible purpose corporation or an abbreviation of those words;
(b) The purpose of the flexible purpose corporation, which must be for the benefit of the long-term and the short-term interests of the flexible purpose corporation and its shareholders;
(c) The purpose of promoting positive short-term or long-term effects of, or minimizing adverse short-term or long-term effects of, the flexible purpose corporation's activities upon any of the following:
  (i) The flexible purpose corporation's employees, suppliers, customers, and creditors;
  (ii) The community and society;
  (iii) The environment; and
(d) A statement that the flexible purpose corporation is organized as a flexible purpose corporation under the Corporate Flexibility Act of 2011.

## Enforcement of the Flexible Purpose Corporation Statute by Non-Shareholder Corporate Constituencies

The flexible purpose corporation statute is different from the corporate constituency statute in the sense that the pursuit of the goal of improving the effects of the flexible purpose corporation's activities upon non-shareholder corporate constituencies is not secondary or subsidiary to the interests of the shareholders. The reality is that just like the purpose of promoting the interests of the corporation and its shareholders, the purpose of promoting or minimising the effects of the corporation's activities upon non-shareholder corporate constituencies is also regarded as an end in itself.

## The Essence of the Benefit Corporation Statutes

In contrast with all the other states that have adopted the benefit corporation statutes, only California introduced not one but two new corporate forms – a flexible purpose corporation and a benefit corporation – pursuant to two competing statutes.

In all the states with benefit corporation statutes, a benefit corporation can be set up much like a traditional, for-profit corporation, but its articles of incorporation must state that it is a benefit corporation, with a general public benefit and optional specific public benefits. A general public benefit is defined as a 'material positive impact on society and the environment, taken as a whole, as assessed against a third-party standard'. The optional specific public benefits can include any of the following:

(1) Providing low-income or underserved individuals or communities with beneficial products or services.
(2) Promoting economic opportunity for individuals or communities beyond the creation of jobs in the ordinary course of business.
(3) Preserving the environment.
(4) Improving human health.
(5) Promoting the arts, sciences, or advancement of knowledge.
(6) Increasing the flow of capital to entities with a public benefit purpose.
(7) The accomplishment of any other particular benefit for society or the environment.

The 'third-party standard' utilised by a benefit corporation refers to a 'standard for defining, reporting, and assessing overall corporate social and environmental performance to which all' of a long list of requirements apply.

Any traditional for-profit corporation can become a benefit corporation simply by amending its articles to state that the entity is a benefit corporation, and likewise, a benefit corporation can terminate its status as a benefit corporation simply by amending its articles to delete such statements. In either case, the amendment requires approval by at least two-thirds of the outstanding shares of each class or series of stock of the corporation, regardless of any limitation stated in the articles or bylaws on the voting rights of any class or series.

In addition, the corporation changing its status must provide dissenters' rights to all shareholders not voting in favour of the proposed change. A benefit corporation may amend, add or delete any additional, specific public benefits identified in its articles by amending its articles, with the approval of at least two-thirds of the outstanding shares of each class or series of its stock (or a higher threshold, if specified in its articles).

## The Essence and the Enforcement of the Benefit Corporation Statutes by Non-Shareholder Corporate Constituencies

A common provision present in all the benefit corporation statutes in relation to the interests of the corporation is to the effect that '[t]he creation of general and specific public benefits . . . shall be in the best interests of the [benefit/ sustainable business] corporation', effectively signifying that the pursuit of public benefits, as opposed to stockholders' interests, is tantamount to the promotion of the best interests of the corporation. This is so regardless of whether the company which adopted those general and specific public benefits is a conventional 'for-profit' corporation. What this means is that contrary to the traditional corporate law proposition which regards the interests of the corporation as equivalent to the interests of the shareholders, it is the general and specific public benefits which constitute 'the interests of the corporation' in a benefit corporation.

The statutes further assert that "[i]n discharging their respective duties, the board of directors, committees of the board and individual directors of a benefit corporation are required to 'consider the impacts of any action or proposed action upon all of the following':

(1) The shareholders of the benefit corporation;
(2) The employees and workforce of the benefit corporation and its subsidiaries and suppliers;
(3) The interests of customers of the benefit corporation as beneficiaries of the general or specific public benefit purposes of the benefit corporation;
(4) Community and societal considerations, including those of any community in which offices or facilities of the benefit corporation or its subsidiaries or suppliers are located;
(5) The local and global environment;
(6) The short-term and long-term interests of the benefit corporation, including benefits that may accrue to the benefit corporation from its long-term plans and the possibility that these interests may be best served by retaining control of the benefit corporation rather than selling or transferring control to another entity; and
(7) The ability of the benefit corporation to accomplish its general, and any specific public benefit, purpose.

In California, the statute expressly provides that no priority should be afforded to any of the constituencies, including the shareholder constituencies, in discharging directors' duties within the benefit corporation. However, other states appear to be ranking corporate constituencies' interests in the same manner accomplished by most corporate constituency statutes discussed above. The only difference, however, appears to be the inclusion of the accomplishment of general and specific public benefits within the category of interests the directors are required, as opposed to permitted, to take into account in corporate decision-making. A typical section in this regard provides that:

(a) In discharging the duties of their respective positions, the board of directors, committees of the board, and individual directors of a sustainable business corporation, in considering the best interests of the sustainable business corporation:
  (1) Shall consider the effects of any action of the sustainable business corporation upon:
    (A) The shareholders of the sustainable business corporation; and
    (B) The accomplishment of *general and specific public benefits* set forth in the sustainable business corporation's purposes; and [emphasis added].
  (2) May consider:
    (A) The employees and workforce of the sustainable business corporation and its subsidiaries and suppliers;
    (B) The interests of customers as beneficiaries of the general or specific public benefit purposes of the sustainable business corporation;
    (C) Community and societal considerations, including those of any community in which offices or facilities of the sustainable business corporation or its subsidiaries or suppliers are located;
    (D) The local and global environment;
    (E) The short-term and long-term interests of the sustainable business corporation, including benefits that may accrue to the sustainable business corporation from its long-term plans and the possibility that these interests may be best served by the continued independence of the sustainable business corporation;
    (F) The ability of the sustainable business corporation to accomplish its general public benefit purpose and any specific public benefit purpose;
    (G) The resources, intent, and conduct of any person seeking to acquire control of the corporation; and
    (H) Any other pertinent factors or *the interests of any other group* that they deem appropriate. [Emphasis added].
(b) A director shall not be personally liable for monetary damages for any action taken as a director if the director performed the duties of the director's office in compliance with the general standards of conduct pursuant to section 414–221. [191]

It is interesting to note that the effects of corporate actions on the interests of shareholders, the sustainability of the business corporation and the accomplishment of general and specific public benefits are mandatory factors that must be considered by the board of directors, committees of the board, and individual directors of a sustainable business corporation in corporate decision-making. The main concern about this section is its indemnification of a director of a sustainable business corporation from personal liability for monetary damages where such a director performs the duties of the director's office in compliance with the general standards of conduct, regardless of the fact that such general standards of conduct place the interests of shareholders above those of any other corporate constituent group, including the accomplishment of general and specific public benefits.

This is clearly in conflict with the statute's declaration that it is the general and specific public benefits which are the interests of the corporation. It is also disconcerting for the statute to allow directors to merely exercise their discretion in deciding whether to take into account other non-shareholder corporate constituency considerations, regardless of the possibility that such considerations may, in fact, form part of the said general and/or specific public benefits.

A clearly misconceived provision regarding enforcement of the benefit corporation statute is found, for example, in section 10 of the Hawaii Sustainable Business Corporation Act, which provides that:

> [T]he shareholders and directors of a sustainable business corporation shall have the right to bring direct or derivative claims to enforce corporate purposes and the standards for directors as set forth in section 414-221(a) and shall have the right to bring direct or derivative claims to enforce the general or specific public benefit purposes of the sustainable business corporation and the standard of conduct for directors pursuant to section 6(a)(1).[192]

While it is understandable for the institution of direct or derivative claims to be limited to the shareholders and directors in respect of the breach of general standards of conduct which endorse the 'shareholder primacy norm', it is inexplicable that such limitation should be extended to the institution of direct or derivative claims to enforce the general or specific public benefit purposes of the sustainable business corporation and the standard of conduct for directors, pursuant to section 6(a)(1).

While it appears that the provisions of section 6(a) and (b) of the New Jersey Benefit Corporation Act envisage some element involving ranking the non-shareholder corporate constituency factors, with those in section 6(a) imposing a mandatory requirement on behalf of the board of directors, as contrasted with the discretionary considerations in section 6(b), this interpretation is expressly countered by the provisions of section 6(c), which provides that:

> [T]he board of directors, committees of the board and individual directors of a benefit corporation shall not be required to give priority to the interests of any particular person or group referred to in subsection a. or subsection b. of this section over the interests of any other person or group unless the benefit corporation has stated its intention to give priority to interests related to a specific public benefit purpose identified in its certificate of incorporation.[193]

The right of action under the New Jersey Benefit Corporation Statute is addressed in an interesting manner, which has the potential to extend legal standing to unconventional litigants where the benefit corporation has identified those potential non-shareholder corporate constituencies as litigants within the corporation's certificate of incorporation or its by-laws. In this regard, section 10(a) and (b) provide that:

> . . . [t]he duties of directors and officers under this act, and the general and any specific public benefit purpose of a benefit corporation, may be enforced only in a benefit enforcement proceeding. No person may bring an action or assert a claim against a benefit corporation or its directors or officers with respect to the duties of directors and officers under this act and the general and any specific public benefit purpose of the benefit corporation except in a benefit enforcement proceeding.
>
> b. A benefit enforcement proceeding may be commenced or maintained only:
> (1) Directly by the benefit corporation; or
> (2) Derivatively by:
> (a) a shareholder;
> (b) a director;
> (c) a person or group of persons that owns beneficially or of record 10% or more of the equity interests in an entity of which the benefit corporation is a subsidiary; or
> *(d) such other persons as may be specified in the certificate of incorporation or by-laws of the benefit corporation.*[194] [Emphasis added].

Although this provision introduces the possible likelihood of non-shareholder corporate constituent groups being vested with the right of action to bring proceedings under the benefit corporation statute, such a right is indirect. It may only be invoked when such non-shareholder corporate constituent groups are specified in the certificate of incorporation or in the by-laws of the benefit corporation.

As far as the right of action to enforce the benefit corporation statutes, almost all states which have enacted these statutes generally follow Delaware common law on issues of shareholder standing,[195] effectively meaning that a shareholder can pursue a claim for an injury that is undifferentiated from other parties, as Delaware courts have expressly rejected the 'special injury' requirement in a corporate context.[196] Christopher Lacovara further observes that 'Delaware's broad interpretation of derivative standing – "one of the most interesting and ingenious of accountability mechanisms for large formal organizations"'[197] – has the potential to provide benefit corporation shareholders (and possibly non-shareholders) with an effective mechanism to enforce fiduciary duties of [benefit corporation] directors, as the possibility exists for shareholders or non-shareholder corporate constituencies to claim that the failure of directors to manage a corporation to achieve its benefit purposes amounts to mismanagement of corporate assets, a claim for which recovery on behalf of the corporation would be appropriate.[198] He argues that since employees and customers rank equally with shareholders as parties whose interests business corporation directors must consider, and the Business Corporation charters state that consideration of their interests is 'in the best interest of the corporation', these non-shareholder corporate constituencies might claim derivative standing as well.[199]

However, the unfortunate bias in favour of shareholders by almost all benefit corporation statutes, insofar as the right of action and enforcement is concerned, reduces the utility of the statutes for the non-shareholder corporate constituent groups as they are, unwillingly, left at the mercy of the shareholders, who may not have the incentive to enforce a general or specific public benefit if such a benefit will not lead to shareholder wealth maximisation, or may prove to be detrimental to the value of their investments.

As one of the mechanisms to resolve this dilemma of non-shareholder corporate constituencies, Christopher Lacovara suggests that '[c]onstitutional standing doctrine provides another avenue for non-shareholder claims of standing'. According to him, 'Constitutional standing doctrine recognizes that statutes may create legal obligations to specific parties that may confer standing on those parties as prospective litigants that they would otherwise lack'.[200] This avenue, however, has its own shortcomings, as a plaintiff who invokes a right created by statute must still demonstrate that the alleged injury 'fall[s] within the zone of interests protected or regulated by the statutory provision invoked in the suit'. In other words, the party seeking judicial relief must also be among those actually injured by the breach of the statutory requirement.

## ANALYSIS OF THE BENEFIT CORPORATION STATUTES OF DELAWARE AND MARYLAND

### Introduction

The importance of the position of Delaware and Maryland in US corporate law cannot be gainsaid. Given its overwhelming preference as the state of incorporation by the majority of corporations with securities listed on the New York Stock Exchange and by more than half of the Fortune 500 companies, Delaware has established itself as the corporate law capital of the United States.[201] In fact, Delaware law is influential in the United States to the extent that its corporate law is, intrinsically, the one '. . . to which other states . . . defer in the absence of local precedent on corporate law'.[202] Moreover, following a complete recodification of the former Article 23 of the Annotated Code of Maryland into the Corporations and Associations Article in 1975, the basic corporation law of Maryland is, admittedly, 'at least as favorable to corporations as Delaware's, and in many instances *(e.g.,* director and officer liability limitation and hostile takeovers) considerably more favorable'.[203] It is in this context that the closer analysis of the relevant provisions of the benefit corporation statutes of both Delaware and Maryland is not only necessary but indispensable, as the effect of any changes to the basic corporation law of the two states, particularly with regard to the corporate objectives for public corporations therein, will have far-reaching ramifications throughout the United States and other parts of the common law world, such as South Africa.

Given the fact that the United States has historically, and largely due to the influence of Delaware and (lately) Maryland, espoused corporate law that has not been structured or tailored to accommodate the pursuit of a social or environmental mission by for-profit companies, it is appropriate to assess whether the adoption of these benefit corporation statutes, particularly in these two states, will mark the beginning of an era in which the United States will move toward a more inclusive approach in corporate decision-making in the private sector, given the influence that these two states have in matters of corporate law.

In order to determine whether these developments will have that effect, the statutes of these two states have to be closely analysed, with the primary objective being establishing whether the measures have the potential to influence change in the determination of corporate purpose, accountability of directors and officers insofar as the broader corporate constituent groups are concerned, the promotion of transparency, and, more importantly, the possible extension of legal standing to encompass non-shareholder corporate constituent groups. It is, therefore, only logical for the assessment of these two statutes to cover the aspects highlighted hereunder if any objective assessment of the impact of the statutes is to be credibly undertaken.

## Purpose

Determining whether the provisions of the statutes in these two states expand the corporate purpose as a matter of law is of particular importance since corporate decision-making in the United States has habitually been justified in terms of creating long-term shareholder value, especially as Delaware had previously stayed clear of corporate constituency statutes. As a result of this legal tradition, and in the absence of any clear statutory prescription, a commitment to pursuing a goal other than profit as an end unto itself is ordinarily viewed in many states as inconsistent with the traditional perspective that a corporation's purpose is to maximise profits for the benefit of its shareholders.

Moving from the premise of the corporation having as its sole purpose the maximisation of financial gain for its shareholders, as was first articulated in *Dodge v Ford Motor Co.* in 1919, would appear to be diametrically opposed to the US corporate law marriage to the concept of 'shareholder primacy', which has come to be widely accepted throughout the US, following judicial reaffirmation of this position in Delaware by courts in cases such as that of *eBay Domestic Holdings, Inc. v Newmark,* in which the Delaware Chancery Court stated that a non-financial mission that 'seeks not to maximize the economic value of a for-profit Delaware corporation for the benefit of its stockholders' is inconsistent with directors' fiduciary duties.

In the context of this state of affairs, it is therefore fitting to assess whether the benefit corporation statutes – particularly those of Delaware[204] and Maryland[205] – do have the possible effect of altering this long-standing position, even if in limited categories of for-profit companies. In brief, the assessment will consider whether the statute accommodates the creation of a general public benefit that can be pursued by 'for-profit' corporations that have adopted the public benefit corporation status. In addition to the general public benefit that may be created by the statute, the analysis will consider whether benefit corporations are afforded the right to name specific public benefit purposes. Finally, the inquiry will not be complete if it is not considered whether the pursuit of such general and specific public benefit purposes is recognised in law as being in the best interests of the benefit corporation.[206]

## Delaware

With regard to the recognition of the possible creation of the general public benefit purpose by the benefit corporation under the Delaware statute, section 362(a) of the Delaware Benefit Corporation Act specifically provides, inter alia, that '[a] public benefit corporation is a for-profit corporation . . . intended to produce a *public benefit or public benefits* and to operate in a responsible and sustainable manner'[207] [emphasis added]. The section continues to stress that 'a public benefit corporation shall be managed in a manner that balances the stockholders' pecuniary interests, the best interests of those materially affected by the corporation's conduct, and the public benefit or public benefits identified in its certificate of incorporation'.[208] In addition, the Delaware statute obliges a public benefit corporation to '(i) identify within its statement of business or purpose . . . one or more specific public benefits to be promoted by the corporation, and (ii) state within its heading that it is a public benefit corporation'.[209]

It remains to be seen whether the Delaware statute considers the pursuit of general and specific public purposes as being synonymous with the pursuit of the interests of the corporation. It appears that this is specifically addressed by the seemingly mandatory provision which states that 'a public benefit corporation *shall* be managed in a manner that balances the stockholders' pecuniary interests, the best interests of those materially affected by the corporation's conduct, and the public benefit or public benefits . . .'[210]

In other words, for a public benefit corporation, the interests of the corporation are not tantamount only to the stockholders' pecuniary interests, as it is the position under the shareholder primacy norm which is pursued in relation to all the other 'for-profit' corporations incorporated under Delaware law.

## Maryland

Notwithstanding that Delaware is not a Model Act state, its overwhelming influence over other states in the determination of corporate purpose with respect to 'for-profit' companies is unwavering. Indeed, its almost immutable association with the 'shareholder primacy norm' has been contagious throughout the United States. The position in Delaware is no different than that pertaining to Maryland, which, although unlike Delaware, possesses a statutory standard of conduct based on the Model Business Corporation Act, requiring its corporate directors to perform their duties in good faith, in a manner they reasonably believe to be in the best interests of the corporation, and with the care of an ordinarily prudent person in a like position under similar circumstances.[211]

This position is not altered by Maryland's adoption of a statute akin to a corporate constituency statute.[212] This is because Maryland's unusual corporate constituency statute is dissimilar to typical corporate constituency statutes, which are of general application. As has already been demonstrated above,[213] Maryland's corporate constituency statute is only applicable to the extent that it has been adopted in a corporate charter. Although this is no different to the way in which public benefit corporation statutes generally become applicable to 'for-profit' companies, this means that in the case of Maryland, its corporate constituency statute never had the impact that can be claimed by other states with such statutes – that of questioning the shareholder primacy norm as the corporate purpose for 'profit corporations'.

Maryland's half-hearted adoption of the corporate constituency statute did not affect its enthusiasm for becoming the first state to adopt a benefit corporation statute, which has largely become a template for other states to follow. Like the statute of Delaware, the Maryland statute clearly envisages the possible alteration of the corporate purpose for 'for-profit companies' that have adopted the benefit corporation status, from being exclusively based on the shareholder primacy norm to the one that is all-inclusive, taking into account both general and specific public purposes.

According to the Maryland Benefit Corporation Statute, 'each benefit corporation *shall* have the purpose of creating a general public benefit which is in addition to, and may be a limitation on, the purposes of the corporation under § 2–101 [of the General Corporation Law]'.[214] The Maryland statute clearly envisages the adoption of one or more specific public benefit purposes in addition to the general public benefit purpose, as it continues to state that 'in addition to its purposes . . . the charter of a benefit corporation may identify as one of the purposes of the benefit corporation the creation of one or more specific public benefits'.[215] It clearly appears from the language of the statute that the general public benefit, as well as specific public benefit purposes, may constitute a limitation on the general corporate purpose characterised by the shareholder primacy norm.[216]

To dispel any doubt as to whether the general and specific public benefit purposes are capable of replacing the traditional corporate purpose within benefit corporations, the Maryland statute expressly provides that '[t]he creation of a general public benefit or specific public benefit . . . is in the best interests of the benefit corporation'.[217]

The above provisions of the two statutes of Delaware and Maryland confirm unequivocally that insofar as benefit corporations are concerned, the general corporate purpose, characterised by the shareholder primacy norm, has been altered. Such a revolution is, however, limited to 'for-profit' corporate entities that have elected to become benefit corporations. As is confirmed under the Maryland statute, '[t]he existence of a provision of [the benefit corporation statute] does not of itself create any implication that a contrary or different rule of law is or would be applicable to a corporation that is not a benefit corporation'[218] and that '[the benefit corporation statute] does not affect any statute or rule of law as it applies to a corporation that is not a benefit corporation'.[219] Relating to the limited application of the public benefit corporation provisions, the Delaware statute also provides explicitly that '[t]his subchapter shall not affect a statute or the rule of law that is applicable to a corporation that is not a public benefit corporation, except as provided'.[220]

## Accountability

Now that the issue of corporate purpose is clear, the next question to be addressed relates to the authority to whom the directors are accountable in corporate decision-making. In other words, we must decide whether accountability is aligned to the corporate purpose or whether there is still misalignment in this regard.

### *Delaware*

Delaware's statute provisions in this regard are, understandably, quite extensive and are found in section 365. Firstly, the section provides that:

> [T]he board of directors *shall* manage or direct the business and affairs of the public benefit corporation in a manner that *balances* the pecuniary interests of the stockholders, the best interests of those materially affected by the corporation's conduct, and the *specific public benefit or public benefits* identified in its certificate of incorporation.[221] [Emphasis added].

Unlike the corporate constituency statutes in many of the states which adopted them, the provision of the Delaware statute relating to accountability does not seek to create a hierarchy of priorities in which the directors have to have regard to managing or directing the business and affairs of the public benefit corporation, with the duty to corporate stockholder taking priority. Instead, the obligation clearly appears to be for those directing or managing the business and affairs of the public benefit corporation to maintain a balance between the three specific interests, with no single interest taking priority. These interests are, firstly, the economic interests of the corporation's stockholders; secondly, the best interests of those materially affected by the corporation's conduct; and thirdly, the specific public benefit or public benefits identified in the corporation's certificate of incorporation.

The section goes on to provide that:

> [A] director of a public benefit corporation *shall not* . . . have any duty to any person on account of any interest of such person in the public benefit or public benefits identified in the certificate of incorporation or on account of any interest materially affected by the corporation's conduct.[222]

While the statute expects directors to manage the public benefit corporation in a manner that balances the interests identified, this sub-section explicitly dispels the existence of any fiduciary duty by the directors of a public benefit corporation toward the beneficiaries of those interests. This is unfortunate because the reality of the situation is that if the directors of public benefit corporations owe no fiduciary duty to any of the beneficiaries in respect of whom the stated interests are applicable, none of those beneficiaries will be able to hold them legally accountable for conduct which is to the detriment of those interests. Furthermore, regarding a decision implicating the balance of the interests referred to above, the statute declares that a director of a public benefit corporation 'will be deemed to satisfy his or her fiduciary duties to stockholders and the corporation if such director's decision is both informed and disinterested and not such that no person of ordinary, sound judgment would approve'.[223] This is clearly the re-enactment of the business judgment rule in favour of directors in respect of public benefit corporations, in the same manner as it applies in respect of for-profit corporations which have not adopted the public benefit status.

Lastly, section 365 empowers public benefit corporations to explicitly provide that any disregard or failure by directors to consider those interests shall not amount to a breach of a duty of loyalty. The relevant sub-section provides that:

> [T]he certificate of incorporation of a public benefit corporation may include a provision that any disinterested failure to satisfy [the balancing of the stated interests] shall not . . . constitute an act or omission not in good faith, or a breach of the duty of loyalty.[224]

If any failure to manage the business and affairs of the public benefit corporation by the corporation's directors in a required manner does not constitute a breach of good faith or loyalty [and does not constitute a breach of the duty to exercise reasonable care, skill and diligence because of the operation of the business judgment rule], this essentially means that none of the beneficiaries of the stipulated interests shall be endowed with legal standing to bring proceedings to enforce the breach or contravention of the required duty.

### *Maryland*

In the beginning, Maryland's statute on the aspect of accountability appears different from that of Delaware and clearly equates the interests of the public benefit corporation with those of a number of corporate constituencies, without clearly according supremacy to the interests of stockholders as it is done in a number of corporate constituency statutes. The relevant section of the statute provides that:

> [I]n determining what the director reasonably believes to be in the best interests of the benefit corporation, [the director] *shall* consider the effects of any action or decision not to act on: (i) the stockholders of the benefit corporation; (ii) the

> employees and workforce of the benefit corporation and the subsidiaries and suppliers of the benefit corporation; (iii) the interests of customers as beneficiaries of the general or specific public benefit purposes of the benefit corporation; (iv) community and societal considerations, including those of any community in which offices or facilities of the benefit corporation or the subsidiaries or suppliers of the benefit corporation are located; and(v) the local and global environment.[225]

While the consideration of the interests stated above appears to be obligatory in the pursuit of the interests of the public benefit corporation, the section goes on to give the directors the discretion to 'consider any other pertinent factors or the interests of any other group that the director determines are appropriate to consider in light of the public benefit described in the charter of the corporation'.[226]

Having extensively described what constitutes the interests of the public benefit corporation, the statute, like that of Delaware, then dispels any duty to any beneficiary of the public benefit purposes by expressly stating that '[a] director of a benefit corporation, in the performance of duties in that capacity, does not have any duty to a person that is a beneficiary of the public benefit purposes of the benefit corporation described in the charter of the corporation'.[227]

## Right of Action

With the mixed messages manifested by the corporate purpose and the accountability provisions of the benefit corporation statutes of the two states, one cannot help but wonder whether the statutes endeavour to alter the traditional shareholder-centric right of action in corporations, which characterised corporate law for many generations in Anglo-American jurisdictions and those with which they share corporate law traditions. The consideration of a possible departure from the traditional corporate law trajectory in the specific area of the right of action is also important for another fundamental reason, which is that the usefulness of benefit corporation statutes, particularly those of the two states under consideration, will only be established if the right of action in respect of benefit corporations is extended to the beneficiaries of general and specific public benefit purposes. It is in this regard that anything less than extended legal standing will add nothing of value to the addition of the public benefit corporation statutes.

### *Delaware*

Delaware statute does not pretend to extend the right of action to any corporate constituent group other than shareholders. In this regard, section 367 authorizes stockholders of public benefit corporations to sue derivatively to enforce the directors' duties under § 365, but only if at the time suit is filed, those stockholders individually or collectively own (i) at least two per cent of the corporation's outstanding shares, or (ii) in the case of corporations with shares listed on a national securities exchange, the lesser of two per cent of the outstanding shares or shares with a market value of at least two million dollars.[228] Other than this right of action provision, Delaware offers no alternative provision in respect of other corporate constituent groups. Perhaps this reflects the director-centric position which is really at the heart of Delaware.

Even before considering the Maryland statute on the aspect of the right of action, one fundamental aberration in the Delaware statute in this regard is immediately discernible. The fundamental strangeness of this provision relates to the expectation that the enforcement of the tri-partite balancing requirement imposed upon directors of a benefit corporation can be better achieved by a corporate constituent group represented by one of the three interests required to be balanced. The requirement for directors of benefit corporation interests to balance (i) the stockholders' pecuniary interests, (ii) the interests of those materially affected by the corporation's conduct, and (iii) a public benefit or public benefits identified in the corporation's certificate of incorporation clearly point to the fact that the economic interests of the stockholders rank equally with those whose interests are materially affected by the corporation's conduct and the beneficiaries of public benefits identified in the corporation's certificate of incorporation. Therefore, to single out a corporate constituent group, which represents just one of those interests, in order to grant that group the exclusive right of action is grossly inapposite and deliberately disregards the fact that because the required balancing requirement is, presumably, 'in the best interest of the corporation', the beneficiaries of the other stated interests are also entitled to claim derivative standing as well.

While it is understandable that the shareholders are properly positioned to monitor the enforcement of the stockholders' pecuniary interests, it is questionable whether the pursuit of the interests of those materially affected by the corporation's conduct and those which are encapsulated within public benefits of the corporation can properly be represented by shareholders, who are likely not to have an incentive to enforce a general or specific public benefit if such a benefit would not lead to shareholder wealth maximisation, or could prove to be detrimental to the value of their investments.

### *Maryland*

The Maryland Benefit Corporation Statute does not have any specific 'right of action' clause applicable to benefit corporations. Moreover, the statute makes it clear that no beneficiary of public benefits has a right of action by explicitly stating that '[a] director of a benefit corporation, in the performance of duties in that capacity, does not have any duty to a person that is a beneficiary of the public benefit purposes of the benefit corporation'.[229]

This speaks volumes of Maryland's continued preoccupation with the protection of directors from liability in an effort to make the state the preferred destination for investment, mainly because of its favourable regulatory environment for directors. This is further reflected in another provision of the benefit corporation statute, which states that '[a] director of a benefit corporation, in the reasonable performance of duties in accordance with the standard provided in this subtitle, shall have the immunity from liability described in § 5–417 of the courts article'.

It, therefore, means that the provisions of the Maryland General Corporation Law relating to conventional business corporations apply in so far as the right of action is concerned. This is confirmed by the existence of a provision within the benefit corporation statute which provides that:

> [T]he provisions of the Maryland General Corporation Law apply to benefit corporations except to the extent that: (1) the context of a provision clearly requires otherwise; or (2) a specific provision of this subtitle or another provision of law governing specific classes of corporations provides otherwise.[230]

In this regard, a director of a Maryland corporation is required to perform his duties in good faith, in a manner he reasonably believes to be in the corporation's best interests and with the care of an ordinarily prudent person in a like position under similar circumstances.[231] A director who complies with this standard is immune from liability.[232] Again, in Maryland, a director's act is presumed to satisfy the standard of conduct,[233] and a director is subject to no higher duty or greater scrutiny because his act relates to or affects an acquisition or potential acquisition of control of a corporation.[234]

As with the relevant Delaware provision which addresses the right of action, insofar as the benefit corporation is concerned, it appears that the apparent obligatory duty imposed upon the directors of the benefit corporation directors to consider the effects of any action or decision not to act on enumerated shareholder and non-shareholder matters[235] is effectively rendered nugatory because the enumerated beneficiaries of the duty have no recourse in the event of breach or failure to consider their interests. In other words, if the violation of or failure to pursue general or specific public benefit is a violation of a duty or standard of conduct, then we must ask why the statute precludes the beneficiaries of the general or specific public benefits from having a right of action to address such a violation or failure.

## Transparency

One of the major purposes of benefit corporation statutes is to promote transparency in a manner that is not achieved by conventional corporate law statutes. While information rights in conventional corporate statutes are generally afforded almost exclusively to shareholders, the question is whether information rights under benefit corporation statutes go beyond those of conventional corporate statutes.

### *Delaware*

In Delaware, the matter of transparency under the benefit corporation statute is addressed in section 366, which provides, among others, that:

> [A] public benefit corporation shall no less than biennially provide its stockholders with a statement as to the corporation's promotion of the public benefit or public benefits identified in the certificate of incorporation and of the best interests of those materially affected by the corporation's conduct. The statement shall include: (i) the objectives the board of directors has established to promote such public benefit or public benefits and interests; (ii) the standards the board of directors has adopted to measure the corporation's progress in promoting such public benefit or public benefits and interests; (iii) objective factual information based on those standards regarding the corporation's success in meeting the objectives for promoting such public benefit or public benefits and interests; and (iv) an assessment of the corporation's success in meeting the objectives and promoting such public benefit or public benefits and interests.[236]

The section continues to provide that:

> [T]he certificate of incorporation or bylaws of a public benefit corporation *may* require that the corporation (i) provide the statement described in subsection (b) more frequently than biennially, (ii) make the statement described in subsection (b) available to the public, and/or (iii) use a third party standard in connection with and/or attain a periodic third party certification addressing the corporation's promotion of the public benefit or public benefits identified in the certificate of incorporation and/or the best interests of those materially affected by the corporation's conduct.[237] [Emphasis added].

While the requirement to make the public benefit statement available to shareholders is mandatory as provided for under § 366(b) of the Act, public benefit corporations merely have the discretion to make the public benefit statement available to the public, provide the statement more frequently than biennially, or attain a periodic third party certification addressing the corporation's promotion of public benefits. Furthermore, this may only be attained if the certificate of incorporation or bylaws of the public benefit corporation requires it. The shortcomings of the statute in failing to empower the beneficiaries of public benefits with the right of action for the purpose of addressing the violation of or failure to pursue general or specific public benefits is worsened by the shareholder-centric transparency provisions encapsulated in section 366. It is, therefore, indisputable that the information rights which are ordinarily contained in conventional corporate law statutes have not been altered or improved for benefit corporations, regardless of the expanded corporate purpose which takes into account general and specific benefit purposes.

### *Maryland*

In Maryland, the relevant benefit corporation statute provision addressing transparency provides that:

> [a] benefit corporation shall deliver to each stockholder an annual benefit report including:
>
> (1) a description of: (i) the ways in which the benefit corporation pursued a general public benefit during the year and the extent to which the general public benefit was created; (ii) the ways in which the benefit corporation pursued any specific public benefit that its charter states is the purpose of the benefit corporation to create and the extent to which that specific public benefit was created; and (iii) any circumstances that have hindered the creation by the benefit corporation of the public benefit; and
>
> (2) an assessment of the societal and environmental performance of the benefit corporation prepared in accordance with a third-party standard applied consistently with the prior year's benefit report or accompanied by an explanation of the reasons for any inconsistent application.
>
> (b) the benefit report shall be delivered to each stockholder within 120 days following the end of each fiscal year of the benefit corporation.
>
> (c) (1) a benefit corporation shall post its most recent benefit report on the public portion of its website, *if any*.
>
> (2) if a benefit corporation does not have a public website, the benefit corporation *shall provide* a copy of its most recent benefit report on demand and without charge *to any person* who requests a copy. [Emphasis added].

In light of the above provision, the question which emerges is whether the information rights provided with regard to the benefit report go beyond the typical conventional corporate law statute. Unlike Delaware, the benefit report in terms of the Maryland benefit corporation statute is not required to be prepared biennially, but annually. However, as regards the corporate constituent group to whom the benefit corporation is obligated to deliver, it is clear that in both Delaware and Maryland, such a report is required to be delivered to shareholders and to no other corporate constituent group.

That said, the Maryland statute, unlike that of Delaware, obligates a public benefit corporation to post its most recent annual benefit report on the public portion of its website, if any. While this might have been an important extension of information rights to corporate constituencies beyond shareholders, it is nevertheless not obligatory for public benefit corporations to have relevant public websites on which to post such benefit reports. To mitigate the optional nature of the public website requirement of Maryland's statute, however, it goes on to provide that in the event of the non-existence of such a public website, a public benefit corporation is obliged to provide a copy of its most recent benefit report on demand and without charge to any person who requests a copy.

At first glance, this might appear to be quite a revolutionary step in terms of the Maryland statute. However, the fact that this information cannot be used by any other corporate constituent group (except shareholders) to call the benefit corporation directors to account since these directors do not have any duty to a person who is a beneficiary of the public benefit purposes, effectively means that this apparent revolutionary measure is effectively worthless.

## Conclusion on the Impact of the Benefit Corporation Statutes in Delaware and Maryland

Benefit corporation statutes could have been a very important addition to corporate social responsibility statutory measures had their effect of extending both the corporate purposes and the duty to act in the best interests of the corporation not been negated by the statutes' continued conservative right of action provisions and the insulation of directors from liability by not making them accountable to beneficiaries of public benefit purposes, particularly as public benefit corporations are special kinds of corporations whose core purposes are general and specific public benefits.

## Observations

### *General Observations Regarding Benefit Corporation and Flexible Purpose Corporation Statutes*

While it may seem that the extensive nature of the considerations required to be taken into account by the corporate leaders is likely to be beneficial to both shareholder and non-shareholder corporate constituencies, having to consider all these factors for every issue that comes before a board of directors, could be a tall order. Moreover, compounding the situation is the fact that the statutes specifically provide that directors are not required to give particular weight to any of these specific factors or interests unless the corporation's articles of incorporation state a preference for particular factors or interests.[238] While this approach provides flexibility, the typical benefit corporation and flexible purpose legislation does not make clear what standards directors should follow in making decisions, resulting in some commentators expressing concern that directors of benefit corporations may have too much discretion and lack accountability to shareholders [or to anyone, for that matter].[239]

Moreover, some statutes give corporate leaders the discretion to consider non-shareholder constituencies' interests, which are additional to those represented by general and specific public benefits. According to these statutes, corporate leaders *may* consider (a) the employees and workforce of the sustainable business corporation and its subsidiaries and suppliers; (b) the interests of customers as beneficiaries of the general or specific public benefit purposes of the sustainable business corporation; (c) community and societal considerations, including those of any community in which offices or facilities of the sustainable business corporation or its subsidiaries or suppliers are located; (d) the local and global environment; (e) the short-term and long-term interests of the sustainable business corporation, including benefits that may accrue to the sustainable business corporation from its long-term plans and the possibility that these interests may be best served by the continued independence of the sustainable business corporation; (f) the ability of the sustainable business corporation to accomplish its general public benefit purpose and any specific public benefit purpose; (g) the resources, intent, and conduct of any person seeking to acquire control of the corporation; and (h) any other pertinent factors or the interests of any other group that they deem appropriate.[240]

A tall order as it may appear to be, the one advantage of this system is that the discretionary consideration of the interests of other non-shareholder corporate constituencies, in addition to those represented by the general and specific public benefits, does not offer any reprieve to corporate leaders, as those additional non-shareholder constituencies may still be represented under the general and specific public benefits.

On a more positive note, however, unlike a typical corporate constituency statute, which mandates the consideration of the interests of the corporation and shareholders ahead of any of those of non-shareholder corporate constituencies, the benefit corporation statute ranks the effects of any action of the corporation upon the shareholders equally with the general and specific public benefits set forth in the benefit corporation's purposes, as reflected in the corporation's articles of incorporation.

## Discharge of Duties Under benefit corporation Statutes and Right of Action and Enforceability

Generally, benefit corporation statutes limit directors' liability for monetary damages for failure of a benefit corporation to create a general or specific public benefit,[241] and state that directors shall owe no fiduciary duties to beneficiaries of the benefit corporation's general or specific public benefit purposes.[242]

Nevertheless, some statutes expressly contemplate that a 'benefit enforcement proceeding' may be brought against a benefit corporation or its directors or officers by the corporation itself or derivatively by shareholders, directors, persons who hold more than 5 per cent of the equity of a parent entity or *other persons specified in the articles or bylaws* of the corporation.[243] [Emphasis added]. However, except for California and New Jersey, as shown above, US statutes contain no provisions for other persons to bring direct or derivative claims to enforce corporate purposes, the standards for directors, and such general or specific public benefit purposes. There does not seem, therefore, to even exist an option for those other persons to be specified in the articles or bylaws of the corporation. Another drawback of the statutes is that while they also specifically require an officer of a benefit corporation to consider the same interests and factors that board members must consider (as described above) whenever an officer has the discretion to act and action may materially impact such interests or factors, such an officer shall, nevertheless, be deemed not to have violated his duties when and in whichever manner he or she so acts.[244]

What appears to be beneficial is that similar to the reporting regime required for flexible purpose corporations, benefit corporations are required to deliver to each shareholder and make publicly available on their website (if they have one) an annual benefit report that (i) details for the applicable year the process and rationale for selecting a third-party standard used to prepare the report, the ways in which it pursued a general public benefit and any specific public benefits and any circumstances that have hindered the creation of such public benefit purposes, (ii) assesses the social and environmental performance of the benefit corporation according to the third-party standard, (iii) identifies any person that owns five percent or more of the corporation, (iv) includes a statement of the corporation's board of directors regarding whether the corporation failed to pursue its public benefit purposes in all material respects during such year, and (v) identifies any connections between the corporation (or its directors, officers or material owners) and the entity (or its directors, officers or material owners) that created the third-party standard used by the corporation to assess the pursuit of its benefit purposes, in any case, that might 'materially affect the credibility of the objective assessment of the third-party standard'.[245] There is no mechanism for a benefit corporation or its shareholders to opt out of these annual reporting and disclosure requirements.

### Concluding Remarks

The striking similarity of these statutes across all the states which have adopted them attests to the likelihood that these measures were hurried through legislative processes with no, or limited, consideration of their specific impact on each state. Regardless of the rush by many states to introduce these measures, as evidenced by a number of states which have already introduced similar measures, it appears that these state legislatures present non-shareholder corporate constituencies with half-hearted measures, the benefit of which consists of the hope that some benefit corporations might entitle persons other than shareholders or directors to bring benefit enforcement proceedings against the benefit corporations, their directors or their officers.

Likely due to the acknowledgement that the corporate constituency statutes are inadequate in ensuring the protection of non-shareholder constituencies' interests, these states have introduced benefit corporation statutes in the hope that they might offer a viable alternative.

## CONCLUSION AND CHAPTER SYNOPSIS

In this chapter, it has been shown that UK common law has traditionally adopted the 'shareholder primacy' norm, which effectively propagates the shareholder value maximisation philosophy, supplemented by shareholder-oriented enforcement mechanisms. It has also been shown that the common law position is characterised by the justifiable lack of an extended legal enforcement framework in the promotion of public benefits or non-shareholder constituencies' interests.

It was also shown that regardless of the existence of a legal authority which is over a century old and more recent dicta favouring the consideration of non-shareholder corporate constituencies' interests, the deliberate unwillingness or inability of the legal system to accommodate enforcement mechanisms embracing those non-shareholder corporate constituencies effectively renders the consideration of any interests other than those of shareholders effectively nugatory.

It was further shown that while legislative measures were adopted as early as 1985 through the enactment of s 309 of the UK Companies Act, allowing for the consideration of employees' interests by corporate directors, the lack of enforcement or monitoring mechanisms to enable the possible enforcement of this enactment also ensured the continued operation of the 'shareholder primacy' norm, effectively side-lining any possible consideration of those employees' interests. The lack of decided cases upholding such employees' interests in corporate decision-making bears testimony to the apparent disregard of the enactment in favour of the continued application of the 'shareholder value maximisation' approach.

It has also been shown that the institutionalisation of the Enlightened Shareholder Value Approach by s 172 of the UK Companies Act of 2006, following the recent corporate law reforms, is at risk of suffering the same fate as s 309 of the 1985 Companies Act, since there are still no enforcement mechanisms to ensure the realisation of non-shareholder constituencies' interests specifically mentioned in that section.

The unavoidable similarity between the Enlightened Shareholder Value Approach, institutionalised by s 172 of the 2006 UK Companies Act, and the Non-Stockholder Constituency Statutes in the United States, along with the continued lack of enforcement mechanisms in favour of the non-shareholder constituencies referred to in such statutes is remarkable; this deficiency has effectively caused the statutes to end up being as ineffectual as the old UK judicial pronouncements and recent dicta, the apparent recognition of employees' interests under s 309 of the 2005 UK Companies Act and the celebrated Enlightened Shareholder Value Approach.

It was, therefore, not far-fetched for one commentator to conclude that the Non-Stockholder Constituency Statutes brought about 'hollow hopes and false fears'.[246] Although the recent developments in the form of flexible purpose and benefit corporation statutes have not been tested as they are relatively new, they too run the same risk of failure due to the continued disregard for the call to extend legal standing to the specified non-shareholder constituencies to enforce the statutory measures. The risk is further increased by the express provisions in many of those statutes that no fiduciary duties are owed to such non-shareholder corporate constituencies and the silence regarding their potential enforcement by any other person.

## NOTES

1. It was previously held, for example, in the case of *Moran v Household Int'l, Inc.*, 500 A.2d 1346, 1356 (Del. 1985), that common law duty-of-loyalty rules include, for example, the standards by which the adoption of tender offer defences

are measured and been developed to account for pervasive directorial self-interest in these types of transactions.

2. At the time of writing this book, more than half of the states of the United States continued to have some form of corporate constituency statute in their statute books. Of late, the number of states which have enacted benefit corporation statutes has increased to 37.

3. As it was pointed out elsewhere, by 2002, more than half of the states of the United States have adopted some form of corporate constituency statute.

4. The Company Law Review Steering Group, *Modern Company Law for a Competitive Economy: The Strategic Framework* (1999), op cit note 41, at 34–35.

5. Ibid., at 37.

6. The Hampel Committee, *Report on Corporate Governance (Final Committee Report)* (1998), op cit note 49, at para 1.17.

7. [1951] Ch. 286.

8. Ibid., at 291.

9. [1962] Ch. 927.

10. Ibid., at 963.

11. *Brady v Brady* [1988] BCLC 20, at 40 (CA); *West Mercia Safetywear Ltd v Dodd* [1988] BCLC 250, at 252–253 (CA); *Lee Panavision Ltd v Lee Lighting Ltd* [1992] BCLC 22, at 31 (CA). In signifying the importance of Britain as an exporter of legal concepts, particularly in the area of common law duties of directors, a court in Australia commented as follows 'In considering whether the actions of directors were *bona fide* in the best interests of the company as a whole, the court is not obliged to look at the company as in some way disembodied from its members', *per* Kirby P in *Darvall v North Sydney Brick & Tile Co Ltd* (1989) 15 ACLR 230 248 CA (NSW). The earliest English case to equate the interests of the company with those of the shareholders is that of *Harris v North Devon Railway Co* (1885) 20 Beav 384; 52 ER 651, in which the court, emphasising that 'the interests of the company' are the interests of all the shareholders when dealing with a power vested in the directors to direct a forfeiture of shares, said, per Sir John Romilly MR, that:

> [T]he forfeiture of shares in this case is . . . a power and discretion in the directors, who are trustees for the benefit of all the shareholders, which is to be exercised for the benefit of all the shareholders in the company; and it is the duty of the directors to direct a forfeiture when it is for the benefit of all the shareholders, and to refrain from doing so when it is not for their benefit. (Ibid.)

12. 'In a solvent company the proprietary interests of the shareholders entitle them as a general body to be regarded as the company when questions of the duty of directors arise'. This was quoted with approval by Dillon LJ in *West Mercia Safetywear Ltd v Dodd* [1988] BCLC 250, at 252–253 (CA). Clearly, what is meant here is not any propriety interests of the shareholders in the company's assets, but their 'proprietary' interests *qua* shareholders in the company.

13. See *Greenhalgh v Arderne Cinemas Ltd* [1951] Ch 286 291; [1950] 2 All ER 1120 1126 (CA).

14. It has been said that the interests of the company are those of both present and future members: see *Gaiman v National Association for Mental Health* [1971] Ch 317 330; [1970] 2 All ER 362 374; *Brady v Brady* [1988] BCLC 20 40 (CA); *Runciman v Walter Runciman plc* [1992] BCLC 1084, at 1097. This means that the directors are entitled to consider the long-term position and must act on the footing that [the company] would be continued as a going concern.

15. In *Re BSB Holdings Ltd (No 2)* [1996] 1 BCLC 155, at 246, one example given to illustrate this was that the exercise by the directors of their power to recommend dividends may be contrary to the interests of the company in the sense of the company as a separate legal entity, 'since . . . it would often be in the interests of the company in that sense to retain profits'. (Ibid.)

16. *Gaiman v National Association for Mental Health* [1971] Ch 317 330; [1970] 2 All ER 362 374; *Howard Smith v Ampol Petroleum Ltd* [1974] AC 821 835; [1974] 1 All ER 1126 1134 (PC); *Glover v Willert* (1996) 20 ACSR 182 SC(Qld).

17. In this regard, see the discussion of the Entity Maximisation and the Sustainability Model (EMS) in Chapter 1 above.

18. Keay, 'Tackling the Issue of Corporate Objective', op cit note 48, at 599.

19. McPherson BH, 'Duties of Directors and Powers of Shareholders' (1977) 51 *ALJ* 460, at 468; Heydon JD, 'Directors' Duties and the Company's Interests' in Finn (ed.), *Equity and Commercial Relationships* (1987) 120, at 125–126 ('it has been basic law that even if the director must consider the shareholders' interests, his fiduciary duty is owed to the company, not to the shareholders, not even to a shareholder owning as many as 99 per cent of the shares'). See also Santow GKF, 'Defensive Measures against Company Take-overs' (1979) 53 *ALJ* 374. It has also been argued that under the general principle of the division of powers, directors may lawfully make decisions contrary to the interests of the majority of the shareholders: see Heydon JD, 'Directors' Duties and the Company's Interests' in Finn (ed.), *Equity and Commercial Relationships* (1987) 120, at 125–126. This not only ignores the fact that the directors are required to act in the interests of all the shareholders, but it also ignores the fact that the directors' duty is to act in what they, the directors, consider to be in the best interests of the shareholders. As I. A. Renard says (Comment in *Equity and Commercial Relationships* ed Finn (1987) 137 139–140) of Heydon's argument:

> [A]rguments of this kind appear to fail to distinguish sufficiently between the present and future needs of existing shareholders as a general body (which I would argue directors are bound to uphold) and the needs and desires of a section, even a majority, of existing members (which the directors are bound, if they perceive the interests of the corporators as a whole requiring a different decision, to set to one side).

20. [1988] BCLC 20 (CA).

21. Ibid., at 40.

22. Writing in 1967, he considered that a reappraisal of this issue was long overdue; and said that 'for the present, the directors especially of large companies find themselves in the position of being expected as a matter of business to consider the claims of any competing interests, while being legally answerable to only one': Sealy LS, 'The Director as Trustee' (1967) *Corporate Law Journal (CLJ)* 83, at 89–90. See

also Walsh JK, 'The Exercise of Powers in the Interests of the Company' (1967) 8 *University of Western Australia LR* 176, at 194.

23. 23 Ch.D. 654.

24. Ibid., at 673.

25. Ibid., at 673.

26. Section 309 of the *Companies Act 1985* provided as follows:

. . .. Directors to have regard to interests of employees

> (1) The matters to which the directors of a company are to have regard in the performance of their functions include the interests of the company's employees in general, as well as the interests of its members.
> (2) Accordingly, the duty imposed by this section on the directors is owed by them to the company (and the company alone) and is enforceable in the same way as any other fiduciary duty owed to a company by its directors.
> (3) This section applies to shadow directors as it does to directors.

27. Section 309(2).

28. See, among others, Dodd 'For Whom are Corporate Managers Trustees?' op cit note 3; Berle, 'For Whom Corporate Managers Are Trustees', op cit note 4; Weiner JL, 'The Berle-Dodd Dialogue on the Concept of the Corporation' (1964) 64 *Columbia LR* 1458; Tarver MT, 'The Arrogance of Corporate Power: A Study of the Evolution of the Fiduciary Duty Owed by Management to the Corporation or its Shareholders' (1967) 42 *Tulane LR* 155; Beuthin RC, 'The Range of a Company's Interests' (1969) 86 *SALJ* 155; Engel D, 'An Approach to Corporate Social Responsibility' (1979) 32 *Stan LR* 1; Werner W, 'Corporation Law in Search of its Future' (1981) 81 *Columbia LR* 1611; Hodes L, 'The Social Responsibility of a Company' (1983) 100 *SALJ* 468; Lord Wedderburn, 'The Legal Development of Corporate Responsibility' in Hopt and Teuber (eds.), *Corporate Governance and the Director's Liabilities* (1986) 3; Lord Wedderburn, 'The Social Responsibility of Companies' (1985) 15 *MULR* 4; Sealy LS, 'Directors' Wider Responsibilities', op cit note 33; Sommer AA, 'Whom Should the Corporation Serve? The Berle-Dodd Debate Revisited Sixty Years Later' (1991) 16 *Delaware Journal of Corporate Law* 33; Romano R, 'The Corporate Stakeholder Debate: The Classical Theory and its Critics' (1993) 43 *University of Toronto Law Journal* 533; Slaughter CM, 'Corporate Social Responsibility: A New Perspective' (1997) 18 *Company Lawyer* 313.

29. For instance, see *Fulham Football Club Ltd v Cabra Estates plc* [1994] 1 BCLC 363, at 392.

30. The 'proper plaintiff principle' was described in the case of *Prudential Assurance v Newman Industries* (1981) Ch 257; [1982] Ch 204 (CA) as:

> [T]he elementary principle that A cannot, as a general rule, bring an action against B to recover damages or secure other relief on behalf of C for an injury done by B to C. C is the proper plaintiff because C is the party injured, and, therefore, the person in whom the cause of action is vested. (Ibid., at 210).

31. *Foss v Harbottle* (1843) 2 Hare 461; 67 ER 189.

32. See Cheffins, BR, 'Reforming the Derivative Action: The Canadian Experience and British Prospects' (1997) *Company, Financial and Insolvency Law Review* (*CfiLR*) 227, at 228.

33. Ibid.

34. Section 172(1) of the UK Companies Act, 2006, for example, requires directors to act in good faith in a manner that is likely to promote the success of the company for the benefit of its members [shareholders] as a whole, while having the discretion to have regard, among others, the interests of the company's employees.

35. As shown in the discussion of the Non-Stockholder Constituency Statutes below, a considerable number of them mandate the consideration of the interests of the corporation and its shareholders while making the consideration of non-shareholder corporate constituencies discretionary. This is in line with 'the shareholders first' philosophy of the Enlightened Shareholder Value Approach.

36. Those considerations are listed in note 114 above.

37. For example, WYO. STAT. ANN. § 17–16–830(e).

38. Keay, 'Tackling the Issue of Corporate Objective', op cit note 48, at 593.

39. Ibid.

40. See, for example, the comments of Lord Justice Neill in *Fulham Football Club Ltd v Cabra Estates plc* [1992] BCC 863 at 876 (Lord Justice Neill).

41. This has been one of the problems with s 309 of the 1985 legislation, as acknowledged by the CLRSG in its deliberations (See The Company Law Review Steering Group, *Modern Company Law for a Competitive Economy*: *The Strategic Framework,* op cit note 41, at 41–42.

42. McDaniel, 'Bondholders and Stockholders', op cit note 154, at 309.

43. UK Department of Trade and Industry, *Company Law Reform: Modern Company Law for a Competitive Economy* (March 1998), op cit note 102, at 14.

44. Section 172(1)(b) of the UK Companies Act, 2006.

45. David Chivers QC, *The Companies Act 2006: Directors' Duties Guidance* (The Corporate Responsibility Coalition, 2007), at 6.

46. The contents of the section are set out in note 114, above.

47. David Chivers QC, *The Companies Act 2006: Directors' Duties Guidance* (2007), op cit note 489, at 6–7.

48. Ibid., at 7.

49. UK Department of Trade & Industry, Ministerial Statements on the Companies Act, 2006 (June 2007).

50. David Chivers QC, *The Companies Act 2006: Directors' Duties Guidance* (2007), op cit note 489, at 7.

51. Ibid. According to Andrew Keay, (Keay, 'Tackling the Issue of Corporate Objective', op cit note 48, at 599):

> [T]he main, and perhaps even the only, benefit [of s 172] is that it would seem to give legislative permission to directors to look at interests other than short-term shareholder interests, and this would alleviate the concerns of some directors who, as reported by Dr Janice Dean in relation to an empirical study she conducted amongst directors of UK public companies, feel that they must operate in a way that is acceptable to society in

a 'common sense' way and take into account the interests of the primary stakeholders. ((2007), op cit note 41, at 599).

52. See, among others, Keay 'Tackling the Issue of Corporate Objective', op cit note 48, at 592; Ho, 'Director's Duty to Promote the Success of the Company', op cit note 17, at 23.

53. Ibid.

54. David Chalmers QC, *Directors' Duties*, an address to the expert meeting on corporate Law and Human rights, held at Osgoode Hall Law School, York University, Toronto, 5 November 2009.

55. Ibid.

56. Ibid.

57. David Chivers QC, *The Companies Act 2006: Directors' Duties Guidance* (2007), op cit note 489, at 7.

58. Keay, 'Tackling the Issue of Corporate Objective', op cit note 48, at 577.

59. Ibid.

60. Ibid.

61. Parliamentary Joint Committee on Corporations and Financial Services, Commonwealth of Australia, *Corporate Responsibility: Managing Risk and Creating Value* (2006) Available at www.aph.gov.au/Senate/committee/corporations_ctte/corporate_responsibility/report/report.pdf at 51, accessed on 25 July 2012.

62. Springer JD, 'Corporate Constituency Statutes: Hollow Hopes and False Fears' (1999) *Annual Survey of American Law* 85, at 104–105.

63. Hanks, 'Playing with Fire', op cit note 7, at 103.

64. Ibid. See also ABA Committee on Corporate Laws, 'Other Constituencies Statutes: Potential for Confusion', (1990) 45 *Business Law* 2253, at 2253; Hanks, 'An Idea Whose Time Should Never Have Come', op cit note 47, at 20.

65. Alabama, Arizona, Arkansas, Connecticut, Florida, Georgia, Hawaii, Idaho, Indiana, Iowa, Kentucky, Maine, Massachusetts, Mississippi, Montana, Nebraska, New Hampshire, North Carolina, Oregon, Rhode Island, South Carolina, South Dakota, Tennessee, Utah, Vermont, Virginia, Washington, West Virginia, Wisconsin, and Wyoming. See Bebchuk L, 'The Case for Increasing Shareholder Power' (2004–5) 118 *Harvard Law Review* 833, 844.

66. Alaska, the District of Columbia and New Mexico.

67. Committee on Corporate Laws, *Model Business Corporation Act: Official Text with Official Comment and Statutory Cross-References Revised through December 2007* (2008), op cit note 508, at ix.

68. The authority for this legal position is § 8.30 (a) of the Model Business Corporation Act (MBCA) 2008, which provides that 'Each member of the board of directors when discharging the duties of a director, shall act: (1) in good faith, and (2) in a manner the director reasonably believes to be in the best interests of the corporation'. The MBCA Official Comment states that '(2) The phrase ''best interests of the corporation'' is key to an explication of a director's duties. The term ''corporation'' is a surrogate for the business enterprise as well as a frame of reference encompassing the shareholder body'. (Ibid., at 8–44–8–45).

69. These are (a) Alabama, (b) Arkansas, (c) Mississippi, (d) Montana, (e) New Hampshire, (f) North Carolina, (g) South Carolina, (h) Utah, (i) Washington, and (j) West Virginia.

70. See Mitchell, 'A Theoretical and Practical Framework', op cit note 6, at 610, note 146. It is not surprising that Delaware is still recognised as the national corporate law because it has been established recently that '[m]ore than 900,000 business entities call Delaware their legal home, with 50% of all public companies and 2/3 of all Fortune 500 companies incorporated in Delaware'. See Delaware Legislation Update, Available at http://www.bcorporation.net/what-are-b-corps/legislation, accessed on 10 July 2013. Following the complete overhaul of the former Article 23 of the Annotated Code of Maryland and its recodification into the Corporations and Associations Article ('the Maryland General Corporation Law') by the General Assembly of Maryland in 1975, Maryland basic corporation law was, according to many members of the bar, catapulted into being 'at least as favorable to corporations as Delaware's, and in many instances *(e.g.,* director and officer liability limitation and hostile takeovers) considerably more favorable'. (See James J Hanks Jr., *Comparison of the Principal Provisions of the Delaware and Maryland Corporation Statutes* (2011), at iv). Moreover, 'Maryland is the second most popular state of incorporation for New York Stock Exchange-listed corporations'. (Ibid.)

71. See, for example, *Paramount Communications, Inc. v Time Inc.* 571 A.2d 1140, at 1150.

72. See, for example, Springer, 'Hollow Hopes and False Fears', op cit note 316, at 95, 114, 118, and 120.

73. 15 Pa. Cons. Stat. Ann. § 1408(B) (Purdon Supp. 1986) (repealed 1986). See also Hale, 'Corporate Law and Stakeholders', op cit note 32, at 833.

74. Ibid., at 831–832.

75. Ibid. See also Anderson JA, 'Maine's Non-Shareholder Constituency Statute', op cit note 117, at 155.

76. Ibid. See also 15 Pa. C.S.A. § 5712.

77. Lipton M, 'Takeover Bids in the Target's Boardroom' (1979) 35 *Business Lawyer* 101.

78. This is yet another invention of Martin Lipton in 1982, as a response to tender-based hostile takeovers. See Harvard Business School, Case Study 9-496–037, at 5.

79. Bisconti A, 'The Double Bottom Line', op cit note 116, at 768, maintains that the following states had some form of a Non-Stockholder Constituency statute by 2009: (a) Arizona, (b) Connecticut, (c) Florida, (d) Georgia, (e) Hawaii, (f) Idaho, (g) Illinois, (h) Indiana, (i) Iowa, (j) Kentucky, (k) Louisiana, (l) Maine, (m) Maryland, (n) Massachusetts, (o) Minnesota, (p) Missouri, (q) Nebraska, (r) Nevada, (s) New Jersey, (t) New Mexico, (u) New York, (v) North Dakota, (w) Ohio, (x) Oregon, Pennsylvania, (y) Rhode Island, (z) South Dakota, (aa) Tennessee, (bb) Vermont, (cc) Virginia, (dd) Wisconsin, and (ee) Wyoming. However, Tyler, 'Negating the Legal Problems of Having "Two Masters"', op cit note 9, at 132) submitted in 2010 that because Nebraska had repealed its statute in 1995 (i.e. NEB. REV. STAT. §

21–2035(1)(c) (repealed 1995)), there were only 31 states with some variation of Non-Stockholder Constituency Statutes by 2010.

80. Mickels A, 'Beyond Corporate Social Responsibility: Reconciling the Ideals of a For-Benefit Corporation with Director Fiduciary Duties in the US and Europe' (2009) 32 *Hastings International & Comparative Law Review* 271, at 290 note 113. The author quoted the following states: (a) Arizona (ARIZ. REV. STAT. ANN. § 10–2702 (West 2008)); (b) Connecticut (CONN. GEN. STAT. § 33–756 (2008)); (c) Florida (FLA. STAT. ANN. § 607.0830(3) (West 2007)); (d) Georgia (GA. CODE ANN. § 14–2–202(b)(5) (2003)); (e) Hawaii (HAW. REV. STAT. § 414–221 (2004)); (f) Idaho (IDAHO CODE ANN. § 30–1602–1702 (2008)); (g) Illinois (805 ILL. COMP. STAT. ANN. 5/8.85 (West 2004)); (h) Indiana (IND. CODE ANN. § 23–1–35–1 (West 2008)); (i) Iowa (IOWA CODE ANN. § 491.101B (West 1999)); (j) Kentucky (KY. REV. STAT. ANN. § 271B.12–210(4) (LexisNexis 2003)); (k) Louisiana (LA. REV. STAT. ANN. § 12:92(G)(2) (2008)); (l) Maine (ME. REV. STAT. ANN. tit. 13-C, § 831 (2009)); (m) Maryland (MD. CODE. ANN. CORPS. & ASS'NS. § 2–104(b)(9) (LexisNexis 2007)); (n) Minnesota (MINN. STAT. ANN. § 302A.251(5) (West 2004)); (o) Mississippi (MISS. CODE ANN. § 79–4–8.30(d) (2000)); (p) Missouri (MO. ANN. STAT. § 351.347 (West 2001)); (q) New Jersey (N.J. STAT. ANN. §§ 14A:6–1(2), 6–14(4) (West 2003)); (r) New Mexico (N.M. STAT. ANN. § 53–11–35(D) (LexisNexis 2004)); (s) New York (N.Y.BUS. CORP. LAW § 717(b) (McKinney 2003)); (t) North Dakota (N.D. CENT. CODE § 10–19.1–50(6) (2007)); (u) Ohio (OHIO REV. CODE ANN. § 1701.59(E) (LexisNexis 2009)); (v) Oregon (OR. REV. STAT. § 60.357(5) (2009)); (w) Pennsylvania (15 PA. CONS. STAT.§ 1715 (West 1995)); (x) Rhode Island (R.I. GEN. LAWS § 7–5.2–8(a) (West 2009)); (y) South Dakota (S.D. CODIFIED LAWS § 47–33–4(1) (2007)); (z) Tennessee (TENN. CODE ANN. § 48–103–202–204 (2008)); (aa) Vermont (VT. STAT. ANN. tit. 11A, § 8.30(a)(3) (West 2007)); (bb) Wisconsin WIS. STAT. ANN. § 180.0827 (West 2002); and (cc) Wyoming (WYO. STAT. ANN. § 17–16–830(e) (2009)).

81. These are (a) Connecticut, (b) Louisiana, (c) Minnesota, (d) Missouri, (e) Nevada, (f) New York, (g) Ohio, (h) Pennsylvania, (i) Tennessee, and (j) Vermont.

82. Keay, 'Tackling the Issue of Corporate Objective', op cit note 48, at 577.

83. Macey, 'An Economic Analysis of the Various Rationales', op cit note 63, at 23.

84. See chapter 1 above. Also refer generally Smith, 'The Shareholder Primacy Norm', op cit note 66.

85. Ibid. See also Millon D, 'Redefining Corporate Law', (1991) 24 *Indiana Law Review* 223, at 277.

86. Connecticut Business Corporation Act, Conn Gen Stat § 33–756*(d)* (2009). See also Springer, 'Hollow Hopes and False Fears', op cit note 316, at 96 (noting that 'most of these . . . statutes are similar in form').

87. Those states whose statutes apply only to directors are: Connecticut, Florida, Idaho, Indiana, Kentucky, Minnesota, Missouri, Nebraska, New Mexico, New York, and Pennsylvania; those which apply to both directors and officers are: Illinois, Maine, Wisconsin.

88. Those states with statutes considering only the best interests of the corporation are: Connecticut, Idaho, Illinois, Kentucky, Minnesota, Nebraska, Indiana, Pennsylvania; those considering both the best interests of the corporation and the shareholders are: Florida, Maine, New Mexico.

89. Those states with statutes considering only interests are: Connecticut, Idaho, Kentucky, and Minnesota; those considering only effects are: Florida, Illinois, Indiana, Missouri, Nebraska, New York, Pennsylvania, Wisconsin; (New Mexico allows consideration of both the interests and effects.)

90. Those states with statutes that allow the consideration of non-shareholder interests on 'any' decision or 'effects' are: Florida, Idaho, Illinois, Indiana, Kentucky, Minnesota, Nebraska, New Mexico, New York, Pennsylvania, Wisconsin; those which limit it to particular instances are: Connecticut (sale of substantially all assets) and Missouri (acquisitions).

91. Those states with such statutes are: Connecticut, Idaho, Kentucky, Minnesota, and New Mexico.

92. Those states are: Indiana (allowing presumption if approval of a majority of disinterested directors, unless not made in good faith after reasonable investigation); Pennsylvania ('absent breach of fiduciary duty, lack of good faith or self-dealing, actions taken as a director shall be presumed to be in the best interests of the corporation'.).

93. Examples of those non-shareholder constituencies used are: employees, customers, creditors, suppliers, communities, economies, and others. Maine's statute includes several of these and contains an 'all other pertinent factors' clause that does not limit the constituencies to those specified.

94. ARIZ. REV. STAT. ANN. § 10–2702 (West 2008)); (b) Connecticut (CONN. GEN. STAT. § 33–756 (2008)); (c) Florida (FLA. STAT. ANN. § 607.0830(3) (West 2007)); (d) Georgia (GA. CODE ANN. § 14–2–202(b)(5) (2003)); (e) Hawaii (HAW. REV. STAT. § 414–221 (2004)); (f) Idaho (IDAHO CODE ANN. § 30–1602–1702 (2008)); (g) Illinois (805 ILL. COMP. STAT. ANN. 5/8.85 (West 2004)); (h) Indiana (IND. CODE ANN. § 23–1–35–1 (West 2008)); (i) Iowa (IOWA CODE ANN. § 491.101B (West 1999)); (j) Kentucky (KY. REV. STAT. ANN. § 271B.12–210(4) (LexisNexis 2003)); (k) Louisiana (LA. REV. STAT. ANN. § 12:92(G)(2) (2008)); (l) Maine (ME. REV. STAT. ANN. tit. 13-C, § 831 (2009)); (m) Maryland (MD. CODE. ANN. CORPS. & ASS'NS. § 2–104(b)(9) (LexisNexis 2007)); (n) Minnesota (MINN. STAT. ANN. § 302A.251(5) (West 2004)); (o) Mississippi (MISS. CODE ANN. § 79–4–8.30(d) (2000)); (p) Missouri (MO. ANN. STAT. § 351.347 (West 2001)); (q) New Jersey (N.J. STAT. ANN. §§ 14A:6–1(2), 6–14(4) (West 2003)); (r) New Mexico (N.M. STAT. ANN. § 53–11–35(D) (LexisNexis 2004)); (s) New York (N.Y.BUS. CORP. LAW § 717(b) (McKinney 2003)); (t) North Dakota (N.D. CENT. CODE § 10–19.1–50(6) (2007)); (u) Ohio (OHIO REV. CODE ANN. § 1701.59(E) (LexisNexis 2009)); (v) Oregon (OR. REV. STAT. § 60.357(5) (2009)); (w) Pennsylvania (15 PA. CONS. STAT.§ 1715 (West 1995)); (x) Rhode Island (R.I. GEN. LAWS § 7–5.2–8(a) (West 2009)); (y) South Dakota (S.D. CODIFIED LAWS § 47–33–4(1) (2007)); (z) Tennessee (TENN. CODE ANN. § 48–103–202–204 (2008)); (aa) Vermont (VT. STAT. ANN. tit. 11A, § 8.30(a)(3) (West 2007)); (bb)

Wisconsin WIS. STAT. ANN. § 180.0827 (West 2002); and (cc) Wyoming (WYO. STAT. ANN. § 17–16–830(e) (2009)).

95. Fla. Stat. Ann. § 607.0830(1) - (3) (Sub-section (1) deals with the core duties of directors and sub-section (3) enacts the corporate constituency statute).

96. The section provides thus:

> (1) A director shall discharge his or her duties as a director, including his or her duties as a member of a committee:
> (a) In good faith;
> (b) With the care an ordinarily prudent person in a like position would exercise under similar circumstances; and
> (c) In a manner he or she reasonably believes to be in the best interests of the corporation
>
> . . .
>
> (3) *In discharging his or her duties, a director may consider such factors as the director deems relevant, including the long-term prospects and interests of the corporation and its shareholders, and the social, economic, legal, or other effects of any action on the employees, suppliers, customers of the corporation or its subsidiaries, the communities and society in which the corporation or its subsidiaries operate, and the economy of the state and the nation.* [Emphasis added].

97. See Trevor S Norwitz, 'The Metaphysics of Time', op cit note 132, at 377–378, in which he maintains that in the absence of a 'non-shareholder constituency' statute, the general rule in US jurisdictions would be that other stakeholder interests can only be taken into account through the lens of shareholder interests.

98. As in the case of Florida, i.e. Fla. Stat. Ann. § 607.0830(1).

99. A typical example is the statute of the state of Hawaii, i.e. Haw. Rev. Stat. § 414–221(b)(1) and (4).

100. As in the cases of Illinois, Indiana and Iowa, . See Ill. Ann. Stat. § 8.85; Ind. Code Ann. § 23–1–35–1(d); Iowa Code § 491.101B(1)(c).

101. As in the case of Florida, Maryland (although subject to the corporation's articles of incorporation), and Hawaii. See Fla. Stat. Ann. § 607.0830 (3); Maryland General Corporation Law, § 2–104 (b) (9); and Haw. Rev. Stat. § 414–221(b)(1) and (4).

102. See Hale, 'Corporate Law and Stakeholders', op cit note 32, at 834.

103. New York (N.Y.BUS. CORP. LAW § 717(b) (McKinney 2003).

104. Ibid.

105. N.Y. Bus. Corp. Law § 717(a) (McKinney Supp. 2003).

106. N.Y. Bus. Corp. Law § 717(a) (McKinney Supp. 2003) (in particular because of the use of the phrase 'without limitation').

107. Letter from Joseph A Grundfest, *Commissioner, Securities Exchange Commission, to Mario Cuomo, Governor of New York* (6 June 1989).

108. A typical example is the corporate constituency statute of the state of New Mexico. See N.M. Stat. Ann. § 53–11–35(d)(1)–(4).

109. Connecticut Business Corporation Act, Conn Gen Stat § 33–756*(d)* (2009).

110. Ibid.

111. Conn. Gen. Stat. Ann. § 33–756(a).

112. Available at http://www.professorbainbridge.com, accessed on 31 July 2012.

113. In the same way a discretionary approach applies in respect of non-shareholder considerations while an obligation is imposed in respect of shareholder considerations, as fully discussed in para 3.3.1.3 above.

114. Hart & Degener, 'Non-Stockholder Constituency Statutes', op cit note 135.

115. Ibid., at 4. This view appears to be also endorsed by the American Bar Association Committee on Corporate Laws, 'Other Constituencies Statutes: Potential for Confusion', (1990), at 2261.

116. Anderson, 'Maine's Non-Shareholder Constituency Statute', op cit note 117, at 167.

117. Playing with Fire, op cit note 7, at 111.

118. Ariz.Rev.Stat.Ann. § 10–1202. However, the Arizona statute is expressly limited to takeovers. See Ariz. Rev. Stat. § 10–2702

119. Haw. Rev. Stat. § 414–221(b)(1) and (4).

120. Idaho Code § 30–1702.

121. Ibid., § 491.101B(1)(c).

122. Nevada, NV. ST. 78.138.4 (a)–(d).

123. KRS § 271B.12–210(4).

124. N.J. Rev. Stat. § 14A:6–1(3) (Supp. 1989).

125. N.M. Stat. Ann. § 53–11–35(d)(1)–(4) (Supp. 1988).

126. Ohio Rev. Code Ann. § 1701.59(E) (1)–(4) (Page Supp. 1988).

127. W.S.A. 180.0827.

128. W.S.A. 180.0827.

129. Ga. Code Ann. § 14–2–202(b) (5).

130. *Maryland General Corporation Law* § 2–104 (b) (9)(i)–(3).

131. Ibid., § 2–104(c).

132. IND. CODE § 23–1–35–1 (d)(f) (1995)

133. Springer, 'Hollow Hopes and False Fears', op cit note 316, at 98.

134. The official comment to Ind. Code Ann. § 23–1–35–1(d), op cit.

135. See Indiana: IND. CODE § 23–1–35–1 (d)(f) (1995) and Pennsylvania: 15 PA. CONS. STAT §§ 515(a)–(b), 516(a) (2002).

136. Keay, 'Tackling the Issue of Corporate Objective', op cit note 48, at 595.

137. Ibid. Keay observes that:

> [T]his is even acknowledged by the Committee on Corporate Laws of the Section of Business Law of the American Bar Association, 'Other Constituency Statutes: Potential for Confusion' (1990) 45 *The Business Lawyer* 2253 at 2262, which was essentially in favour of shareholder primacy (Ibid.)

138. Springer, 'Hollow Hopes and False Fears', op cit note 316, at 108.

139. Iowa Code § 490.101B.

140. Ibid., § 491.101B(2).

141. Ibid.

142. Ibid.

143. This view is supported by Springer, 'Hollow Hopes and False Fears', op cit note 316, at 99.

144. *Unocal Corp. v Mesa Petroleum Co* 493 A.2d 946 (Del.1985).

145. *Revlon, Inc. v MacAndrews & Forbes Holdings, Inc.* 506 A.2d 173 (Del.1986).

146. Nevada, NV. ST. 78.138.5.

147. Nevada, NV. ST. 78.138.6.

148. Nevada, NV. ST. 78.138.1.

149. See Me. Rev. Stat. Ann. tit. 13-A, § 716 (West Supp. 1990–1991).

150. Me. Rev. Stat. Ann. tit. 13-A, § 716.

151. 727 F. Supp. 31 (D. Me. 1989).

152. Ibid., at 33.

153. Anderson, 'Maine's Non-Shareholder Constituency Statute', op cit note 117, at 154.

154. Ibid., at 160.

155. James B Zimpritch, *Maine Corporation Law and Practice* (Supp. 1991) § 7.7(f), at 286.

156. *Model Business Corporation Act* § 8.30, Official Comment (2008), at 8–35.

157. Op cit note 535. See the Committee on Corporate Laws, op cit note 554, at 2267 (quoting 15 PA. Cons. Stat. Ann. § 1408(B) (Purdon Supp. 1986) (repealed 1986)).

158. W.S.A. 180.0827.

159. 708 F. Supp. 984 (E.D. Wis. 1989) (interpreting Wisconsin law).

160. Ibid., at 1013.

161. See also James J Hanks, 'An Idea Whose Time Should Never Have Come', op cit note 47, at 21.

162. Anderson, 'Maine's Non-Shareholder Constituency Statute', op cit note 117, at 169.

163. See *Georgia-Pacific Corp. v Great Northern Nekoosa Corp.*, op cit note 569.

164. *Amanda Acquisition Corp. v Universal Foods Corp.*, 877 F.2d 496 (7th Cir.1989).

165. Ibid., at 500.

166. Ariz.Rev.Stat.Ann. § 10–1202. However, the Arizona statute is expressly limited to takeovers. See Ariz. Rev. Stat.§ 10–2702.

167. WYO. STAT. ANN. § 17–16–830(g) (i)–(v) (2009).

168. For example, Model Business Corporation Act, § 8.30 and WYO. STAT. ANN. § 17–16–830(a) (2009).

169. See Adams & Matheson, 'A Statutory Model for Corporate Constituency Concerns', op cit note 175, at 1088.

170. Model Business Corporation Act 2008 (2008), op cit note 508, at ix.

171. The Hampel Committee, Report on Corporate Governance (Final Committee Report) (1998), Para 1.17.

172. Hale, 'Corporate Law and Stakeholders', op cit note 32, at 836.

173. Playing with Fire, op cit, note 7, at 111.

174. Ibid.
175. *Baron v Strawbridge & Clothier* 646 F. Supp. 690 (E.D. Pa. 1986) (interpreting Pennsylvania law).
176. Ibid.
177. Ga. Code Ann. § 14–2–202(b)(5).
178. Op cit note 535.
179. Ibid., at 697.
180. Ibid., at 8–35.
181. For example, in La. Rev. Stat. Ann. § 12:92 (G).
182. American Bar Association Committee on Corporate Laws, 'Other Constituencies Statutes: Potential for Confusion', (1990), op cit note 554, at 2261.
183. Mitchell LE, 'A Theoretical and Practical Framework', op cit note 6.
184. Springer, 'Hollow Hopes and False Fears', op cit note 324.
185. Mitchell, 'A Theoretical and Practical Framework', op cit note 6, at 581–582.
186. Ibid., at 582.
187. Springer, 'Hollow Hopes and False Fears', op cit note 324, at 85, 122–124.
188. Ibid., at 85.
189. Ibid.
190. See Gibson, Dunn & Crutcher, 'California Adopts Two New Corporate Forms to Advance Social Benefits', available at http://www.gibsondunn.com.
191. For example, Hawaii Sustainable Business Corporations Act (2011), § 6.
192. HAW. REV. STAT. (*Sustainable Business Corporations*) (2011), op cit note 457, § 10.
193. New Jersey Benefit Corporation Act (2011), § 6b.
194. New Jersey Benefit Corporation Act (2011), § 10a and b.
195. This point is emphatically made by Lacovara C, 'Strange Creatures: A Hybrid Approach to Fiduciary Duty in Benefit Corporations' (2011) 3 *Columbia Business Law Review*, 815, at 854.
196. *Tooley v Donaldson, Lufkin & Jenrette, Inc.,* 845 A.2d at 1035 (rejecting earlier holdings that required a shareholder bringing a direct action to demonstrate a 'special injury . . . "separate and distinct from that suffered by other shareholders . . . or a wrong involving a contractual right of a shareholder . . .."' (quoting *Moran v Household Int'l, Inc.* 490 A.2d 1059, 1070 (Del. Ch. 1985), *affd,* 500 A.2d 1346 (Del. 1986))).
197. Op cit note 472, at 856.
198. Ibid.
199. Ibid.
200. Ibid.
201. In particular, ever since the decision of *Revlon, Inc. v MacAndrews & Forbes Holdings, Inc.* 506 A.2d 173 (Del. 1986) in 1986, most of the states in the United States readily subscribe to the shareholder-centric corporate law objective for public corporations as established in the state of Delaware, more especially in relation to the change of control transactions, such as takeovers. (See, among others, Bisconti, 'The Double Bottom Line', op cit note 116, at 779). Writing as recently as 2011, James J Hanks Jr. stated that 'Maryland is the second most popular state of incorporation for

New York Stock Exchange-listed corporations' [after Delaware]. (See James J Hanks Jr. *Comparison of the Principal Provisions of the Delaware and Maryland Corporation Statutes* (2011), at iv.).

202. See, in particular, Springer, 'Hollow Hopes and False Fears', op cit note 324, at 91.

203. See James J Hanks Jr., *Principal Provisions of the Delaware and Maryland Corporation Statutes,* op cit, at iv.

204. The state of Delaware has introduced public benefit corporations by amending Title 8 of the Delaware Code relating to the General Corporation Law and, specifically, by adding Subchapter XV entitled 'Public Benefit corporations. For the purposes of this book, reference will be made to the relevant sections of the Delaware General Corporation Law when referring to the sections affecting public benefit corporations.

205. In the same manner, the state of Maryland has enacted for public benefit corporations by adding to the Corporations and Associations Article of the Maryland Code the new subtitle 6C entitled 'Benefit Corporations'.

206. This is also relevant in the context of a broader enforcement framework under the South African corporate statute, which may be justified by the statute's recognition of the need to promote compliance with the Bill of Rights in the application of company law. See s 7(a) of the Companies Act, 2008.

207. Delaware General Corporation Law, § 362(a).

208. Ibid.

209. Delaware General Corporation Law, § 362(a) (i) and (ii).

210. Delaware General Corporation Law, § 362(a).

211. Maryland General Corporation Law, § 2–405.1(a).

212. See Para 3.3.1.5 above.

213. Ibid.

214. Maryland General Corporation Law, § 5–6C–06. (A)(1).

215. Maryland General Corporation Law, § 5–6C–06. (B)(1). § 5–6C–01 (D) defines specific public benefit to include: (1) providing individuals or communities with beneficial products or services; (2) promoting economic opportunity for individuals or communities beyond the creation of jobs in the normal course of business; (3) preserving the environment; (4) improving human health; (5) promoting the arts, sciences, or advancement of knowledge; (6) increasing the flow of capital to entities with a public benefit purpose; or (7) the accomplishment of any other particular benefit for society or the environment.

216. Maryland General Corporation Law, § 5–6C–06. (A)(2).

217. Maryland General Corporation Law, § 5–6C–06. (C).

218. Maryland General Corporation Law, § 5–6C–02. (C)(1).

219. Maryland General Corporation Law, § 5–6C–02. (C)(2).

220. Delaware General Corporation Law, § 368.

221. Delaware General Corporation Law, § 365(a).

222. Delaware General Corporation Law, § 365(b).

223. Ibid.

224. Delaware General Corporation Law, § 365(c).

225. Maryland General Corporation Law, § 5–6C–07. (A)(1).
226. Maryland General Corporation Law, § 5–6C–07. (A)(2).
227. Maryland General Corporation Law, § 5–6C–07. (B).
228. Delaware General Corporation Law, § 367.
229. Maryland General Corporation Law, § 5–6C–07. (B).
230. Maryland General Corporation Law, § 5–6C–02. (A).
231. Maryland General Corporation Law, § 2–405.1(a).
232. Maryland General Corporation Law, § 2–405.1(c); Courts & Judicial Proceedings Article ('CJP') of the Annotated Code of Maryland, § 5–417. Furthermore, In Maryland, a director's duty does not require him to accept, recommend or respond on behalf of the corporation to any proposal by an acquiring person; to authorize the corporation to redeem any rights under, modify or render inapplicable a stockholder rights plan; to elect or refrain from electing on behalf of the corporation to be subject to any or all of the unsolicited takeover provisions of Subtitle 8 of Title 3; to make a determination under the business combination or control share acquisition statutes; or to act (or fail to act) solely because of the effect that the action (or failure to act) may have on an acquisition or potential acquisition of control of the corporation or because of the amount or type of any consideration that may be offered or paid to stockholders in an acquisition. (See Maryland General Corporation Law, § 2–405.1(d)).
233. Maryland General Corporation Law, § 2–405.1(e).
234. Maryland General Corporation Law, § 2–405.1(1).
235. See Maryland General Corporation Law, § 5–6C–07. (A)(1).
236. Delaware General Corporation Law, § 366(b).
237. Delaware General Corporation Law, § 366(c).
238. Ibid. See, for example, Part 13 of the California *Corporations Code*, op cit note 644 § 14620(d).
239. Gibson, Dunn & Crutcher, 'California Adopts Two New Corporate Forms to Advance Social Benefits', available at http://www.gibsondunn.com, accessed on 2 February 2012.
240. For example, see Hawaii Sustainable Business Corporations Act (2011), § 6(a)(2)(A)–(H).
241. See, for example, California Business Corporation Act (2011), § 14620(f) and the Hawaii Sustainable Business Corporations Act (2011), § 6(b).
242. See, for example, California Benefit Corporations Act (2011), § 14620(1).
243. Ibid, § 14623(a) and (b). Although an indirect right of action by non-shareholder corporate constituencies, both the Californian and the New Jersey statutes expressly recognise it.
244. For example, California Benefit Corporation Act (2011), § 14622.
245. Ibid., § 14630(a)(1)–(5).
246. Springer, 'Hollow Hopes and False Fears', op cit note 324, at 85, 122–124.

*Chapter 3*

# The Legal Basis for Protection of Company's Legal Interests

## INTRODUCTION

This chapter demonstrates that the breach of fiduciary obligations forms the basis for protecting the legal interests of the company. It argues that what invariably leads to the need to protect the interests of the company through derivative actions is the breach of fiduciary obligations and the duty of care, skill and diligence by the directors.[1] In other words, since derivative actions essentially entail the redress of wrongs committed against the company by the directors, it is the breach of the common law duties of directors which will be at issue when these proceedings are instituted. In this context, the chapter then argues that since the fiduciary obligations and the duty of care, skill, and diligence concern the supervision of the use of corporate powers for an overarching purpose of minimising or eradicating directorial self-serving misconduct, these duties cannot possibly be owed exclusively to shareholders, thus the justification for a broad legal standing to institute derivative actions.

Under conventional corporate law, the almost unwavering legal standing of shareholders to derivatively enforce compliance with corporate law duties by directors is justified on the basis that they (i.e. the shareholders) are the personification of the company in the context of 'the best interests of the company.[2] The corollary is that other corporate constituent groups are not owed any legal duties and, naturally, cannot be vested with legal standing to enforce compliance with corporate law.[3] Arguments as to why non-shareholder corporate constituencies are not owed any duties by the directors include the assertion that the protection of non-shareholder corporate constituencies should be left to market forces and private ordering, rather than corporate law.[4]

This preference of shareholders as the beneficiaries of directorial duties is based on the assumption of their 'ownership' of corporate entities.[5] Notwithstanding the fact that Easterbrook and Fischel noted as far back as 1983 that a 'number of scholars have pointed out that [s]hareholders are no more the owners of the firm than are other constituencies [and as such, the right to vote could logically involve a number of different constituencies]',[6] Luis A. Aguilar insisted as recently as 21 February 2013 that shareholders are not only investors but also owners of corporations.[7] It is this reasoning, a longstanding justification for the existing corporate legal enforcement framework, which became entrenched, among others, as a jurisprudential justification for making shareholders exclusive beneficiaries of directors' fiduciary obligations.

Corporate ownership by shareholders was not the only legal justification for the existing corporate legal enforcement framework characterised by shareholder favouritism. Another legal justification is based on the recognition of shareholders as residual rights investors. Quoting, with approval, the words of Dean Robert Clark[8] of Harvard Law School, James J. Hanks Jr. insisted that 'although the corporation has numerous and perhaps all-encompassing duties to . . . others, it is the shareholders who [only] have the claim on the residual value of the enterprise'.[9]

As though the justifications for anchoring the corporate legal enforcement framework to shareholders were not enough, the exclusion of non-shareholder corporate constituencies from the conventional corporate legal enforcement framework was further justified on the basis of the perceived bargaining power allegedly enjoyed by non-shareholder corporate constituencies based on the law of contract. The argument here is that many of the non-shareholder corporate constituent groups are already protected by contracts defining their rights against the corporation and, as such, need no further protection through extended legal standing to enforce compliance.[10]

Another argument advanced for the sustenance of the conventional corporate legal enforcement framework is predicated upon the readily accepted efficacy of market forces in privately ordering any necessary cost allocations within companies. It is expected that each of the legal justifications advanced above can be overwhelmingly dismissed as plausible for the continued retention of the conventional corporate legal enforcement framework in the twenty-first century.

## SHAREHOLDERS AS 'OWNERS' OF COMPANIES

Regardless of the fact that case law in the developed world had previously established that shareholders are not the owners of companies, the continued dominance of the property conception of the public company effectively meant that the company continued to be seen as the private property of its 'shareholder-owners'. According to this conception, the company's purpose is to advance the purposes of these owners, which, in the words of Ronald Hampel, boils down to 'the preservation and the greatest practicable enhancement over time of . . . shareholders' investment'.[11] According to this conception, therefore, the function of the directors amounts to no more than acting as agents of the shareholder-owners in advancing their financial interests.[12]

It is this conception of ownership of the corporation by shareholders that has for a long time been regarded as the basis for the shareholders' solely held standing to bring derivative suits.[13]

The view of corporate ownership by shareholders is entrenched in corporate law circles within Anglo-American jurisdictions, so much so that at the time of the introduction of corporate constituency statutes within many states of the United States, one member of the American Bar Association found the idea of accommodating corporate constituencies in corporate decision-making so radical that he vehemently argued against the inclusion of a constituency provision in the Revised Model Business Corporation Act, primarily on the basis that the idea effectively suggested that 'decisions about ownership can disregard the best interests of the owners'.[14]

While some notable corporate governance scholars cogently argued, even as early as the 1980s, that the concept of ownership is irrelevant to the theory of the firm,[15] it was still acknowledged a decade later that the restriction of derivative standing to shareholders was based on the idea of shareholders as corporate owners.[16] Moreover, courts in the United States have maintained a much more traditional approach to corporate law than have corporate scholars.[17]

It is on the basis of company ownership by the shareholders that shareholders alone are said to possess the means to assert directors' fiduciary duties and redress their violation. This right has led to the conclusion that the duty is owed to the shareholders rather than to other corporate constituent groups. In other words, the law continues to assert that shareholders are the only corporate constituent group that can enforce these fiduciary duties because they are owed to them. As correctly observed by Mitchell:

> [T]hat stockholders are the enforcers of the [fiduciary duties] is not itself a necessary result of the existence of the [duties], but rather is the product of nineteenth-century ownership concepts and the doctrinal confusion of different types of fiduciary duties owed by directors and controlling stockholders.[18]

Notwithstanding the clear purpose of fiduciary duties as a mechanism for prohibiting self-serving misconduct on the part of the directors, the courts in

South Africa and the United States have consistently and (virtually) unanimously limited such standing to shareholders.[19]

Interestingly, most of the cases that limited the legal standing to bring derivative suits to shareholders have, almost invariably and without analysis, concluded that ownership is the basis for fiduciary duties, not the prohibition of self-serving conduct by the directors.[20]

Mitchell acknowledges that the days when fiduciary duties were automatically assumed to be designed specifically for the protection of shareholders, merely because they are corporate owners, are long gone and that '[t]he central corporate law focus on the problems engendered by the separation of ownership and control has led to a concentration on restraining managerial self-dealing [as] the clear objective of both statutory and common law rules of the duty of loyalty'.[21]

Moreover, the special treatment of shareholders, one of the many investors within a corporation, on the basis that shareholding as a form of investment entitles investors to corporate ownership status, is questionable. This is because, on the basis of the alleged existence of a 'nexus of contracts' among shareholders, employees, creditors and suppliers, none of the corporate constituent groups owns the corporation. Under this view, each of the corporate constituent groups, including shareholders, merely owns an input of supply or a corresponding output.[22] This does not mean that shareholders are not part of the equation in determining the ambit of stakeholders' protection pursuant to corporate law. In fact, the 'nexus of contracts' theory does not envisage the exclusion of shareholders completely from the equation, but it acknowledges that the exclusive protection of shareholders at the expense of other corporate constituencies cannot be sustained since each of the corporate constituent groups owns nothing more than an input of supply or a corresponding output, not the corporation.[23]

Ascribing ownership of the company to the shareholders is arguably predicated upon the almost always analytically incoherent nineteenth-century judicial opinions and common law rules dealing with the requirement for the utilisation of the assets in the treasury of an incorporated enterprise for the ultimate (or residual) benefit of the contributors to such corporate treasury, that is, the shareholders.

At the turn of the twentieth century, and increasingly during the early twenty-first century, policymakers and legislators woke up to the realisation that the investor who buys shares in an incorporated enterprise and the investor who lends money to the incorporated enterprise are, as a matter of economics, engaged in the same kind of activity and are motivated by the same objectives. They are both making a capital investment; they both expect or hope to get their investment back in the long run, either by liquidating payout or by sale of the security; and they both expect and hope to receive income from their investment in the interim before their capital is returned to them in full.[24] Moreover, the nature of investment instruments today is such that these instruments are not monolithic and that hybrid instruments, bearing the attributes of equity and debt at the same time, are very common. It is in this context that regarding the shareholders as the only investors to whom 'ownership' of the company vests is inconsistent with the economic understanding of the reality of a twenty-first-century public company.

A number of recent corporate law developments, particularly in South Africa, appropriately suggest that the imposition of strict capital rules and requirements as the jurisprudential basis for the universally accepted 'shareholders-as-owners' paradigm is implicitly being challenged.

## SHAREHOLDERS AS 'RESIDUAL RIGHTS INVESTORS'

Robert Clark forcefully argued as early as 1986 that:

> It is the shareholders who have the claim on the residual value of the enterprise, that is, what's left after all definite obligations are satisfied, and the managers have an affirmative open-ended obligation to increase this residual value, rather than the wealth of some other affected group (including themselves).[25]

Using Clarke's reasoning, James J. Hanks Jr. was scathing in his opposition to the arguments that the residual wealth of the corporation – what is left over after suppliers, lenders, employees, and governments have been paid pursuant to either statutory or contractual obligations of the corporation – should also devolve to non-shareholders whose statutory and contractual claims have already been fully satisfied. He maintains that these arguments are unsustainable as they are based on the mere existence of some unspecified form of relationship with a corporation entitling a person not only to whatever the law entitles him by statute and whatever he is able to negotiate by contract but also to the right to receive a piece of whatever is left over after all other non-shareholders' claims have been paid. He concludes that this does not explain how additional wealth would be created for the non-shareholders without taking it from the stockholders.[26]

The argument of shareholders as residual rights holders is at the core of the shareholder primacy norm, as discussed in chapter 1. It is used as a justification for the conclusion that fiduciary duties are only owed to shareholders and, consequently, are the only corporate constituencies vested with legal standing to institute derivative suits.

As shown in chapter 1, the argument made by those who favour the shareholder primacy norm is that since the obligation of directors is to increase only the shareholders' residual value, rather than the wealth of other corporate constituencies (including themselves as directors), any argument that directors can be held to account by non-shareholder corporate constituencies must accordingly fail.

It has also been argued that allowing more corporate constituencies as residual rights owners will introduce an almost unlimited number of potential new competitors for the residual assets of the corporation and, therefore, for the directors' attention.[27]

At the heart of arguments insisting that shareholders are the only ones who are residual rights investors lies two primary justifications; one relating to the nature of the risk assumed and the other, more persuasive, relating to the profit motivation of the shareholders.

Regarding the first justification referred to above, the residual rights theory claims that a person would not assume the risk of a variable return based on corporate performance without insisting on control. This argument can easily be deflected because of, among others, speculators who trade in stock derivatives such as options and indexes; non-voting ordinary shareholders; participating debt-instrument holders, and profit-sharing employees. In other words, a person whose return depends on corporate performance may prefer that another person who has more expertise is less risk averse, or has less to lose, should control the company. Therefore, assuming that shareholders will automatically insist on control and that the corporate legal enforcement regime should thus be designed for their exclusive benefit loses sight of this important consideration. Unsurprisingly, shareholders have often delegated their voting rights and, more particularly, their investment decisions to financial intermediaries.

It was observed by Lynn L. Dallas in 1995 that even the so-called persuasive argument for considering shareholders as residual rights holders, that is, the profit motivation, is not at all convincing.[28] The author observes that the assumption made by those who support this justification is that shareholders should have control because, as owners of the residual value, they have the greatest incentive to maximise the value of the corporation. Dallas argues that this assumption is fallacious since, among other things, the motivation and the ability of the shareholders to maximise the value of the corporation, as alleged, is greatly diminished by the number of shareholders in a single corporation, the increase in the size and complexity of the corporation, the minuscule investment by shareholders in any one corporation, and the professionalisation of the investment function.

Finally, what James J. Hanks Jr. and others who support the argument of shareholders as residual rights investors want us to believe is that because of the statutory and contractual obligations of the public corporation to non-shareholder corporate constituencies, the corporate legal enforcement regime should effectively discount them, and shareholders should be the only beneficiaries of any such corporate legal enforcement regime. What this argument fails to appreciate is that it is exactly these statutory and contractual ties with the corporation that may necessitate the expansion of the corporate legal enforcement regime to benefit the non-shareholder corporate constituencies. As regards the statutory obligations of public corporations, corporate constituency statutes and public benefit corporation statutes offer a perfect example of obligations to non-shareholder corporate constituencies that require these constituencies to have a part in their enforcement, rather than relying on shareholders to enforce them on their behalf. Shareholders would not have the incentive or the desire to do this on behalf of other corporate constituent groups because doing so only advances the promotion of public benefit or non-shareholder objectives and does not necessarily maximise shareholder value within the corporation. Using the argument of shareholders as residual rights investors and, thus, beneficiaries of corporate law protection even when public benefit objectives are being implicated does not make sense. In a situation where the objective of the enforcement is the enhancement of shareholder value, it is perfectly logical to empower shareholders, even to the possible exclusion of non-shareholder corporate constituent groups. The reality is that the latter corporate constituent groups may not be actively incentivised to promote objectives that do not promote their interests and may, possibly, have the effect of diminishing their investment.

As far as the sufficiency of the contractual obligations in discounting the non-shareholder corporate constituencies from the corporate legal enforcement regime, the assumption is that legal enforcement is completely taken care of by the contractual obligations of the corporations, and this also presupposes that there exists parity in bargaining power between contracting parties, something which is effectively dealt with in the section hereunder. The argument also assumes that it is standard for such contractual arrangements to incorporate the corporate legal enforcement regime, which grants other corporate constituencies a footing within the corporate legal enforcement regime, entitling them to legal standing to enforce compliance with any conduct by directors that does not endanger or prejudice such constituencies' interests. This assumption cannot be further from the truth about the reality of the current state of affairs.

## THE INADEQUACY OF BARGAINING POWER AS A PROTECTION FOR NON-SHAREHOLDER CORPORATE CONSTITUENCIES

As observed by David Millon, at the heart of the arguments by those who support the view that non-shareholder corporate constituencies are able to support themselves through contract is a fundamental assumption, based on the libertarian idea, that consent should be the sole basis for obligation since it is, presumably, the equalizing plumb line.[29] James J. Hanks Jr. unapologetically concludes that '[t]here is no need to confer on [non-shareholder corporate constituencies] a gratuitous additional opportunity to share in the assets of the corporation after their statutory and contractual claims have already been satisfied',[30] effectively implying that whatever statutory contractual arrangements are in existence are more than enough to take care of these constituencies' interests, even though these arrangements may not consist of legal measures to enable those corporate constituencies to address the promotion of non-shareholder or public benefit objectives, in respect of which these corporate constituencies are the primary beneficiaries.

In what appears to be his response to the undeniable reality that the current contractual arrangements fall short of addressing the difficulty inherent in those corporate constituencies not being able to correct any failure by these arrangements to ensure compliance by corporate controllers, Hanks then argues that '[i]n recent years . . . many lenders now include in their loan documents so-called "event risk" provisions protecting them in the event of a restructuring that substantially increases debt or otherwise depresses the value of the lenders' debt securities'. [31]

The reality is that while some powerful lenders may be able to impose such contractual obligations upon corporations, this is not true for all corporate constituencies, many of whom are effectively at the mercy of the corporation and have no choice but to settle for 'the crumbs that fall from the master's table', as bargaining capability is a function of wealth. This cannot be classified as meaningful bargaining. Therefore, since the playing field is not level in these contractual arrangements, there should be a continued pursuit by other corporate constituent groups, within the confines of universal pragmatic and legal constraints, to ensure the normalisation of the contractual bargaining process, even if it means that the corporate legal enforcement framework has to be reformed. Arguing that the levelling of the playing field in this regard can be addressed by changing contract law and not corporate law is disingenuous on the part of the supporters of the shareholder primacy theory, as they use the alleged adequacy of contractual arrangements to reject any possible consideration of non-shareholder corporate constituencies' interests in corporate law enforcement.

As articulated by David Millon, '[u]nless shareholders have consented to limit their wealth maximization efforts, they should be under no obligation to temper those pursuits for the sake of non-shareholder interests'.[32] The author concludes that in the absence of such consent, 'obligation [by shareholders] becomes a matter of coercion [which] offends liberty [since] nothing more than a vaguely articulated libertarianism is offered as the basis for [the] insistence on the primacy of contract in defining all intracorporate relationships'.

## THE INADEQUACY OF MARKET FORCES AND PRIVATE ORDERING

Another argument raised against the kinds of legal intervention which are aimed at empowering non-shareholder corporate constituencies with legal standing to access corporate law remedies is based on the reasoning that contracting and market processes are sufficient to redress any externalities that might arise.[33] The argument is to the effect that these contracting and market processes will restore equilibrium in the sense that all participants in a legal transaction will realise fair value, and, as a result, there is no need for any legal infrastructure other than one that facilitates contracting and market efficiency.[34] It is also argued that the introduction of legal rules empowering non-shareholder corporate constituencies will work to everyone's detriment by diminishing corporate wealth.[35] This argument erroneously assumes that every corporate suit by non-shareholder corporate constituencies will be successful and that measures to deter frivolous and vexatious suits are deficient or nonexistent.

Again, certain corporate lawsuits by non-shareholder corporate constituencies, particularly derivative suits aimed at promoting general and specific public benefit purposes of corporations, are likely to benefit, rather than be detrimental to the corporation, since the pursuit of such public benefit purposes is for the benefit of all corporate constituencies, as such purposes are recognised in all benefit corporation statutes, for example, as being in the best interests of those corporations. The market forces argument also presupposes perfect bargaining processes and, as has already been demonstrated, bargaining power disparities in contracting processes effectively necessitate law reform aimed at addressing bargaining outcomes that are substantially unfair.

At any rate, even if these market mechanisms work well in the sense that they inevitably ensure a baseline result along the lines of 'you get what you pay for', according to Lawrence Mitchell, 'this end is not the sole function of legal rules'.[36] Mitchell concludes, correctly in my view, that the 'law abdicates its function as a socializing tool when it leaves the redressing of individual and societal wrongs to the forces of competition',[37] which is what market mechanisms endeavour to achieve.

## DIRECTORIAL DUTIES AS THE BASIS FOR RESTRAINING DIRECTORIAL OR MANAGERIAL SELF-DEALING

The continued insistence of traditional corporate law in anchoring its corporate legal enforcement framework on the basis of shareholder wealth maximisation is oblivious to the centrality of restraining directorial or managerial self-dealing as the proper basis for fiduciary obligations and, thus, the resultant legal enforcement framework.[38]

Common law rules developed in relation to fiduciary obligations have led to the incorrect conclusion that these obligations are owed exclusively to shareholders and that they are the only corporate constituent group entitled to enforce compliance therewith.[39] Given the fact that the real role of these obligations is to restrain or prohibit directorial or managerial self-dealing for the benefit not only of the shareholders but of all corporate constituencies whose financial well-being is linked to the success of the company, particularly in a modern public company with so many corporate constituencies, it is no wonder that latching the powers to enforce corporate law remedies on the assumption that it is only the shareholders to whom fiduciary obligations are owed is fundamentally flawed.[40] The development of this dysfunctional equation was, as I shall demonstrate, inter alia, based on the assumption of shareholders as corporate owners. With the realisation that shareholders are another group of corporate investors in twenty-first-century corporate law, the reasoning behind this dysfunctional construct no longer applies.

Since the primary concern of fiduciary obligations is not, as is universally accepted, the exclusive protection of shareholders, continuing to use fiduciary obligations as a basis for the current enforcement framework in corporate law is illusory.[41] The continued insistence of corporate law in regarding shareholders as the only legitimate beneficiaries of the enforcement framework is, therefore, inextricably linked to the status of shareholders as notional owners of companies. The relaxation of the rules relating to corporate voting and other corporate governance rules under modern corporate law effectively renders the current corporate law enforcement arrangements questionable.

Closer scrutiny of the common examples of common law fiduciary obligations reveals that the primary concern of fiduciary obligations is not the exclusive protection of the shareholders but the restraining of the managerial or directorial self-dealing on the part of those vested with the power for corporate decision-making.

While the Companies Act of 2008[42] in South Africa provides for the partial codification of the directors' standards of conduct or common law directors' duties,[43] it appears that these standards of conduct continue to be determined in accordance with common law interpretation accorded as to their meaning.

The language of ss 75-78 arguably perpetuates the continued application of common law rules affecting directors' duties, even in the aftermath of the introduction of statutory standards of conduct.[44] The common law rules, developed over many years of judicial precedent, indicate that a number of duties which must be observed by company directors are divided into two broad categories (a) fiduciary obligations and (b) duties of care, skill and diligence. The appearance of the continued application of the common law notwithstanding, the availability of the extended corporate legal enforcement framework under the Companies Act, 2008 may be indicative of the legislature's intention to extend the meaning of what constitutes 'the best interests of the company'. This is also arguably borne out by section 7 of the Act, which clearly provides for a broad purpose of company law.

The analysis in this section proceeds from the premise that common law duties are not unitary and are, thus, not immutable mechanisms for the exclusive protection of shareholders at all times. It is acknowledged, however, that in some contexts, directors do indeed owe duties exclusively to shareholders.[45] That said, however, it needs to be appreciated that common law duties, particularly fiduciary obligations, are designed to deal with a variety of different types of conflict of interest.[46] It is therefore critical that a proper understanding of the effects and the intended beneficiaries of each of the commonly known variants of these obligations be presented. This analysis is obviously undertaken with the aim of dispelling the myth that the purpose of all fiduciary obligations is the exclusive protection of the corporate shareholder constituent group. A proper understanding of these duties requires that they be carefully matched with the conflicts they are designed to address.

The reality is that some of the fiduciary obligations are designed to restrain directors from self-dealing at the expense of the company.[47] Others are purposed to prevent interference by directors with corporate transactions to protect their interests.[48] Others still are designed to restrain directors from dealing in the company's shares at the expense of shareholders.[49] Based on this analysis, it is clearly evident that the conventional corporate law rules relating to the corporate legal enforcement regime readily and erroneously assume that all fiduciary obligations address the last-mentioned purpose above.

The indiscriminate conglomeration of fiduciary obligations as a corporate law mechanism for keeping directors in check and additionally behaving as the gatekeepers for the exclusive protection of shareholders has led to the continued application of the apparently invariable shareholder-oriented legal enforcement framework, something which is lamentable, as it unjustifiably excludes other non-shareholder corporate constituent groups from accessing these corporate law remedies, even in situations where they may be beneficiaries of fiduciary obligations.[50] From the above analysis of the distinct purposes of fiduciary obligations, the better view is that the overwhelming concern of these duties is the prohibition of self-dealing on the part of directors. It is this view of the fiduciary duties which conforms to the new recognition of the pluralistic nature of the company and thus is a major step toward the creation of a more realistic model of the corporation. If this view is accepted, as it should be, the corporate legal enforcement framework will appropriately be reformed from its deficient position of being concerned with affording legal standing exclusively to shareholders.

When all is said and done, the purpose of the fiduciary obligations imposed on the fiduciary is to protect the beneficiary[51] from vulnerability, which largely results from self-interested conduct on the part of the fiduciary.[52] While the common law readily concludes that such beneficiaries are exclusively shareholders, the analysis of case law, particularly in other Anglo-American jurisdictions, demonstrates that other corporate constituencies may well be the beneficiaries, depending on the conflicts of interest presented by the fiduciary obligations in question.[53]

## ASSESSMENT OF THE JURISPRUDENTIAL BASIS FOR THE ALL-INCLUSIVE ENFORCEMENT FRAMEWORK

Writing as recently as 2012, Lynn A. Stout forcefully argued that:

> [T]he philosophical case for shareholder value maximization . . . rests on incorrect factual claims about the economic structure of corporations, including the mistaken claims that shareholders [understood as equity investors] 'own' corporations, that they have the only residual claim on the firm's profits, and that they are 'principals' who hire and control directors to act as their agents.[54]

She concludes that 'shareholder value ideology is based on wishful thinking, not reality [and] [a]s a theory of corporate purpose, it is poised for intellectual collapse'.[55]

It is this theory, discussed in detail in chapter 1, which unjustifiably focuses directorial fiduciary obligations on – and limits enforcement powers to – shareholders. As it is the shareholder value theory that perpetuates the current dispensation of corporate law remedies, the conclusion that this theory is jurisprudentially flawed in corporate law effectively means that 'an all-inclusive theory', which can be jurisprudentially defended, is needed in order to justify a legal enforcement framework that is broadly inclusive of all corporate constituent groups.

The common perception that fiduciary obligations are owed only to shareholders has been conclusively proven to be jurisprudentially untenable, as it disregards the significance of restricting directorial or managerial self-dealing as an overarching concern for fiduciary obligations.

Since shareholder value is clearly inappropriate as the jurisprudential basis for the legal enforcement framework that enables non-shareholder corporate constituencies to access corporate law remedies, as it is preoccupied exclusively with equity investors as the sole beneficiaries of corporate law remedies,[56] the question remains as to which of the other approaches are best suited to provide such a jurisprudential justification. In the same manner, the limited nature of both the Enlightened Shareholder Value Approach and the Entity Maximisation and Sustainability Model means that these, too, are doomed to failure, as the only possible way in which they could be able to facilitate access to corporate law remedies by non-shareholder corporate constituencies is by means of derivative action proceedings. As has been shown in chapter 1,[57] this is grossly unsatisfactory, as such a remedy could only possibly benefit the company, rather than the non-shareholder corporate constituencies.

This leaves the Actionable Enlightened Shareholder Value Approach as the only possible alternative mechanism through which an all-inclusive legal enforcement framework can be made available for the time being, given the present circumstances. It was conceded at least twenty-one years ago that an all-inclusive legal framework approach was possible even within the context of the requirement that 'directors [should continue] to act in the interests of maximizing stockholder wealth'.[58] No jurisprudential justification exists for the legal enforcement framework affording non-shareholder corporate constituencies access to corporate law remedies beyond derivative action proceedings, except for the Actionable Enlightened Shareholder Value Approach (AESVA).

The traces of an all-inclusive enforcement framework, even within the context of the overall objective of maximising shareholder value, emanate from the 1992 article by Lawrence E. Mitchell.[59] According to this approach, which is made up of numerous procedural steps outlined hereunder, the basic presumption is that 'directors are to act [ultimately] in the interests of maximizing stockholder wealth'.[60] This purpose, however, does not exempt the directors from being required to take into account the extent to which their actions harm a range of corporate constituents affected by their actions.[61] Having said that, it is not sufficient that directors are required to take into account affected corporate constituencies; members of each such corporate constituent group have standing to challenge corporate actions that they claim have injured them.[62]

## CONCLUSION AND CHAPTER SYNOPSIS

It has been clarified that the need for legal intervention in providing corporate remedies for non-shareholder corporate constituencies should not be inhibited by the jurisprudentially and pragmatically unjustifiable status of shareholders as 'owners' of corporations. As has been argued, the alleged position of shareholders as residual rights investors is similarly unjustifiable as an impediment to deflect arguments for law reform aimed at addressing the inadequacy of the corporate legal enforcement framework. The bargaining power and market forces arguments have also been shown to be deficient in explaining away the continued need for legal intervention towards enabling the re-design of the corporate legal enforcement regime to better accommodate non-shareholder corporate constituencies.

Furthermore, it is argued that if the current corporate legal enforcement framework is based on the alleged indebtedness of directors to shareholders solely on the basis of fiduciary obligations, then that framework is fundamentally flawed, as the central purpose of those fiduciary obligations is not the exclusive protection of shareholders, but the prohibition of directorial or managerial self-dealing for the benefit of the broader spectrum of corporate constituencies.

The chapter has also shown that recent corporate law developments, particularly in South Africa, which remove, at last, some of the tightly held legal and pragmatic justifications for the conventional corporate legal enforcement regime, signify the acceptance of the pluralistic nature of a public company in the twenty-first century.

## NOTES

1. Regardless of the fact that the language of section 165 (2) makes no explicit reference to the common law duties as the basis for derivative actions, the violation of the legal interests of the company invariably takes place through breach of directorial common law duties.

2. In this regard, see, among others, Havenga M, 'Directors' Fiduciary Duties Under Our Future Company-law Regime' (1997) 9 *SAMLJ* 310, at 317.

3. Ibid. Speaking in relation to loyalty and good faith as intrinsic elements of fiduciary duties, Havenga maintained that 'It cannot be stated as a categorical rule that these requirements exists in the relationships between directors and various groups [of stakeholders]'. Ibid., at 320.

4. See, among others, Carney WJ, 'Does Defining Constituencies Matter?' (1990) 59 *University of Cincinnati Law Review* 385, at 389; and Macey JR, 'Externalities, Firm-Specific Capital Investments, and the Legal Treatment of Fundamental Corporate Changes', (1989) *DUKE Law Journal* 173, at 174.

5. Even the definition of 'shares' in the Model Business Corporation Act as 'the units into which the proprietary interests in a corporation are divided' essentially denotes corporate ownership by shareholders (See §1.40(22) of the Model Business Corporation Act).

6. Easterbrook FH & Fischel DR, 'Voting in Corporate Law' (1983) 26 *The Journal of Law and Economics* 395, at 396.

7. Aguilar, LA, 'Shareholders Need Robust Disclosure to Exercise Their Voting Rights as Investors and Owners' *The CLS Blue Sky Blog*, Columbia Law School's blog on Corporations and the Capital Markets. Available at http://columbia.us4.list-manage.com/track/click?u=5cbcaa004e7ddae22916ab50e&id=5bf6654d42&e=67a733c7b2, accessed on 5 September 2013.

8. Clark R, *Corporate Law* (1986), 17–19.

9. Hanks, 'Playing with Fire', op cit note 7, at 108.

10. See, among others, Hanks, Ibid., at 115.

11. The Hampel Committee, *Report on Corporate Governance (Final Committee Report)* (1998), op cit note 49, at para 1.17.

12. William T Allen, 'Our Schizophrenic Conception of the Corporation' (1992) 14 *Cardozo Law Review* 261, at 265.

13. See, for example, ALI Principles of Corporate Governance (1988) (Rent. Draft No. 8), § 7.02.

14. ABA (Reg. &L. Rep (BNA)) Model Act Panel Rejects Other-Constituencies Measures, (17 Aug. 1990), 1217, at 1218.

15. See, for example, Fama EF, 'Agency Problems and the Theory of the Firm' (1980) 88 *Journal of Political Economy* 288, at 289.

16. See, inter alia, Mitchell LE, 'The Fairness Rights of Corporate Bondholders' (1990) 65 *New York University Law Review* 1165, at 1192–1193. The Delaware Court of Chancery also applied the traditional model of shareholder ownership in 1990 in the case of *Stahl v Apple Bancorp*, 579 A.2d 1115, 1121 (Del. Ch. 1990).

17. The case of *Kusner v First Pennsylvania Corp.*, 395 F. Supp. 276, 280 (E.D. Pa. 1975) referred to share ownership as a 'proprietary interest in the corporate enterprise' and noted that damage to that interest may be redressed by a derivative lawsuit. The court relied on the case of *Kauffman v Dreyfus Fund, Inc.*, 434 F.2d 727, 735 (3d Cir. 1970), which quoted *Ashwander v Tennessee Valley Auth.*, 297 US 288, 321 (1936) as authority. Also, the case of *Simons v Cogan*, 542 A.2d 785, 791 (Del. 1987) held the same, relying on Harffv. Kerkorian, 324 A.2d 215, 218–219 (Del. Ch. 1974), which noted that stock is evidence of ownership of corporate assets and that stockholders can sue for mismanagement of the corporation.

18. Mitchell, 'A Theoretical and Practical Framework', op cit note 6, at 603.

19. In South Africa, the application of the English common law on derivative action necessitated the introduction of legal standing for the exclusive benefit of shareholders in derivative suits. Firstly, as a result of the relaxation of the rule in *Foss v Harbottle* by the English and South African courts, it became very clear that of all corporate constituent groups within a company, it was only the shareholders who were vested with legal standing in derivative suits. Also, the wording of the previous statutory derivative action under the Companies Act of 1973 in South Africa expressly made it clear that the initiation of proceedings on behalf of a company was to be undertaken by a member (see s. 266 of the Companies Act, 1973). As a justification for the relaxation of the common law rule in *Foss v Harbottle* to accommodate shareholders and no other corporate constituencies, Blackman observed in *The Law*

*of South Africa (LAWSA)* First Reissue, (1996) Vol. 4, Part 2, at para 210, that one of the reasons for the introduction of the limited statutory derivative action was 'the need for adequate deterrents to inhibit frivolous and vexatious proceedings' (ibid.). See also *TWK Agriculture Ltd v NCT Forestry Co-operative Ltd and Others* 2006 SA 20 (N), at 16, para 42, where the court noted that '[t]he courts have recognised a member's [or a shareholder's] standing to bring a derivative action without first having proposed a resolution that the company institute action where such a proposal would have been an exercise in futility'. See also *Moti v Moti and Hassim Moti Ltd* 1934 TPD 428; *Gundelfinger v African Textile Manufacturers Ltd and Others* 1939 SA 314 (AD); *McLelland v Hulett and Others* 1992 (1) SA 456 (D&CLD) and *Fedsure Life Assurance Co Ltd v Worldwide African Investment Holdings (Pty) Ltd and Others* 2003 (3) SA 268. In the case of the US, see, for example, the case of *Metropolitan Life Ins. Co. v RJR Nabisco*, 716 F. Supp. 1504, 1524 (S.D.N.Y. 1989), which held that the plaintiff creditors were protected by the terms of their contracts, and did not have the requisite property right or equitable interest to impose a fiduciary duty on the defendants. Again, in the case of *Dorfman v Chemical Bank*, 56 F.R.D. 363, 364 (S.D.N.Y. 1972), it was held that debenture holders lacked shareholder standing to maintain a derivative suit. On the same note, the case of *Harff v Kerkorkian*, 324 A.2d 215, 219 (Del. Ch. 1974) held that convertible debenture holders did not have standing as stockholders for purposes of a derivative action suit. Another case, *Haberman v Washington Public Power Supply System*, 744 P.2d 1032, 1061 (Wash. 1987), held that, because '[s]tanding to bring a stockholder derivative claim requires a proprietary interest in the corporation whose right is asserted', plaintiff bondholders had no right to bring a derivative action.

20. See, for example, *Simons v Cogan*, 549 A.2d 300, 304 (Del. 1988).

21. Mitchell, 'A Theoretical and Practical Framework', op cit note 6, at 632.

22. See, for example, Alchien A and Demsetz H, 'Production, Information Costs, and Economic Organization' (1972) 66 *American Economic Review* 777, at 789 note 14.

23. Ibid. See also Easterbrook & Fischel 'Voting in Corporate Law', op cit note 527, at 396.

24. See Bayless Manning and James J Hanks Jr., *Legal Capital* (3rd ed.) (1990), at 13.

25. Clark R, *Corporate Law* (1986), at 19.

26. Playing with Fire, at 112.

27. Ibid.

28. Lynne L Dallas, 'Working Toward a New Paradigm' in Lawrence E. Mitchell (ed.), *Progressive Corporate Law* (1995), at 47.

29. Millon, 'Communitarianism in Corporate Law', op cit note 91, at 7.

30. Hanks, 'Playing with Fire', op cit note 7, at 116.

31. Ibid.

32. Millon, 'Communitarianism in Corporate Law', op cit note 91, at 7.

33. See, for example, Carney 'Does Defining Constituencies Matter?' op cit note 525, at 389; and Macey, 'Externalities', op cit note 526, at 174.

34. Ibid.

35. Mitchell, 'A Theoretical and Practical Framework', op cit note 6, at 640.

36. Ibid., at 641.

37. Ibid.

38. In chapter 1, both the 'shareholder primacy' and the 'Enlightened Shareholder Value' theories rely on directors' fiduciary obligations as the basis for holding that shareholders are exclusively or primarily the beneficiaries of the corporate law enforcement framework. Even in chapter 2, corporate law developments in the United Kingdom and the statutory corporate constituency mechanisms put in place in the United States to justify corporate law enforcement by corporate constituencies are premised on the centrality of fiduciary obligations as the basis for designing a legal enforcement framework under corporate law.

39. It was forcefully argued, as far back as 1995, by William W. Bratton that the corporate fiduciary law battle during the 1970s and 1980s was settled through a compromise position which recognised the significance of 'the self-dealing prohibition' as the primary concern of corporate fiduciary law. Although admittedly, the projected era of shareholder-enforced corporate governance was acknowledged as being the unsatisfactory part of this compromise. (See William W Bratton, 'Game Theory and the Restoration of Honor to Corporate Law's Duty of Loyalty' in Lawrence E. Mitchell (ed.), *Progressive Corporate Law* (1995), 139, at 139–140.) Bratton acknowledges that because the compromise view accepts the centrality of the prohibition against self-dealing in corporate fiduciary law, it 'disfavors normative intervention . . . [but propagates] a revised fiduciary regime in which judges review corporate processes used to approve transactions, rather than the transactions themselves'. (Ibid., at 140).

40. Lawrence E. Mitchell argues that treating directors' fiduciary duties as a unitary concept masks the differences in the nature of the underlying conflicts those duties are meant to mediate and leads to a faulty analysis of the purpose and significance of different fiduciary rules, that is, the fiduciary fallacy. (Mitchell, 'A Theoretical and Practical Framework', op cit note 6, at 593). A brief study of Justice Douglas's famous opinion in *Pepper v Litton* 308 US 295 (1939) illustrates that corporate fiduciary rules focus primarily on the issue of self-dealing and only secondarily on the stockholder interest side of the equation.

41. Although fiduciary duties have been readily assumed to be concerned with the exclusive protection of shareholders, the tendency of fiduciary duty in corporate law has been toward the development of situational rules designed to regulate certain types of undesirable conduct by directors.

42. The Companies Act (Act No. 71 of 2008) in South Africa only became the official corporate legislation with effect from 01 May 2011. That said, however, transitional arrangements in Schedule 5 effectively ensured the continued operation of the Companies Act, 1973 (Act No. 61 of 1973) through constitutional arrangements put in place by companies in line with that 1973 Companies Act. The supremacy of these constitutional arrangements came to an end on 30 April 2013, thereby making the effective date for the full operation of the 2008 Companies Act to be 01 May 2013.

43. These are primarily found in ss 75 and 76 of the Companies Act, 71 of 2008.

44. In particular, the narrow application of s 75 only to the disclosure of directors' personal financial interests in transactions clearly shows that the common law

rules regulating the broader aspect of conflict between director's duty and interests continue to apply. Furthermore, reference to 'good faith' and 'a proper purpose' in s 76(3) (a) clearly envisages the continued application of common law rules of 'good faith', which is the cornerstone of 'fiduciary duties'. This is the case even in the absence of a provision similar to s 42(2) of the Close Corporations Act, 69 of 1984, which, in essence, provides that the list of members' duties enumerated in that section apply '[W]ithout prejudice to the generality of the expression "fiduciary relationship" . . .'. Moreover, mere restatement, in s 76 (3) (b) of the Act, of the common law duty to exercise the powers and perform the functions of director . . . 'in the best interests of the company' without an attempt to give statutory meaning to 'the interests of the company' is another example of the continued application of the common law rules in this regard. Further examples of the continued application of the common law in the aftermath of the 2008 Companies Act include s 77(2)(a) and (b) and s 78(5), all of which clearly envisage such common law rules.

45. See Havenga M, 'Directors Fiduciary Duties Under Our Future Company-law Regime', op cit note 519, AT 317–323. There are also a few examples of from the United States, and they include *Diamond v Oreamun,* 248 N.E.2d 910, 914 (N.Y. 1969), which held that the sale of corporate stock by officers who acquired inside information regarding corporate finances was an abuse of those officers' fiduciary relationship with the corporation's stockholders; *Essex Universal Corp. v Yates*, 305 F.2d 572, 575 (2d Cir. 1962), which established that selling corporate control, by itself, violates New York state law; *Perlman v Feldmann*, 219 F.2d 173, 174–175 (2d Cir.) and 349 US 952 (1955), which held that a director who sold controlling stock to the corporation's customers was accountable to the minority stockholders; *Gerdes v Reynolds*, 28 N.Y.S.2d 622, 629–630 (N.Y. Sup. Ct. 1941), which decided whether officers and directors of an investment trust who sold their majority share were accountable for the purchaser's waste and improper application of the trust's assets.

46. This point is convincingly made by Mitchell ('A Theoretical and Practical Framework', op cit note 6, at 590).

47. According to Mitchell (ibid., at 590), conflicts of interest intended to be addressed by these fiduciary obligations are called vertical conflicts. According to Mitchell (ibid.), '[t]hese conflicts occur between virtually omnipotent managers and relatively powerless constituents of the corporation (or the corporation itself)' According to Mitchell (ibid.), '[v]ertical conflicts present the problem of restraining the board from acting in its own self-interest to the detriment of these less powerful groups'. Examples include the fiduciary obligation of directors not to exceed their powers. Within the US context, see Williamson O, 'Corporate Governance', 93 *YALE Law Journal* 1197, 1200–1205 (1984), in which these corporate governance conflicts are discussed in terms of transaction costs. See also *Irving Trust Co. v Deutsch,* 73 F.2d 121, 123 (2d Cir. 1934), 294 US 708 (1935); *Guth v Loft, Inc.*, 5 A.2d 503, 505–508, 510 (Del. 1939); and *Klinicki v Lundgren*, 695 P.2d 906, 920–921 (Or. 1985).

48. In this regard, the trend-setting Delaware case of *Unocal Corp. v Mesa Petroleum Co.*, 493 A.2d 946, 955 (Del. 1985) observed that a defensive, selective stock repurchase plan must not be motivated by the directors' desires to self-perpetuate

their positions. Furthermore, the rules designed to prevent directors from taking decisions or benefiting from transactions in which their interests conflict, or may potentially conflict, with their duties are aimed at addressing this purpose of fiduciary obligations.

49. Mitchell (op cit note 6, at 590) refers to these as 'intra-class horizontal fiduciary duties'. Horizontal conflicts exist among two or more relatively powerless groups that have interests in the corporation. A primary example in this regard is the fiduciary obligation of directors not to exercise their powers for collateral or improper purposes. Other examples of these conflicts are the expropriation of wealth from bondholders by shareholders and the layoff of employees as a cost-cutting measure designed to assure the repayment of debt assumed to finance a leveraged takeover. See also *Dirks v SEC,* 463 US 646, 653 (1983).

50. Particularly in benefit corporations, where the pursuit of non-shareholder-oriented general and specific public benefit purposes is regarded as being tantamount to the pursuit of the interests of the corporation concerned.

51. In the context of directors, such beneficiaries are regarded by common law as company shareholders. This assumption is simplistic and extremely general, as in some instances, beneficiaries of these fiduciary obligations may be the company itself or other corporate constituencies whose financial well-being is tied to the success of the corporation.

52. In *Frame v Smith* (1987) 42 DLR (4th) 81, Wilson J said (98–99) that:

> Relationships in which a fiduciary obligation have been imposed seem to possess three general characteristics: (1) the fiduciary has scope for the exercise of some discretion or power. (2) The fiduciary can unilaterally exercise that power or discretion so as to affect the beneficiary's legal or practical interests. (3) The beneficiary is peculiarly vulnerable to or at the mercy of the fiduciary holding the discretion or power.

These are typically consequences of a relationship where one person undertakes, assumes or is otherwise legally required to act in the interests of another.

53. See, among others, *Irving Trust Co. v Deutsch,* 73 F.2d 121, 123 (2d Cir. 1934), 294 US 708 (1935); *Guth v Loft, Inc.*, 5 A.2d 503, 505–508, 510 (Del. 1939); *Klinicki v Lundgren*, 695 P.2d 906, 920–921 (Or. 1985); *Unocal Corp. v Mesa Petroleum Co.*, 493 A.2d 946, 955 (Del. 1985); and *Dirks v SEC,* 463 US 646, 653 (1983).

54. Lynn A Stout, *The Shareholder Value Myth: How Putting Shareholders First Harms Investors, Corporations, and the Public* (2012), at 18.

55. Ibid.

56. Lynn A Stout (op cit note 639) further argues that the shareholder primacy norm gets corporate law, corporate economics and the empirical evidence wrong and, as such, it is 'the dumbest idea in the world'. (Ibid.)

57. See chapter 1.

58. Mitchell, 'A Theoretical and Practical Framework', op cit note 6, at 635–636.

59. Ibid.

60. Ibid., at 635.

61. Ibid.

62. Ibid., at 635–636.

# *Chapter 4*

# The Enforcement Framework Under the 2008 Companies Act

## INTRODUCTION

Just like the Anglo-American jurisdictions with which it shares company law traditions, South Africa hails from a very conservative, individualistic background concerning legal standing, particularly in the area of corporate law. In recent times, however, South Africa has substantially liberalised its legal standing, and its corporate law is exemplary as far as this liberalisation trend is concerned. To a large extent, the modernisation of legal standing in the area of corporate law has been influenced by developments in constitutional law.

While the procedural standards favouring non-shareholder corporate constituencies have been appropriately legislated, judicially affirmed, and modernised in South Africa, what appears to be lacking is the precise articulation of the normative goals underpinning such procedural standards.

## PROCEEDING TO RESTRAIN THE COMPANY FROM DOING ANYTHING INCONSISTENT WITH THE COMPANIES ACT

### The Content of the Mechanism

Departure from conventional legal standing rules in corporate law is exemplified by, among others, the provisions of section 20(4), which deals with the powers to interdict conduct by the company in contravention of the Act. According to this section:

> One or more shareholders, directors or prescribed officers of a company, or a trade union representing employees of the company, may apply to the High

Court for an appropriate order to restrain the company from doing anything inconsistent with this Act.[1]

## The Jurisprudential Basis for the Mechanism

In its simplest form, the conventional common law rule concerning legal standing comes down to the question of whether the person claiming legal standing has a direct and substantial interest or competence to claim a particular relief. At common law, this direct and substantial interest does not include mere financial interest, which is taken to be an indirect interest.[2] In other words, within the context of the matter dealt with in this section, the question is whether the claimant has a direct and substantial interest in the interdict sought. The section lists the three categories of persons who may be entitled to make an application for an order restraining the company from doing anything inconsistent with the Act – that is, shareholders, directors and prescribed officers, and a trade union representing the employees of the company – determining whether any of those categories of persons has *locus standi* at common law is considered with reference to the relief they seek and the right on which they base their claim.[3]

Shareholders, directors and prescribed officers can base their claim to restrain the company from doing anything inconsistent with the Act on their right to be part of corporate decision-making, either pursuant to their right to participate and vote in general meetings, in accordance with the principles of the majority rule (in the case of shareholders) or in accordance with the 'internal management principle', which vests directors and prescribed officers with managerial control in accordance with the corporate constitution.[4] It would thus appear that insofar as the employees are concerned, their right at common law has nothing to do with corporate decision-making and consists only of the right to reasonable remuneration.[5] Therefore, according to the common law, a trade union representing the employees of the company will ordinarily not have *locus standi* to bring proceedings to restrain the company from doing anything inconsistent with the Companies Act since the right on which they will be basing their claim amounts to no more than a mere financial interest and not a direct and substantial interest as required.

It is, therefore, clear that granting employees, as represented by a trade union, the *locus standi* to bring proceedings to restrain the company from doing anything inconsistent with the Companies Act is a departure from the common law. This departure is jurisprudentially justified, *inter alia*, on the basis that the Companies Act, 2008, specifically enjoins its interpretation and application 'in a manner that gives effect to the purposes set out in section 7'.[6]

Some of the relevant purposes of the Act, as specifically stated in section 7, are to—

(*a*) promote compliance with the Bill of Rights as provided for in the Constitution, in the application of company law;[7]
(*b*) promote the development of the South African economy by . . . encouraging transparency and high standards of corporate governance as appropriate, given the significant role of enterprises within the social and economic life of the nation;[8]
(*d*) reaffirm the concept of the company as a means of achieving economic and social benefits;[9]
(*f*) promote the development of companies within all sectors of the economy, and encourage active participation in economic organisation, management and productivity;[10] and
(*j*) encourage the efficient and responsible management of companies . . ..[11]

As the *locus standi* provisions under section 20(4) clearly point to the need for the advancement of the above purposes as opposed to the perpetuation of the common law standing rules, the inclusion of the trade union representing the employees of the company as one of the categories of persons that is capable of bringing proceedings to restrain the company from doing anything inconsistent with the Companies Act is jurisprudentially justified.

In light of the justification for the inclusion of trade unions representing the employees of the company in restraining the company from doing anything inconsistent with the Act, there may not seem to be a reason why other non-shareholder corporate constituencies, over and above trade unions, cannot be included in the legal standing. However, the legislature's clear intention to limit the remedy's accessibility to trade unions may have been influenced by rational considerations. For one, since there is no cause of action requirement, except for the likelihood of the Act's contravention by the company, there may be a real threat of possible abuse of the remedy if the legal standing is extended beyond the current specifically mentioned constituencies in section 20(4).[12]

It is also doubtful whether the court's inherent power to dismiss any legal proceedings that are frivolous, vexatious and without merit[13] can be helpful if the legal standing is overly broad and the cause of action is so easily accessible.

## The Opportunity to Have a Director Declared Delinquent in the Content of the Mechanism

Regardless of the fact that the provisions of the Companies Act, 2008, under section 162, introduce a new corporate law remedy which never existed under the previous corporate law statutes, the application of the common law rules of standing clearly indicates that the granting of legal standing to certain corporate constituent groups is not supported, given their lack of direct or substantial interest in connection with the nature of the relief provided for. In terms of section 162(2):

> A company, a shareholder, director, company secretary or prescribed officer of a company, a registered trade union that represents employees of the company or another representative of the employees of a company may apply to a court for an order declaring a person delinquent or under probation if—
>
> *(a)* the person is a director of that company or, within the 24 months immediately preceding the application, was a director of that company; and
> *(b)* any of the circumstances contemplated in . . . subsection (5)*(a)* to *(c)* apply, in the case of an application for a declaration of delinquency; or . . . subsections (7)*(a)* and (8) apply, in the case of an application for probation.[14]

Depending on the severity of the grounds for a declaration of delinquency or probation, the punishment may subsist for the lifetime of the person, for seven years, or such longer period as determined by the court at the time of making the declaration, in the case of an order for delinquency,[15] or may subsist for a period not exceeding five years as determined by the court at the time it makes the declaration, in the case of a probation order, and may be made subject to any conditions the court considers appropriate.[16]

## The Jurisprudential Basis for the Mechanism

Since at common law, a company secretary, a registered trade union that represents employees of the company, or another representative of the employees are not ordinarily vested with the power to appoint company directors, which would obviously give rise to the relief to declare the director delinquent or under probation, such persons lack *locus standi* under the conventional rules of legal standing as they have no direct and substantial interest in the matter. As emphasised previously under the discussion concerning the relief to restrain the company from doing anything inconsistent with the Act, the test for determining competence to claim relief at common law is whether the claimant possesses the right which gives rise to the relief sought and that such a right has been infringed, or there existed a threat to infringe it.[17] The relief to which the aggrieved party is entitled depends on the infringed right and is consequential to such infringement. Such relief must fall within the scope of the right.[18]

With the introduction of the Companies Act on 1 May 2011, this common law position lost its significance with regard to the relief provided for under this section. As discussed in chapter 3, while the common law associated corporate voting almost exclusively with shareholders, particularly in connection with the appointment of directors, the 2008 Companies Act has completely changed the rules of the game by recognising that corporate voting is not the exclusive domain of shareholders. In connection with the appointment of directors, in particular, the Act recognises that the company may extend this right to any of the corporate constituencies.

The classic example of the indication of this course of action under the Act is provided under s 66(4), which provides that '[a] company's Memorandum of Incorporation . . . may provide for . . . the direct appointment and removal of one or more directors by any person who is named in, or determined in terms of, the Memorandum of Incorporation . . ..'[19] As the right to appoint and remove directors can effectively be accorded to any of the corporate constituencies, it consequently makes no sense for the relief to apply for a director to be declared delinquent or under probation to be reserved for the shareholders, directors, and prescribed officers. The Companies Act, 2008 appropriately recognises this state of affairs, and it has expanded the categories of persons who may approach the High Court for this relief, as depicted under s 162 (2).

As corporate constituencies such as a company secretary, a registered trade union that represents employees of the company, or another representative of the employees of a company are no longer strangers to the direct appointment and removal of one or more directors within a company, reserving the *locus standi* only for the shareholders and directors to seek delinquency and probation relief under s 162 will not only be jurisprudentially indefensible but will also logically incoherent. To argue that the extension of categories of persons entitled to this relief beyond shareholders would be chaotic, as is usually argued against any extended legal standing attempts, would be to disregard the common law inherent powers of the courts to dispose of any frivolous and vexatious proceedings.[20]

## THE POWER TO INSTITUTE DERIVATIVE LITIGATION PROCEEDINGS TO RECOVER LOSSES DIRECTLY FROM DIRECTORS ON BEHALF OF THE COMPANY IN CIRCUMSTANCES WHERE THE DIRECTORS ARE GUILTY OF WRONGDOING AGAINST THEIR COMPANIES

### The Content of the Mechanism

Derivative proceedings constitute an important right, typically provided to the shareholders, to vindicate the rights of a company. John F. Olson observed in 2010 that 'the Companies Act [of South Africa] is unusual in the constituencies to which it grants the power to bring a derivative action'.[21] In addition to abolishing any right at common law of a person other than a company to bring or prosecute any legal proceedings on behalf of that company, section 165 provides, inter alia, that:

> [A] person may serve a demand upon a company to commence or continue legal proceedings, or take related steps, to protect the legal interests of the company if the person . . . *(a)* is a shareholder or a person entitled to be registered as a shareholder, of the company or of a related company; *(b)* is a director or prescribed officer of the company or of a related company; *(c)* is a registered trade union that represents employees of the company, or another representative of employees of the company; or *(d)* has been granted leave of the court to do so, which may be granted only if the court is satisfied that it is necessary or expedient to do so to protect a legal right of that other person.[22]

The section goes on to provide that:

> [A] person who has made a demand in terms of subsection (2) may apply to a court for leave to bring or continue proceedings in the name and on behalf of the company, and the court may grant leave only if . . .; *(b)* the court is satisfied that . . .; (i) the applicant is acting in good faith; (ii) the proposed or continuing proceedings involve the trial of a serious question of material consequence to the company; and (iii) it is in the best interests of the company that the applicant be granted leave to commence the proposed proceedings or continue the proceedings, as the case may be.[23]

## The Jurisprudential Basis for the Mechanism

Derivative proceedings are effectively concerned with the enforcement of rights or remedies vested in a company as a matter of substantive law[24] and, since such enforcement invariably relates to the breach of directorial duties which, at common law, are readily assumed to be for the exclusive protection of shareholders, the *locus standi* is always vested with these shareholders.

In Anglo-American jurisdictions with which South Africa shares company law traditions, the practice of derivative actions being traditionally regarded as a right solely entrusted to shareholders is primarily a result of the development of common law in equating shareholders' interests with the interests of the company. This exclusive preference for shareholders, as a result of the equation of the shareholders' interests with those of the company, is the unfortunate and unnecessary consequence of the interaction of fiduciary rules prohibiting directorial self-dealing with the narrowly conceived enforcement mechanisms of shareholder voting and derivative litigation.

As shown in chapter 3, because of the established principle that directors' fiduciary duties are owed primarily to (or at least for the benefit of) shareholders, standing rules concerning derivative proceedings are universally and almost invariably skewed in favour of shareholders and no other corporate constituency.

It is clear that instead of dismissing extended derivative action standing rules under the Companies Act solely on the basis of the indiscriminate blending of the different types of restraint targeted by fiduciary obligations together with limited enforcement mechanisms, a process which will invariably perpetuate the continuation of the exclusive preference that (incorrectly) focuses enforcement powers exclusively on shareholders, it is preferable to assess whether the current extended standing rules are likely to be of effective utility to non-shareholder corporate constituencies.

In addition to granting *locus standi* to shareholders or persons entitled to be registered as shareholders of the company or of a related company; directors or prescribed officers of the company or of a related company; any registered trade union that represents employees of the company, or another representative of employees of the company, the section further empowers any other person or corporate constituency if such an actor has been granted leave of the court to commence or continue derivative litigation proceedings to protect the legal interests of the company. The granting of the leave is subject to a number of conditions, which are analysed hereunder.

Firstly, such leave of the court will be granted only if the court is satisfied that it is necessary or expedient to do so to protect the legal right of that other person. Furthermore, general conditions which apply to all potential applicants under this section also need to be satisfied before the court can grant leave for legal proceedings to be commenced or continued. These conditions are that the court should be satisfied that (a) the applicant is acting in good faith; (b) the proposed or continuing proceedings involve the trial of a serious question of material consequence to the company, and (c) it is in the best interests of the company that the applicant be granted leave to commence the proposed proceedings or continue the proceedings.

Before the conditions for the granting of leave of the court can be individually analysed, it is appropriate to assess the jurisprudential basis for such conditions from the theoretic basis. The fundamental observation that should be made with respect to these conditions is that they are not as restrictive as the conventional scheme of enforcement, which grants exclusive legal standing to shareholders. This is because, unlike the shareholder-orientated conventional scheme under the common law and the previous corporate legislation in the form of s 266 of the Companies Act, 1973, these conditions for the court to grant leave to any person to institute derivative proceedings are not premised on the misguided assumption that fiduciary obligation rules are designed exclusively or primarily for the benefit of shareholders. If that were the case, the extension of *locus standi* for derivative suits would not have been so expansive, as reflected within the provisions of s 165(2) of the Act.

What remains apparent from these conditions, however, is the legislature's somewhat overzealous intention to stem the supposed tide of litigation resulting from the liberalisation of these derivative proceedings standing rules. This overzealously pursued agenda is based on the incorrect assumption of the possible impact of the relaxation of these standing rules. The built-in qualifications characterised by the nature of these proceedings are seemingly disregarded or ignored. Firstly, given that it is the rights of the company that are being vindicated in derivative litigation, this is a limiting factor on its own. Further, the fact that the remedy in such suits belongs to the company is also a limitation on the possible floodgate of litigation, something which has clearly been overlooked. Since in a successful derivative action recovery is the right of the company,[25] imposing qualifications for extended standing merely on the basis of false fears of possible heightened levels of legal proceedings instigated by non-shareholder corporate constituencies is plainly short-sighted.

While it is a procedural requirement that leave must be sought from the High Court before derivative proceedings by persons other than shareholders, directors, prescribed officers, and employee representatives may be indisputable, the question that remains is whether all the other additional conditions imposed under section 165 of the Act are necessary.

Those additional conditions are now discussed in turn:

> Whether it is necessary or expedient to do so to protect a legal right of that other person:
>
> In the absence of a decided case in South Africa regarding the circumstances which will render it necessary or expedient to protect the legal right of the person making the application, it is not yet clear as to how this condition will be interpreted. What makes matters even more unpredictable is the fact that while derivative litigation proceedings are instituted for the purpose of protecting the *legal interests* of the company, it is questionable why the necessity or expediency of the protection of the *legal right* of the person making an application for leave should be a cause for contention.

This requirement is arguably unnecessary within the context of derivative proceedings, which are particularly aimed at the protection of the legal interests of the company. If a person wants to protect his or her personal right, why would the person want to do it through derivative litigation proceedings when it would be easier to do so under the common law direct action? In a direct action, it is the claimant's personal rights that are being vindicated and not those of the company. This means that the remedy also belongs to the claimant and does not indirectly flow through the company.

While it is not impossible for the protection of legal rights of the applicant to be contemporaneous with the need for the protection of the legal interests of the company, the two are not necessarily interdependent, and they are often mutually exclusive.[26] It is therefore not clear why the legislature found it necessary to make this a condition for the granting of leave of the court to a non-shareholder corporate constituency to institute or continue derivative litigation proceedings.[27] Cassim et al. express optimism that 'the courts will adopt a permissive approach that will make s 165 more accessible and will promote its use, as opposed to a narrow and restrictive interpretation that will stultify the use of the derivative action'.[28]

Whether the applicant is acting in good faith:

> This condition reinforces the right of the company, in terms of s 165(3), to apply to a court to set aside the demand by any of the persons referred to in s 165(2) for the company to institute or proceed with derivative action on the grounds that it is frivolous, vexatious or without merit.[29] This is an appropriate safeguard, as the risk of a collateral purpose on the part of the applicants for derivative action is great. A better view is that South African courts are very likely to consider the Australian approach,[30] in terms of which the courts ask, firstly, whether the applicant genuinely believes that there is a good cause of action that has a reasonable prospect of success, and, secondly, whether the applicant has a collateral purpose or is bringing the application in pursuit of a private interest rather than the interests of the company.[31] While this interpretation is appropriately restrictive, the reality is that it is not prohibitive like the common law rules which associated enforcement with a breach of shareholder-oriented fiduciary obligations.

The imposition of restrictions, rather than a complete ban, on derivative action by non-shareholder corporate constituencies is not only consonant with the Entity Maximisation and Sustainability Model discussed in chapter 1, but it is also supported by the Actionable Enlightened Shareholder Value Approach. Since the Actionable Enlightened Shareholder Value Approach also envisages the need for directors to consider non-shareholder interests, it would be a travesty if enforcement of those interests were to be virtually non-existent, particularly as a broadly inclusive normative statement of the Enlightened Shareholder Value Approach is of little value without the complementary enforcement framework.

Whether the proceedings involve the trial of a serious question of material consequence to the company:

This condition further reinforces the power of the court to set aside proceedings upon application by the company on the grounds that the demands for derivative proceedings by any other person are frivolous, vexatious and without merit.

Although this requirement has not yet been interpreted by courts in South Africa and has thus not been tested as yet, the experience in Australia points to the fact that this condition should be subjected to a low threshold in company law. Under Australian law, the requirement of a serious question to be tried is interpreted to mean that the applicant needs merely to establish that the derivative proceedings ought to be commenced or continued rather than proving the substantive issues.[32] Austin and Ramsay observe that the courts will not normally enter into the merits of the proposed derivative action to any great degree.[33] It has already been confirmed in Australia that the applicant has the same relatively low hurdle to clear as in the case of an application for an interlocutory injunction.[34]

It is clear that in a *prima facie* case the legal interests, or even rights, of the company have been negatively affected by those acting on behalf of the company and that any failure to redress the wrong will affect the company in a significant way will suffice in order to satisfy this requirement. It is further apparent from the language of the section that this requirement should apply equally to non-shareholder corporate constituencies and shareholder litigants. The low procedural threshold that has to be surmounted under this condition does not necessarily mean that the law has effectively opened the floodgates for possible spurious litigation, as the courts still have the residual power to dismiss frivolous and vexatious litigation. It would, however, serve no necessary purpose to impose such restrictive conditions that even the limited number of possible litigants, no matter who they are, would be seriously disincentivised to bring derivative proceedings. That approach would be so prohibitive that even the common law rule in *Foss v Harbottle*[35] would seem preferable, effectively quashing any possibility of the vindication of corporate interests where the wrongdoers are in control of the company.

Whether it is in the best interests of the company that the applicant be granted leave:

This is the last requirement for the court to grant leave and it is submitted that it need not be interpreted in accordance with the common law equation of the best interests of the company with those of the shareholders. A dangerous presumption that is readily made by this common law interpretation of the best interests of the company is that the non-shareholder corporate constituencies invariably have neither the will nor the wherewithal to launch any legal proceedings to protect the legal interests of the company. The corollary is that only the shareholders have the will and the motivation to undertake such proceedings on behalf of companies.

The reality is that even with the shareholder-oriented enforcement system of derivative litigation proceedings, the targeted potential litigants – that is, shareholders – are and continue to be reluctant and, in some instances, disincentivised to undertake such proceedings. For starters, the prevalent portfolio diversification phenomenon leads to the problem of free-riding. As potential shareholder litigants in derivative proceedings are, justifiably, institutional shareholders who invest in equity in a number of different companies, they would naturally not be greatly compelled to institute proceedings on behalf of one of the many companies in which their company owns equity.[36]

Moreover, given the fact that in a derivative action, recovery is the right of the company, and any benefit that could accrue to a plaintiff shareholder accrues only if the success of the action leads to a substantial increase in the value of the company's shares, shareholders tend to free-ride in the hopes that others undertake the proceedings. The prospect of the success of such action is further not guaranteed, and even in the event of such success, the shareholder who instituted proceedings would not be left better off than fellow shareholders who made no effort to support the litigation.[37] Even though the shareholders own too little equity in any one of the many companies in which they are investing to be incentivised to bring derivative litigation proceedings, the common law nevertheless entrusts them with the power to undertake such proceedings.

Furthermore, the increase in the separation of ownership and control within the corporate landscape of Anglo-American jurisdictions and those with which they share company law traditions decreases, even further, the incentive for shareholders to pursue derivative legal proceedings largely due to, *inter alia*, their insulation from a company's affairs through their use of various intermediaries, such as professional managers.

Importantly, because of the corporate landscape described, shareholders would rather resort to alternative means for keeping wayward directors in check rather than disciplining them through derivative litigation proceedings. Within the context of the system of ownership and control characterised by the removal of the traditional owners (i.e. shareholders) from corporate decision-making, corporate governance developments within Anglo-American jurisdictions and those with which they share company law traditions are deliberately designed to foster the improvement of managerial accountability standards, rather than the protection of corporate constituencies such as minority shareholders. This appears to satisfy policymakers and the judiciary regarding the undesirability of the relaxation of standing rules concerning derivative litigation proceedings.

Given the impact of the state of the corporate landscape on shareholders as outlined above, it is, at best, fanciful to suppose that it is the shareholders who are naturally suited to be vested with the power to bring derivative proceedings, to the exclusion of other corporate constituencies. In the final analysis, the determination of what constitutes the best interests of the company for the purpose of granting leave to bring derivative litigation proceedings should not, for valid reasons, continue to be linked exclusively to the protection of the interests of the shareholders. Rather, this condition should only acknowledge that there may be sound business reasons for companies to decline to pursue legal proceedings such as in which the loss to the company may have been insignificant, where the costs of proceedings may outweigh the potential benefit, where the time spent on litigation might be more profitably used elsewhere, or where the inability of the wrongdoers to meet the judgment will be real, even if the litigation is successful.[38]

## DOES THE ACT FAIL TO RECOGNISE CREDITORS AS POTENTIAL LITIGANTS IN DERIVATIVE ACTIONS?

The section's failure to specifically mention creditors within the list of persons that may commence or continue legal proceedings to protect the legal interests of the company may raise a question of whether creditors are, in fact, allowed to bring derivative litigation proceedings. An argument may be made that since s 165(2) specifically enlists potential litigants for derivative action proceedings and creditors are not specifically mentioned, then they are not envisaged as potential plaintiffs in these proceedings. That argument, however, will not be sustainable given the standing of creditors in corporate law and their apparent inclusion via s 165(2)(d) of the Act. As regards creditors' standing in corporate law, Hansmann and Kraakman maintain that while the most efficacious legal mechanisms for protecting non-shareholder constituencies lie outside corporate law, creditors are an exception.[39] They argue that corporate law should directly regulate some aspects of the relationship between a business corporation and its creditors as there are unique problems of creditor contracting which, because of the existence of limited liability in a corporate form, should afford creditors the opportunity to limit shareholders' ability to use the characteristics of the corporate form opportunistically to exploit creditors.[40] It is in the context of this realisation that the main, if not the only, possible litigant who can avail himself or herself to the provisions of s 165 (2)(d) – allowing the protection of the company's legal interests to be in addition to the protection of the legal right of the litigant[41] – is the creditor. Although it is possible that other non-shareholder constituencies may seek to protect the company's legal interests contemporaneously with their own legal rights,[42] it is the creditors who will almost always find themselves in a situation where the protection of the company's legal interests is, at the same time, the protection of their own legal right as the breach of directorial duties – the primary reason for the institution of derivative actions – usually involves the violation of creditors' rights.

## THE OPPORTUNITY FOR CORPORATE CONSTITUENCIES TO AVAIL THEMSELVES OF EXTENDED STANDING PROVISIONS TO APPLY FOR REMEDIES UNDER THE COMPANIES ACT

### The Content of the Mechanism

The Companies Act, 2008 introduces what appears to be a revolutionary standing rule under corporate law, following closely in the footsteps of a similarly worded provision under South Africa's progressive Constitution. This revolutionary standing provision in corporate law is set out in s 157(1), which provides that:

> [W]hen, in terms of this Act, an application can be made to, or a matter can be brought before, a court, the Companies Tribunal, the Panel or the Commission, the right to make the application or bring the matter may be exercised by a person—
>
> *(a)* directly contemplated in the particular provision of this Act;
> *(b)* acting on behalf of a person contemplated in paragraph *(a)*, who cannot act in their own name;
> *(c)* acting as a member of, or in the interest of, a group or class of affected persons, or an association acting in the interest of its members; or
> *(d)* acting in the public interest, with leave of the court.[43]

> Section 157(3) continues to contextualize this standing rule by stating that: [F]or greater certainty, nothing in this section creates a right of any person to commence any legal proceedings contemplated in section 165(1), other than—
>
> *(a)* on behalf of a person entitled to make a demand in terms of section 165(2); and
> *(b)* in the manner set out in section 165.[44]

### The Jurisprudential Basis for the Mechanism

What is striking about this provision is that in addition to confirming the conventional personal legal standing for a person to institute legal proceedings directly in their personal capacity to vindicate their own rights,[45] for the first time in company law, it also provides for representative actions on behalf of persons who cannot act in their own names[46] and on behalf of, or in the interests of, a group or class of affected persons, or by an association in the interests of its members.[47] The extension of standing rules also envisages the possibility of any other person acting in the public interest, with leave of the court.[48]

It is indisputable that South Africa comes from a background of extremely conservative and highly individualised legal standing rules, particularly in corporate law. It is, therefore, encouraging to witness the entrenchment of, in particular, representative and public interest actions under corporate law.

As this extended standing provision appears for the first time in company law in South Africa, its interpretation will invariably have to be undertaken in the context of the broad approach to *locus standi* in matters relating to the Bill of Rights in terms of s 38 of the Constitution.

That comparable provision of the Constitution provides that:

> [A]nyone listed in this section has the right to approach a competent court, alleging that a right in the Bill of Rights has been infringed or threatened, and the court may grant appropriate relief, including a declaration of rights. The persons who may approach a court are—
>
> (a) anyone acting in their own interest;
> (b) anyone acting on behalf of another person who cannot act in their own name;
> (c) anyone acting as a member of, or in the interest of, a group or class of persons;
> (d) anyone acting in the public interest; and
> (e) an association acting in the interest of its members.[49]

This provision is strikingly similar to the one under section 157(1) of the Companies Act, 2008, the only difference being that while the constitutional standing provision relates to the infringement or the threatened infringement of a right in the Bill of Rights, the extended standing provision under the Companies Act relates to the breach of personal rights of individuals, of members of a group or a class, of members of an association, or to the protection of the public interest. The fact that the latter section does not extend to the protection of the interests of the company is made clear by s 157(3) of the Act.

In relation to the recent interpretation of the class actions under s 38 of the Constitution, where the Supreme Court of Appeal laid out procedural requirements which had to be satisfied before class actions under the section could be sustained, the Court clarified that those requirements are the same whether the right implicated is in terms of the Bill of Rights or in terms of any other area of law.[50]

## THE POSSIBLE IMPACT OF THE EXTENDED STANDING TO APPLY FOR CORPORATE LAW REMEDIES

To understand whether the new extended legal standing provisions, which have been influenced by the South African Constitution in relation to the vindication of personal and collective rights, have had any impact on the development of the corporate legal enforcement framework, it is important to consider the historical development of corporate legal standing rules in the recent past.

The conservative nature of the corporate legal enforcement framework in empowering only the shareholders to be able to access corporate law remedies, particularly derivative action suits, is largely based on the indiscriminate blending of the different types of restraint targeted by fiduciary obligations and the misconstruction of the role of these fiduciary obligations as being the exclusive protection of shareholders when, in fact, they have been designed primarily to restrain directorial self-dealing.[51] This unfortunate mingling of the different types of restraint targeted by fiduciary obligations and the confusion over the primary role of these obligations invariably perpetuates the upholding of the exclusive preference that (incorrectly) focuses enforcement powers exclusively on shareholders rather than on all corporate constituencies, depending on the specific restraint implicated by the fiduciary obligation in question. Another reason for the entrenchment of this skewed corporate legal enforcement framework is the fear of potential floodgates of litigation if corporate law remedies were also made available to non-shareholder corporate constituencies. Nowhere is this conservative approach to the corporate legal enforcement framework more prevalent than in the context of the two primary corporate law remedies of derivative action proceedings and of personal action proceedings emanating from oppressive and/or unfairly prejudicial conduct by, or on behalf of, companies. Section 252 of the Companies Act, 1973, made it very clear that the remedy in the case of oppressive or unfairly prejudicial conduct was reserved to members – interpreted in the case of 'for-profit companies' as shareholders – while s 163 of the Companies Act, 2008, makes the remedy available to shareholders and directors alone.[52] Furthermore, the liberalisation of the common law 'proper plaintiff rule' under the previous 1973 Companies Act merely witnessed the recognition of shareholders as the only litigants in derivative litigation proceedings.[53] This apparent reluctance of the 1973 Companies Act to extend corporate law standing to non-shareholder corporate constituencies, such as the employees, the creditors, the suppliers, the community, the public at large, and any other person who may legally be entitled to a remedy, is clearly predicated on the undeniable need to curb or eliminate frivolous and vexatious litigation.

To argue that the extension of categories of persons entitled to this relief beyond shareholders would be chaotic, as is usually articulated as the argument against any extended legal standing attempts, would be to disregard the power of the courts inherent to the common law of disposing of any frivolous and vexatious proceedings – a notion which is constantly bolstered by statutory provisions.[54]

As regards the inclusion of non-shareholder corporate constituencies within the derivative action remedy in corporate law, the combined impact of the expansive role of fiduciary obligations and the modern perception of the purpose of corporate statutes means that the possibility exists for both shareholders and non-shareholder corporate constituencies to claim that the failure of directors to manage a corporation to achieve its purposes amounts to mismanagement of corporate assets, a claim for which recovery on behalf of the company would be appropriate.

Regarding the granting of leave to a person to serve a demand upon a company to commence or continue legal proceedings to protect the legal interests of the company (i.e. derivative action proceedings), such leave will be granted only if the court is satisfied that the conditions stated in s 165 (1)(d) and (5)(b), as discussed in paragraph 5.4.2 above, have been satisfied.

## CONCLUSION AND CHAPTER SYNOPSIS

Different standing provisions under the Companies Act, 2008, demonstrate a sustained intention by the legislature in this country to part ways with the previous conservative and highly individualised legal standing rules under common law, particularly in the area of corporate law. In this chapter, different remedies that are available specifically to non-shareholder corporate constituencies were discussed in detail. What this chapter endeavours to demonstrate is that all the remedies discussed have certain requirements that have to be met, as reflected in the Companies Act, 2008. In other words, it has been shown that while the reform of the corporate legal enforcement framework is absolutely necessary for the accommodation of any statement of the normative or substantive goals that favour the inclusion of non-shareholder corporate constituencies, it is equally important that such liberalisation of the corporate legal enforcement framework should be properly measured and be subject to jurisprudentially justifiable conditions without being practically dismissive of the necessary reform of the common law rules concerning legal standing. At the same time, the chapter has shown that a 'free-for-all' system of corporate legal enforcement will equally be doomed to fail.

It is indisputable that the granting of legal standing to non-shareholder corporate constituencies, particularly when the recognition of such constituencies' interests is legally permissible can no longer be ignored if the vision to offer a clear and reasonably enforceable scheme of responsibilities to parties other than shareholders is to be achieved, as conceived by Adolf A. Berle in 1932.[55]

That clear and reasonably enforceable scheme is arguably brought about by the different legal standing provisions under the South African Companies Act, 2008, as discussed in this chapter. As reflected throughout this book, the main objection to the liberalisation of the corporate legal enforcement regime in order to bring about a clear and reasonably enforceable scheme of responsibilities to persons other than shareholders is largely based on the fear of possible consequent floodgates of litigation, with the potential to destabilise the smooth operation of public, corporate enterprises.

This fear is, however, appropriately accommodated by the scheme brought about by the Companies Act, 2008. The Act shows, for example, that the extension of legal standing for the institution of proceedings to restrain the company from doing anything inconsistent with the Act and to declare directors delinquent or under probation is appropriately constrained by the courts' residual power to dismiss proceedings that are frivolous, vexatious and without merit.

Again, the extended legal standing for the possible institution of derivative litigation proceedings is also not without constraint, as the indisputable need for stemming the possible tide of litigation is taken care of by the requirement for leave of the court before such proceedings may be undertaken by corporate constituencies other than shareholders, directors (and prescribed officers), and employee representatives. Additionally, further constraints are imposed to ensure that the proceedings are necessary or expedient to protect the legal rights of the litigants, in addition to the company's legal interests; that the litigants are acting in good faith; that the proceedings involve the trial of a serious question of material consequence to the company; and that it is in the best interests of the company that the applicants be granted leave to institute these proceedings. It has also been shown that these necessary constraints imposed by the Act exist in addition to the inevitable, remedy-specific constraints which are perpetuated, in the main, by the fact that in these proceedings, recovery is the right of the company and not of the litigants in their personal capacities.

Finally, it has been shown that the extended legal standing provisions under s 157 of the Companies Act, particularly representative actions, are appropriately constrained by the judicially affirmed requirements for a class action, which include (a) the certification of an action as a class action by the court, (b) the definition of a class, (c) a cause of action raising a triable issue, (d) the existence of common issues of fact or law, and (e) that the applicants are acting as members of, or in the interest of, a class.

All these constraints attest to the viability of the possible introduction of a clear and reasonably enforceable scheme of responsibilities to corporate constituencies other than shareholders. If this clearly and reasonably enforceable potential scheme continues to be ignored, any corporate constituency statutory mechanisms, like the corporate constituency statutes, benefit corporation statutes, and the statutory Enlightened Shareholder Value Approach, are doomed to fail.

The liberalised corporate legal enforcement regime in South Africa is further demonstrated by the ability of a broader range of stakeholders to bring civil remedy proceedings under s 218(2) of the Companies Act, 2008, which provides that any person who contravenes any provision of the Act is liable to another person for any loss or damage suffered by that person as a result of that contravention.[56] The sub-section was recently tested in the Supreme Court of Appeal case of *Venator Africa (Pty) Ltd v Watts and Another*,[57] which concerned a judgment regarding the personal liability of directors to creditors. Notwithstanding the seemingly sweeping reach of s 218(2), the Companies Act does not expressly provide for director liability to third parties (creditors) for loss or damage suffered.

The case involves an appeal by *Venator Africa (Pty) Ltd* (the plaintiff) against the decision of the KwaZulu-Natal Division of the High Court (Pietermaritzburg), in which the court upheld an exception by Lloyd Mason Watts, one of the directors of Siyazi Logistics and Trading (Pty) Ltd (Siyazi), to the plaintiff's particulars of claim. In this case, the plaintiff contracted with Siyazi for clearing and forwarding services and subsequently paid Siyazi a total of R66,395,006.27 in disbursement accounts for payments to the South African Revenue Service (SARS). However, Siyazi only paid R31,353,697.27 to SARS, resulting in a shortfall of R34,612,576.19.[58]

The plaintiff alleged that this short payment occurred due to fraud, theft, or reckless and negligent conduct by Siyazi's employees or directors, in contravention of Section 22(1) of the Companies Act, which prohibits a company from carrying on its business recklessly or with gross negligence.[59] The plaintiff sought to hold the directors of Siyazi, including Watts, jointly and severally liable for the loss under Section 218(2) of the Companies Act. Watts filed an exception, arguing that Section 22(1) imposes duties on the company and not its directors and that the plaintiff failed to aver a breach of any obligation imposed on the directors by the Act.

On appeal from the decision of the High Court in KwaZulu-Natal, which upheld the exception, finding that Section 22(1) does not impose obligations on directors and that the Act does not expressly provide for director liability to third parties for loss or damage suffered,[60] the Supreme Court of Appeal provided a detailed interpretation of the relevant provisions of the Companies Act and concluded that Section 22(1) imposes duties on the company and not its directors. The court also highlighted the separate legal personality of a company and the default immunity of directors from liabilities of the company. The court upheld the High Court's decision, dismissing the plaintiff's appeal and confirming the order granting leave to amend the particulars of the claim. The court found that Section 22(1) of the Companies Act imposes duties on the company and not its directors, and that the Act does not expressly provide for director liability to third parties for loss or damage suffered. The court emphasised the separate legal personality of a company and the default immunity of directors from company liabilities.[61]

This court demonstrated that notwithstanding the apparent width of s218(2) in empowering any person to sue any other person for loss or damages suffered as a result of the latter's breach of any provision of the Companies Act, the Court clarified that, ultimately, the plaintiff must demonstrate the existence of a contravention by the director, who is being sued, of an obligation upon such a director, imposed by the Companies Act.[62]

## NOTES

1. Section 20(4) of the Companies Act, 2008.
2. *Henri Viljoen (Pty) Ltd v Awerbuch Brothers* 1953 (2) SA 151 (O) at 169 and *United Watch & Diamond Co (Pty) Ltd and Others v Disa Hotel Ltd and Another* 1972 (4) SA 409 (C) and *Aquatus (Pty) Ltd v Sacks and Others* 1989 (1) SA 56 (A) at 62.
3. *Wood and Others v Ondangwà Tribal Authority and Another* 1975 (2) SA 294 (A) at 312F.
4. See, among others, Cheffins, 'Reforming the Derivative Action', op cit note 285, at 228.
5. See, for example, Sharrock R, *Business Transactions Law* (8th ed., 2011), at 449.
6. Section 5(1) of the Companies Act, 2008, specifically provides that '[t]his Act must be interpreted and applied in a manner that gives effect to the purposes set out in section 7'.
7. Section 7(a) of the Companies Act, 2008.
8. Section 7(b)(iii) of the Companies Act, 2008.
9. Section 7(d) of the Companies Act, 2008.
10. Section 7(f) of the Companies Act, 2008.
11. Section 7(j) of the Companies Act, 2008.
12. Here, the threat of abuse of the remedy is more real than imagined.
13. In the two recent cases of *Haitas & Others v Port Wild Props 12 (Pty) Ltd 2011 (5) SA 562 (GSJ)* and *Boost Sports Africa (Pty) Ltd v South African Breweries Ltd 2014 (4) SA 343 (GP),* courts confirmed that they were vested with inherent power to regulate their own processes, including the power to guard against vexatious, reckless and unmeritorious litigation.

14. Section 162(2) of the Companies Act, 2008.

15. As demonstrated by the Gauteng High Court case of *Organisation Undoing Tax Abuse NPC and Another v Myeni and Another* [(15996/2017) [2019] ZAGPPHC 957)] in which the former chairperson of the South African Airways (SOC) Ltd was declared a delinquent for life.

16. Section 162(5)–(9) of the Companies Act, 2008.

17. See, for example, *Director of Education, Transvaal v McCagie and Others* 1918 AD 616 at 621.

18. In the case of *Graaff-Reinet Municipality v Van Ryneveld's Pass Irrigation Board* 1950 (2) SA 420 (A), the court observed, at 424, that "the stage of actionable maturity . . . is the stage at which an infringement of the legal rights of one of the parties . . . gives the other a right to claim consequential relief".

19. Section 66(4)(a)(i) of the Companies Act, 2008.

20. In this regard, see *inter alia, Haitas & Others v Port Wild Props 12 (Pty) Ltd 2011 (5) SA 562 (GSJ)* and *Boost Sports Africa (Pty) Ltd v South African Breweries Ltd 2014 (4) SA 343 (GP)*, op cit note 615.

21. John F. Olson, 'South Africa Moves to a Global Model of Corporate Governance but with Important National Variations' in Tshepo H. Mongalo (ed.), *Modern Company Law for a Competitive South African Economy* (2010), at 246.

22. Section 165(2) of the Companies Act, 2008.

23. Section 165(5)(b) of the Companies Act, 2008.

24. See Cheffins, 'Reforming the Derivative Action', op cit note 285, at 228.

25. Among the many case authorities across the entire Anglo-American jurisdictions, *Spokes v Grosvenor Hotel Co* 1991 BCLC 279 is authority for the proposition that with successful derivative litigation only the company will be entitled to a remedy. See also *Wallersteiner v Moir* (2) [1975] 1 ALL ER 849 (CA).

26. It has been submitted that '[t]he intention of this provision presumably is that a court may grant standing to other persons whose legal rights are indirectly affected by virtue of a violation of the company's legal interests' (See Cassim et al., *Contemporary Company Law* 2ed (2012), at 780).

27. This appears to be the reflection of the legislature's buckling under pressure from the business constituency's concern during the NEDLAC consultations (from 2004–2008) that overly permissive derivative actions pose a risk of applicants bringing frivolous or vexatious proceedings or of using the proceedings for 'strike suits' or 'greenmail' in order to extract personal benefits for themselves as opposed to the company.

28. Cassim et al., *Contemporary Company Law* (2nd ed., 2012), at 777.

29. See s 165(3) of the Companies Act, 2008.

30. This is because the provisions of s 165(5)(b) of the Companies Act, 2008, are similar to those under the equivalent Australian provision, which is s 237 of the Corporations Act 2001.

31. See, in particular, *Swansson v R A Pratt Properties Pty Ltd* (2002) 42 ACSR 313 and *Magafas v Carantinos* [2006] NSWSC 1459.

32. Austin RP and Ramsay IM, *Ford's Principles of Corporations Law* (12th ed., 2005), at 653–654.

33. Ibid., at 654.

34. This was held in the case of *Swansson v R A Pratt Properties Pty Ltd* (2002) 42 ACSR 313.

35. (1843) 2 Hare 461; 67 ER 189.

36. See A Global Picture of Business, at 276.

37. See, among others, Elizabeth J. Boros, *Minority Shareholders Remedies* (1995), at 32. See also Tshepo Mongalo (ibid.)

38. See, for example, Cassim et al., *Contemporary Company Law (*2nd ed., 2012), at 787.

39. Hansmann & Kraakman, 'Toward A Single Model of Corporate Law?' op cit note 67, at 58.

40. Ibid.

41. Section 165(2)(d) of the Companies Act, 2008, provides that:

> A person may serve a demand upon a company to commence or continue legal proceedings, or take related steps, to protect the legal interests of the company if the person . . . has been granted leave of the court to do so, which may be granted only if the court is satisfied that it is necessary or expedient to do so to protect a legal right of that other person.

42. As in the case of a consumer seeking to protect his constitutional right at the same time as protecting the company's legal interests.

43. Section 157(1) of the Companies Act, 2008.

44. Section 157(3) of the Companies Act, 2008.

45. Section 157(1)(a) of the Companies Act, 2008.

46. Section 157(1)(b) of the Companies Act, 2008.

47. Section 157(1)(c) of the Companies Act, 2008.

48. Section 157(1)(d) of the Companies Act, 2008.

49. Section 38 of the Constitution of the Republic of South Africa (Act. No. 108 of 1996).

50. *Children Resource Centre Trust and Others v Pioneer Food (Pty) Ltd and Others* 2013 (2) SA 213 (SCA).

51. This is explained in detail in chapter 3 above.

52. Compare s 252 (1) of the Companies Act, 1973, and s 163 (1) of the Companies Act, 2008.

53. Section 266 of the Companies Act, 1973, is the best example of such limited liberalisation.

54. See *Haitas & Others v Port Wild Props 12 (Pty) Ltd* 2011 (5) SA 562 (GSJ) and *Boost Sports Africa (Pty) Ltd v South African Breweries Ltd* 2014 (4) SA 343 (GP), op. cit. note 615.

55. Berle, 'For Whom Corporate Managers Are Trustees', op cit note 4, at 1367–1368.

56. Section 218(2) of the Companies Act, 2008.

57. (053_2023) [2024] ZASCA 60 (24 April 2024).

58. Para [4] of the SCA judgment, ibid.

59. Section 22(1) of the Companies Act, 2008.

60. Para [7] to Para [13], SCA Judgment, op cit note 626.

61. Paras [14] to [24] of the SCA Judgment, op cit note 626.

62. Paras [26] to [27] of the SCA Judgment, op cit note 626.

# Conclusion

## *Summary and Recommendations*

### REVIEW OF RESEARCH CONDUCTED

This book investigated the reasons for the failure of statutory corporate constituency mechanisms in selected Anglo-American jurisdictions and found that the wholesale failure of such corporate constituency mechanisms is largely a result of the identified lack of extended standing for non-shareholder corporate constituent groups to apply for corporate law remedies. The focus was on specific statutory corporate constituencies' protection mechanisms introduced in key Anglo-American jurisdictions in the last thirty years, beginning in 1983 in Pennsylvania.

These statutory corporate constituency mechanisms were discussed and evaluated as they were applied in the United Kingdom and in a number of states of the United States. These corporate constituency mechanisms were also considered to be a means to channel the possible distribution of corporate benefits to all legitimate corporate constituencies within public companies. As we have seen, too often the statutory corporate constituency mechanisms have been punted as some kind of Holy Grail of revolutionary, trend-setting phenomena when they were first introduced. But as reality struck during the attempted implementation of those mechanisms, it became clear that the lack of a clear and reasonable enforcement framework made it impossible for the proponents of these mechanisms to back up these grandiose, trend-setting claims.

At the outset, it was stated that the problem, which was thought to be resolved following the Berle-Dodd debate of the early 1930s, remains far from being settled, even as corporate law develops within key Anglo-American jurisdictions in the twenty-first century. It was stated at the beginning of the book that the primary concern of the research was to determine if the current Anglo-American corporate law scheme of responsibilities to corporate constituencies other than shareholders offered a clear and reasonably enforceable solution to adequately empower those non-shareholder corporate constituencies, as was previously demanded of such a scheme by Adolf A. Berle. Consequently, the research question at the heart of the book was set out as being whether the failure by the current statutory corporate constituency mechanisms is capable of being resolved by the extension of legal standing to the relevant non-shareholder corporate constituent groups to access corporate law remedies previously reserved for the shareholder group of corporate constituencies. It was also shown that this extension of corporate law remedies is necessary, especially since the resolution of conflicting interests between different corporate constituencies' interests will almost always be in the best interest of the company as a going concern.

To that effect, the research had to consider, first, whether such an extension of legal standing is theoretically grounded in corporate law. Second, the book considered whether the existing common law and statutory corporate constituency mechanisms are amenable to the possible accommodation of the extended legal standing scheme. Third, the book considered whether the justification for the retention of the one-and-a-half centuries-old corporate legal enforcement framework is so sacrosanct as to be not accommodative of the required shift to a more inclusive corporate legal enforcement framework. Finally, the research considered whether the inclusive corporate legal enforcement framework, as exemplified under the South African Companies Act of 2008, can be justified under modern corporate legal dispensation, underpinned by constitutional and corporate legal developments applicable, particularly, in South Africa.

In order to answer these questions, the following matters were addressed. In chapter 1, a theoretical foundation was provided concerning, first, theories supporting the traditional corporate law view of tying corporate law enforcement to the equation linking the interests of the company exclusively with those of shareholders, thereby leading to the inevitable design of a shareholder-centric enforcement scheme. Second, the chapter set out an alternative theory which theoretically and practically accommodates non-shareholder corporate constituencies. Third, the chapter analysed theories supporting the extension of legal standing for non-shareholder corporate constituencies to access corporate law remedies. The setting out of this theoretical foundation was undertaken with a view to determining which theories are amenable to an all-inclusive corporate legal enforcement framework and which are inimical to such an inclusive framework. A new theory, broadly accommodative of the inclusive corporate legal enforcement framework, was proposed, termed the 'Actionable Enlightened Shareholder Value Approach'.

Chapter 2 provided a comparative analysis by identifying and examining the common law and statutory corporate constituency mechanisms of the United Kingdom and a large number of US states. In relation to the United Kingdom, an emphasis was placed on the relevant corporate constituency provisions under the 1985 and the 2006 Companies Acts, while with respect to the United States, the focus was on corporate constituency statutes and, in relation to more recent developments, those states which have enacted benefit corporation statutes.

The main reason for considering these jurisdictions is that South Africa shares the same corporate law traditions, particularly in relation to the corporate law enforcement regime. The entrenchment of the shareholder-centric corporate law enforcement regime in corporate law in the United Kingdom was considered through common law developments endorsed by numerous judicial pronouncements. Further, the apparent limited transition from the shareholder primacy model to the Enlightened Shareholder Value Approach was considered; first, through the analysis of the relevant provision under the consolidated Companies Act of 1985, and secondly, through the Enlightened Shareholder Value model as institutionalised through section 172 of the UK Companies Act, 2006. In the United States, a global analysis of the corporate constituency statutes, which were enacted in more than 28 states by 2012, was undertaken by first providing an overview of the statutes. Second, the impact of the inclusion of corporate constituency measures through core corporate law statutes rather than through separate specific statutory instruments was considered. Third, with regard to corporate constituency statutes, the impact of the creation of priority of interests (with shareholder interests generally assuming pre-eminence) in a number of statutes was also considered, with a view to determining whether this trend specifically (or intentionally) excludes the possibility of extended legal standing for non-shareholder corporate constituent groups to access corporate law remedies. Fourth, the analysis regarding corporate constituency statutes reviews whether 'the consideration of the possibility that the long-term, as well as the short-term interests of the corporation and its shareholders, may be served by the continued independence of the corporation', as provided for in a large number of statutes, has any impact on the possible extension of legal standing to non-shareholder corporate constituencies. Fifth, the analysis considers whether the existence of limited instances of optional adoption of corporate constituency measures through corporations' articles of incorporation, as provided for by some statutes, enhances or reduces the efficacy of the corporate constituency statutes in the relevant jurisdictions. Sixth, the significance of the provision that 'the effects of a proposed action on any particular corporate constituent group or interest should not be considered as a dominant or controlling factor' in some statutes is considered with a view to determining whether such a provision has any impact on the possible reform of the corporate legal enforcement framework in the relevant jurisdictions. Further, the chapter considers the possible effect, if any, of limited case law on the possible reform of corporate objectives by the concerned corporate constituency statutes. Finally, the analysis of corporate constituency statutes considers the impact of the disparity of the statutes with regard to the enumeration of categories of the relevant corporate constituent groups, concluding with the global analysis of all the factors relevant to the corporate constituency statutes.

Chapter 2 also considers the impact of benefit corporation statutes, enacted in at least 18 states by the time of the completion of this research, on the possible reform of the corporate law enforcement regime in the jurisdictions concerned. This part of the chapter starts off by undertaking an all-encompassing analysis of the relevant statutory provisions of the 18 states which have enacted these statutes. This is followed by the analysis of the statutes of the two leading corporate law states in the United States (i.e. Delaware and Maryland) by considering the impact of each of the statutes on (a) the corporate purpose, (b) accountability, (c) right of action, and (d) transparency.

In chapter 3, the justifications for the continued acceptance of shareholders as the sole or exclusive beneficiaries of directors' fiduciary obligations are questioned. In particular, the chapter questions the continued jurisprudential and pragmatic validity of the recognition of shareholders as 'owners of public companies' and as residual rights investors in public companies. The chapter further questions the justification for the exclusion of non-shareholder corporate constituencies from protection in terms of fiduciary obligations, based on the supposed adequacy of 'bargaining power' as a protection for those non-shareholder corporate constituencies. The chapter also questions the adequacy of market forces and private ordering as a viable protection for the interests of non-shareholder corporate constituencies. The chapter then provides a justified account of the restraining of directorial or managerial self-dealing, and not the exclusive protection of shareholders, as the primary basis for directors' fiduciary obligations. The chapter concludes by summarising the new corporate law approach in South Africa, which questions the basis for the continuation of the conventional corporate legal enforcement framework by specifically pointing out the erosion of the legal basis for corporate ownership by shareholders and the abandonment of the exclusive corporate voting under corporate law. In the final analysis, the chapter assesses the jurisprudential basis for the all-inclusive enforcement framework in corporate law.

Chapter 4 critically analyses the enforcement framework under South Africa's 2008 Companies Act in a relatively detailed manner. The chapter starts off by showing that the conservative, individualistic corporate law enforcement regime applicable under traditional corporate law can no longer be sustained under modern corporate law. The chapter indicates that this is particularly true if the retention of this conservative, individualistic corporate legal enforcement regime is anchored upon the need to minimise or prevent frivolous and vexatious litigation and to protect shareholders, 'mistakenly', as the exclusive beneficiaries of fiduciary obligations of directors.

The first remedy considered in this chapter deals with proceedings to restrain the company from doing anything inconsistent with the Companies Act of 2008. In this chapter, the broad coverage of constituencies who can avail themselves of this remedy is justified on the basis that the relief sought and the right on which the claim is based are required to be interpreted and applied in a manner that gives effect to the purposes set out in s 7 of the Act, one of which concerns the need to promote the development of the South African economy by 'encouraging transparency and high standards of corporate governance as appropriate, given the significant role of enterprises within the social and economic life of the nation'. It is also acknowledged that the continued application of the courts' inherent power to dismiss any legal proceedings that are frivolous and vexatious reduces the need for any further restriction of access to this remedy.[1]

The chapter further critically analyses the remedy to have a director declared delinquent or under probation, which is accessible not only to shareholders but also to a company secretary and a registered trade union that represents employees of the company or another representative of the employees. The chapter justifies the development of this approach on the basis that any further restriction of access to this remedy would make no sense as the corollary fundamental right to appoint and remove directors, upon which the relief sought may be justified, can effectively be accorded to any of the corporate constituencies (in addition to shareholders) pursuant to the company's Memorandum of Incorporation. Moreover, to argue that the extension of the categories of persons entitled to this relief beyond shareholders would open floodgates of unnecessary litigation would be to unjustifiably disregard the continued application of the common law-based inherent powers of the courts to dispose of any frivolous and vexatious proceedings.[2]

As regards the extension of the right to institute derivative proceedings beyond shareholders and directors to include registered trade unions representing employees of the company or another representative of employees of the company, and any person who has been granted leave of the court to do so, the chapter maintains that this cautiously expanded list of categories of qualifying corporate constituencies is justifiable as the established principle that fiduciary duties are owed exclusively to shareholders has been proved to be unsustainable and jurisprudentially unsound.

As the relevant provision of the Act dealing with derivative proceedings has further in-built restrictions on the ability to bring these proceedings, any further restriction on the ability of non-shareholder corporate constituencies to bring these proceedings would constitute overkill. Furthermore, as the granting of the leave of the court to bring these proceedings is subject to further conditions, compliance with which is monitored by the court in line with statutorily established criteria, any further restriction of access will not be jurisprudentially or pragmatically justifiable. Again, the chapter shows that because of the nature of derivative proceedings, in terms of which the right of recovery and the accompanying remedy belongs to the company, the retention of the common law restrictions of access to this remedy would clearly and unjustifiably disregard the built-in qualifications associated with these proceedings.

Furthermore, the chapter shows that the common law rules concerning the granting of legal standing for derivative litigation suits exclusively to shareholders mistakenly assume that only shareholders would have the will and the wherewithal, as opposed to non-shareholder corporate constituencies, to launch legal proceedings to protect the legal interests of the company. As argued in the chapter, this assumption is misplaced, as shareholders can equally be reluctant and disincentivised as with non-shareholder corporate constituencies, to bring derivative litigation proceedings since, first, it is the legal interests of the company (not of the shareholders directly) which are being protected in these proceedings and, second, the resultant remedy belongs to the company and no-one else. It is also shown in chapter 4 that the somewhat tangential prospect of an increase in the value of shares as a result of successful derivative litigation proceedings is not a sufficiently satisfactory incentive to encourage shareholders to institute these proceedings.

The last aspect relevant to legal standing considered in the chapter is the extended legal standing provisions, under s 157(1) of the Companies Act, 2008, to apply for remedies. In essence, these provisions reform standing rules in respect of representative actions, the most common of which are class actions. The chapter succinctly shows that the new trajectory pursued by the reformed approach to class actions, as abundantly exemplified in the case of *Children Resources Trust and Others v Premier Foods and Others*, is cognisant of the reality that the fear of possible floodgates of litigation occasioned by broadly inclusive standing rules cannot be addressed by the continued pursuit of the traditional and conservative common law restriction to legal standing. Moreover, it is shown that the constitutional imperative endorsed by s 38 of the Constitution of the Republic of South Africa, 1996, cannot be ignored merely because of the need to curb the possibility of floodgates of litigation, as similarly acknowledged by Justice Froneman in the *Ngxuza* case. Thus, the best approach to achieving the goal of curbing possible floodgates of litigation, as argued in chapter 4, can be the requirement for leave to be granted by the court before these proceedings can be embarked upon, rather than the restriction of legal standing to a single corporate constituent group. The discussion in the chapter regarding this aspect further acknowledges that the inherent power of the courts to curb frivolous and vexatious litigation cannot be ignored as an adequate protection against possible floodgates of litigation in respect of class actions as well.

## FINDING AND CONCLUSIONS

### A Theoretical Foundation

Chapter 1 provides a theoretical foundation on theories in company law relevant to corporate legal enforcement. These theories have been considered on the basis of their amenability, or otherwise, to an all-inclusive enforcement framework. The shareholder primacy theory, the Enlightened Shareholder Value Approach, the Stakeholder/Pluralist Theory, and the Entity Maximisation and Sustainability Model were discussed.

Both the shareholder primacy theory and the Enlightened Shareholder Value Approach underscore the centrality of the shareholder position in corporate decision-making insofar as the design of a suitable legal enforcement framework is concerned. The only difference between the two is that while the former endorses the exclusivity of the position of the shareholders, the latter emphasises the pre-eminence of the shareholder corporate constituent group. While the exclusivity of the position of shareholders invariably means that there is no room for a broadly inclusive legal enforcement scheme, the pre-eminence of the shareholders, as propagated by the Enlightened Shareholder Value Approach, is capable of being compatible with a broadly inclusive legal enforcement scheme, although shareholders are first in line in such a scheme. This caveat notwithstanding, the current version of the latter approach, as implemented under § 172 of the UK Companies Act, 2006, is, surprisingly, dismissive of such a broadly inclusive enforcement framework. This then leads to the perpetuation of the exclusivity of the corporate legal enforcement framework propagated by the shareholder primacy theory.

While the Pluralist/Stakeholder Theory is sympathetic to the argument that all stakeholders are residual rights claimants as they all contribute to the capital of the company, albeit through different means, it is, nevertheless, not forthcoming when it comes to a clear statement of the broadly inclusive legal enforcement framework comparable to that which applies in the case of the shareholder primacy theory.

In contrast to the Stakeholder/Pluralist theory, the Entity Maximisation and Sustainability Model, which emphasises the significance of the separateness of the corporate entity when it comes to determining what constitutes the interests of the company, only propagates the possible enforcement by non-shareholder corporate constituencies of indirect legal actions aimed at protecting the interests of the company as a separate legal person (i.e., derivative litigation proceedings).

## RECOMMENDATION: AN ACTIONABLE ENLIGHTENED SHAREHOLDER VALUE APPROACH (AESVA)

Arguments for and against the continued preservation of the conventional corporate legal enforcement framework, linked to the centrality of shareholder interests, were discussed. The shortcomings of the conventional corporate legal enforcement framework were considered in the context of the framework's apparently inextricable link to the assumed exclusivity of corporate privileges (particularly corporate voting and the right of action in derivative action proceedings) and their association with shareholders alone.

It has been argued throughout this book that the continued association of the above corporate privileges exclusively with shareholders, particularly when determining an appropriate legal enforcement scheme, is seriously flawed. This is because modern corporate law developments clearly show that the privileges of corporate voting are capable of being extended to non-shareholder corporate constituencies as well. Further, as regards the exclusivity of the right of action for derivative litigation proceedings purposes, the realisation that the primary purpose of fiduciary obligations is the restraint of directorial self-serving misconduct, rather than the exclusive protection of shareholder interests, strongly militates against the retention of the conventional corporate legal enforcement framework, as the shareholders are not the only beneficiaries of the restraint of directorial self-serving misconduct.

It was in this context that the conventional corporate legal enforcement framework has been found to be inadequate and unsuitable. The book then proposes the possible adoption of the Actionable Enlightened Shareholder Value Approach (AESVA), which acknowledges the limited utility of the apparent inclusion of non-shareholder interests by the current Enlightened Shareholder Value Approach (ESVA), without a complementary right of action to the beneficiaries of those non-shareholder interests. The AESVA takes cognisance of the possible danger of floodgates of litigation that might be occasioned by overly liberal standing rules and, as a result, endorses the incorporation of reasonable limitations within extended legal standing rules, as is undertaken in the new South African Companies Act of 2008. Integral to such limitations are the conditions relating to the need for court certification prior to the commencement or continuation of court proceedings and the need for the leave of the court subject to the satisfaction of specific pre-conditions prior to the institution of derivative litigation proceedings. The AESVA also acknowledges the existence of in-built limitations within particular legal proceedings, such as the entitlement to remedies and the right of recovery in derivative litigation proceedings. Finally, the AESVA also acknowledges and endorses the significance of the inherent powers of the court, under common law, to dismiss frivolous and vexatious proceedings.[3]

## CORPORATE CONSITUENCIES' PROTECTION MECHANISMS IN THE UNITED KINGDOM

The United Kingdom's corporate law developments concerning non-shareholder corporate constituencies are discussed in the comparative analysis chapter. In this regard, the UK law is considered with reference to the apparent transition from the shareholder primacy theory to the ESVA. The significance of such a transition is then considered in detail. What is made clear in this part of the book is that although some traces of reasoning which are in accordance with the Enlightened Shareholder Value Model's principles could be found in earlier judicial pronouncements, which served as a beacon of hope for a reformed legal enforcement framework, the dominance of the shareholder primacy theory in determining the applicable corporate legal enforcement regime basically ensured that all hopes for possible reform towards a broadly inclusive legal enforcement framework were dashed. The analysis also shows that statutorily, the ESVA started to make its appearance in the 1985 Companies Act and not, as widely believed, under the 2006 Companies Act. The last aspect of this discussion reveals that the transition notwithstanding, the continued influence of the shareholder primacy theory in the design of the corporate legal enforcement framework effectively ensured that the reform towards a broadly inclusive legal enforcement regime in corporate law in the United Kingdom remains a pipe dream. Had the design of the corporate legal enforcement regime been influenced by the ESVA, the United Kingdom would most probably have ended up with a broadly inclusive corporate legal enforcement framework, which would be in keeping with the new normative standards clearly set out in s 172 of the Companies Act, 2006. Central arguments made in each of the sections relevant to the UK Company Law developments are discussed hereunder.

## THE APPARENT TRANSITION FROM THE SHAREHOLDER PRIMACY TO THE ENLIGHTENED SHAREHOLDER VALUE MODEL

The analysis of the UK Company Law developments in chapter 2 shows that even after an uncharacteristically progressive approach adopted as early as 1883 in the case of *Hutton v West Cork Railway*, subsequent judicial pronouncements on the corporate objective required to be pursued by companies in the United Kingdom reverted to a very exclusive shareholder primacy theory. This development is particularly exemplified in the two oft-quoted cases of *Greenhalgh v Arderne Cinemas* and *Parke v Daily News Ltd*. However, long before the Labour government sanctioned the Corporate Law Review process and the establishment of the CLRSG in the latter part of the twentieth century, the legislature in that country had already endorsed the policy wisdom of allowing directors to consider not only shareholders in corporate decision-making, although such an extension was only with respect to company employees. This policy shift was reflected in s 309(1) of the Companies Act, 1985. However, because of the non-existent impact of this policy change on the legal enforcement framework, not much notice was given to this limited extension of corporate constituencies in corporate decision-making, and the law continued to be interpreted as hitherto settled. Indeed, it was not until the completion of the Corporate Law Review process, which culminated in the enactment of the Companies Act of 2006, that the significance of the extension of corporate constituencies in corporate decision-making was given so much attention. As shown above in chapter 2, the formal recognition of non-shareholder corporate constituencies' interests in terms of s 172(1) of the UK Companies Act, 2006, effectively brought the reformed policy shift to the forefront of corporate law developments the world over. Particularly due to the breadth of coverage of non-shareholder corporate constituencies' interests, this statutory provision received much acclaim when it was enacted.

## THE SIGNIFICANCE OF THE TRANSITION FROM SHAREHOLDER PRIMACY MODEL TO ENLIGHTENED SHAREHOLDER VALUE APPROACH

Regardless of the acclaim accorded to the greatly expanded ESVA, as reflected under s 172(1) of the Companies Act, 2006, its inability to influence the reform of the corporate legal enforcement framework effectively means that it is of no greater value than its predecessor, s 309(1) of the Companies Act, 1985. It has been argued that the permissive language of both the statutory provisions of the 1985 and the 2006 laws accounts for the apparent retention of the conventional corporate legal enforcement framework in the United Kingdom. Arguments have been made that because directors are permitted, as opposed to being required, to have regard to the non-shareholder corporate constituencies, any failure on the part of the directorate to have regard to those corporate constituencies in corporate decision-making is not legally subject to remedy by the beneficiaries of any of the non-shareholder corporate constituencies' interests. If the seemingly directory language of the statute has been motivated by the acceptance that shareholders are the only residual rights claimants, that they are the exclusive beneficiaries of the privileges of corporate voting and that they are the exclusive beneficiaries of the fiduciary obligations, then the statutory formulation is clearly based on an erroneous legal underpinning and is, as such, jurisprudentially unjustifiable. It would, therefore, have been jurisprudentially justifiable for the transition to ESVA to also be complemented by a broadly inclusive legal enforcement regime.

## CORPORATE CONSTITUENCIES' PROTECTION MECHANISMS IN THE UNITED STATES

Chapter 2 also shows that in the United States, corporate law has, ever since the creation of the union, been the prerogative of state legislatures, and the significance attached to capital formation in each of the states has ensured the entrenchment of the shareholder primacy theory in each of the corporate statutes of those states. This entrenchment was subsequently underscored by the similarly influenced Model Act, which has been adopted substantially entirely by over half of the states in that country. To this very day, the corporate legal enforcement framework in each of the states of the United States continues to be influenced by the shareholder-oriented shareholder primacy theory. Even after the adoption of the corporate constituency statutes and benefit corporation statutes by a large number of the states of the United States, the corporate landscape continues to be entirely dominated by a shareholder-oriented corporate legal enforcement framework. While most, if not all, corporate constituency statutes endeavoured to be broadly encompassing of the non-shareholder corporate constituent groups, as exemplified by the sometimes expansive language of the specific statutory enactments, the legal underpinning remains that of the shareholder primacy theory, as all but one are permissive in nature and none of them is supplemented by right of action in favour of any of the specified non-shareholder corporate constituent groups.

## CORPORATE CONSTITUENCY STATUTES AND THE ENTRENCHMENT OF THE SHAREHOLDER PRIMACY MODEL

In the enactment of corporate constituency statutes, state legislatures immediately faced the dilemma of the possible introduction of a broadly inclusive corporate objective within corporate law, while those corporate constituency measures continue to be included within core corporation statutes and not in specific self-standing statutory instruments. This effectively ruled out the possibility of introducing divergent corporate objectives, as this would invariably fit poorly with the objective that characterises the core duties of directors.

Furthermore, the analysis of corporate constituency statutes in chapter 2 reveals that the almost universal creation of priority of interests in each of those statutes, with shareholder interests assuming pre-eminence, effectively gives an indication that the maintenance of the status quo is preferred and that possible reform of the corporate objective is ruled out.

Again, the inclusion of the need to consider 'the possibility that the long-term, as well as the short-term interests of the corporation and its shareholders, may be best served by the continued independence of the corporation' in almost all the statutes clearly signalled the entrenchment of the shareholder primacy theory.

The existence of limited instances of optional adoption of the corporate constituency measures through corporate charters in some states additionally pointed towards the possible insignificance of the measures.

While in some states, the inclusion of the language that 'the effects of a proposed corporate action on any particular corporate constituent group or interest should not be considered as a dominant or controlling factor' could have had the revolutionary impact of displacing shareholder interests as the yardstick in conventional corporate law, the reality is that this language appears to be applicable to corporate constituencies other than shareholders and, thus, perpetuates the status quo.

Even the existence of limited case law, which represents a significant departure from the established and accepted conventional corporate objective has had no effect in influencing the reform of the corporate legal enforcement framework.

Finally, the lack of uniformity with regard to the categories of corporate constituencies to be taken into account by the directors does not help matters.

## BENEFIT CORPORATION STATUTES AND THE MISSED OPPORTUNITY TO CHART A NEW PATH

What sets benefit corporation statutes apart, as shown above, is the realisation that the pursuit of general and specific public benefit objectives identified by the specific benefit corporation constitutes the advancement of the interests of that corporation. That said, however, chapter 2 shows that the continued preference shown towards shareholders when it comes to the right of action, even with respect to public benefit objectives, effectively erodes any perceived gains that may have been made by the categorisation of public benefit objectives as 'interests of the corporation'. While it is understandable that the law should reserve for shareholders the right of action in relation to the enforcement of objectives aimed at promoting shareholder value within the benefit corporation, it defeats the logic that almost all benefit corporation statutes continue to empower only shareholders with regard to the enforcement of public benefit objectives, even when it is clear that it is non-shareholder corporate constituencies who are the primary, if not the only, beneficiaries of those objectives. The categorisation of public benefit objectives as being tantamount to 'the interests of the corporation' in almost all benefit corporation statutes presented a perfect opportunity for the empowerment of the beneficiaries of those public benefit objectives. It is, therefore, lamentable that such categorisation notwithstanding, very few states have empowered the beneficiaries of public benefit objectives with the right of action. Even in states which have empowered such non-shareholder corporate constituencies, the empowerment is afforded only if specifically incorporated in the corporation's Certificate of Incorporation and/or by-laws.

## JURISPRUDENTIAL UNERPINING OF INCLUSIVE CORPORATE LAW REMEDIES

As it has been shown throughout the book, and particularly in chapters 3 and 4, the retention of the conventional shareholder-oriented corporate legal enforcement framework is anchored on the justification that any broadly inclusive legal enforcement framework is undesirable because, first, corporate constituencies other than shareholders are incapable of having their personal and/or collective rights directly affected or harmed by corporate action, and allowing non-shareholder corporate constituencies the right of action would lead to undesirable floodgates of litigation. Coupled with that, the danger of burdening companies with the unenviable task of having to prioritise or balance competing interests of corporate constituencies appears to loom large as the justification for the retention of the conventional corporate legal enforcement regime, although this danger has been shown to be either more perceived than real or not impossible of resolution.[4] Second, the conventional corporate legal enforcement framework in the area of indirect actions, such as derivative suits, is anchored on the justification that core corporate privileges (such as corporate ownership and entitlement to be residual rights claimants, as well as corporate voting) and the entitlement to benefits flowing from fiduciary obligations (the foundation for derivative suits) are the exclusive preserve of the shareholders.

As it has been argued in chapter 4, these justifications are not legally and pragmatically sustainable and, thus, as the basis for the corporate legal enforcement framework, they are fundamentally unsustainable. For starters, the assumption that non-shareholder corporate constituent groups cannot have their personal or collective rights negatively affected as a result of corporate decision-making, which would necessitate the institution of legal remedies to address preceding oppressive and unfairly prejudicial conduct, is jurisprudentially misplaced. Many examples of situations in which corporate conduct may have possibly harmed the personal and/or collective rights of non-shareholder corporate constituent groups (most of which are beyond the scope of this book) come readily to mind. These instances of corporate harm have the potential to negatively affect the personal rights and/or interests of varied corporate constituencies within companies. It, therefore, goes without saying that the continued perpetuation of the conventional personal legal standing for a person to institute legal proceedings directly in their personal capacity to vindicate their own rights cannot be limited to shareholder corporate constituencies.[5] Corporate law needs, therefore, to also provide for representative actions on behalf of persons who cannot act in their own names[6] and on behalf of, or in the interests of, a group or class of affected persons, or by an association in the interests of its members.[7] The extension of standing rules should also envisage the possibility of any other person acting in the public interest, with leave of the court.[8] The extension of standing in relation to the vindication of personal rights of corporate constituencies as proposed above will, therefore, reflect the entrenchment of, in particular, representative and public interest actions under corporate law, something which is unavoidable in the quest to appropriately empower non-shareholder corporate constituent groups.

It has also been shown that arguments in favour of shareholders as corporate owners and residual rights claimants prove to be seriously flawed, particularly in the context of public companies. Again, corporate law developments in many Anglo-American jurisdictions clearly reveal that the wisdom of the exclusivity of corporate voting has been questioned, and some recent corporate law statutes[9] have reached further in creating an environment to support the possible extension of corporate voting privileges to corporate constituencies other than shareholders.

As regards the justification of shareholders as the exclusive beneficiaries of fiduciary obligations, it has been shown that, in fact, the primary preoccupation of fiduciary obligations is not with the exclusive protection of shareholders, but the restriction of directorial self-serving misconduct, the enforcement of which will not only benefit shareholders but also non-shareholder corporate constituent groups.

As was shown in the book, retaining the highly individualistic and conservative legal standing, merely because non-shareholder corporate constituencies have no personal and/or collective rights to assert against unfavourable corporate conduct, are not corporate owners and/or residual rights claimants, are not entitled to corporate voting privileges, and are not the beneficiaries of fiduciary obligations, is not jurisprudentially sustainable.

## JURISPRUDENTIAL UNDERPINNING OF THE EXTENDED STANDING FOR DERIVATIVE LITIGATION SUITS

As regards indirect corporate law remedies, derivative action proceedings are at the centre thereof, as it is the company's interests which are being vindicated. Even in the area of derivative proceedings, conventional Anglo-American corporate law gives the exclusive right of enforcement to equity investors, presumably on the basis that they are the exclusive beneficiaries of directorial fiduciary obligations and corporate voting. Both these justifications for the exclusive preference of equity investors to bring derivative proceedings are questionable. With regard to equity investors as the exclusive beneficiaries of directorial fiduciary obligations, the reality of the broad nature of the corporate purpose of public corporations, coupled with the recognition of non-shareholder corporate constituencies' interests as falling within the scope of the interests of corporations in some corporate statutes of even some Anglo-American jurisdictions in recent years, renders the arguments for the exclusive nature of directorial fiduciary obligations questionable. Further, the extension of corporate voting privileges to constituencies beyond equity investors in some modern corporate statutes seriously puts into question the justifiability of the exclusivity of corporate voting as the jurisprudential justification for making equity investors the only constituent capable of enforcing derivative proceedings.

A recent example of the extension of legal standing to constituencies other than equity investors in derivative action proceedings is South Africa, in the form of s 165 (2) of the 2008 Companies Act, which recognises creditors, employees, and any persons acting in the public interest as possible litigants in derivative action proceedings, in addition to shareholders and directors.

Furthermore, the perpetuation of conventional legal standing rules in derivative action proceedings disregards the inbuilt safeguards against the abuse of these proceedings, some of which include the fact that courts are vested with inherent powers to dismiss frivolous and vexatious proceedings and the fact that in these proceedings, any remedy obtained rightly belongs to the company and to no-one else.

## ACCEPTABLE LIMITATIONS TO EXTENDED STANDING TO APPLY FOR REMEDIES

For direct and indirect corporate law remedies, doing away with the conservative conventional limitations concerning standing and accommodating broader categories of corporate constituent groups will potentially lead to a substantial increase in legal suits, but this book argues that continuing to make such legal suits the exclusive domain of shareholders is not the preferred solution. As has been argued in the book, there are sufficient safeguards to counter possible floodgates of litigation, and it would not be advisable to continue with the exclusive, conservative, and largely individualistic standing rules attached to corporate law remedies merely because of the risk of increased litigation.

As regards the possible extension of standing in relation to the vindication of personal rights of corporate constituencies as proposed above, the book argues that 'the possibility of unjustified litigation can be curtailed by making it a procedural requirement that leave must be sought from the . . . Court to proceed . . . prior to actually embarking on that road'.[10] In determining whether leave should be granted, courts may take into account jurisprudentially acceptable reasons for denying such leave, but may not dismiss proceedings merely because of the form of investment made by the potential litigant. Thus, leave should not be refused merely because the potential litigant is not a shareholder or an equity investor, as is invariably the conventional practice. The enforcement of collective rights by non-shareholder corporate constituencies can also be subject to the certification process and, as established by the South African Supreme Court of Appeal in relation to class actions,[11] the requirements for such leave of the court include (a) the certification of the action

> [the requirement of which] involves the definition of the class; the identification of some common claim or issue that can be determined by way of a class action;

> some evidence of the existence of a valid cause of action; the suitability of the representative to represent the members of the class; and the determination that a class action is the most appropriate procedure to adopt for the adjudication of the underlying claims'.[12]

Further, requirements, as established by the Court, include (b) the definition of a class,[13] (c) a cause of action raising a triable issue,[14] (d) the existence of common issues of fact or law,[15] and (e) that the applicants are acting as members of, or in the interest of, a class.[16]

As regards limitations to the derivative suits, the most reasonable limitations, as exemplified under the South African Companies Act, 2008[17] and discussed above,[18] include (a) the requirement by the prospective litigant to serve a demand upon a company to commence or continue legal proceedings, or take related steps, to protect the legal interests of the company, (b) the granting of leave of the court prior to the institution or continuation of the proceedings, which may be granted only if the court is satisfied that it is necessary or expedient to do so to protect a legal right of that other person, (c) the prior appointment by the company of an independent and impartial person or committee to investigate the demand and report to the board on various matters establishing the desirability of derivative litigation proceedings, (d) the satisfaction by the court that – (i) the applicant is acting in good faith, (ii) the proposed or continuing proceedings involve the trial of a serious question of material consequence to the company, and (iii) it is in the best interests of the company that the applicant be granted leave to commence or continue the proceedings.[19]

Any limitation based on the identity of the potential litigant (whether shareholder or not), which is currently at the heart of the conventional corporate legal enforcement framework in Anglo-American jurisdictions, can no longer be the sole, or even the primary, justification for denying non-shareholder corporate constituencies access to derivative litigation proceedings. Moreover, this limitation is based on the unsubstantiated presumption that the interests of the company can best be protected by shareholders and that the non-shareholder corporate constituencies invariably have neither the will nor the wherewithal to launch any legal proceedings to protect the legal interests of the company. While it is undeniable that non-shareholder corporate constituencies may not always be motivated to take measures to protect the interests of the company any more than the shareholders may be inclined to do, the reality is that even shareholders are, and continue to be, reluctant and, in some instances, disincentivised to undertake derivative litigation proceedings. The main reason is that shareholders who invest in equity in a number of different companies would naturally not be greatly compelled to institute proceedings on behalf of one of the many companies in which they own equity.[20]

Again, given the fact that in a derivative action, recovery is the right of the company, and any benefit that could accrue to a plaintiff shareholder accrues only if the success of the action leads to a substantial increase in the value of the company's shares; shareholders tend to free-ride in the hope that others undertake the proceedings. Consequently, limiting access to derivative suits by shareholders alone fails to address the primary concern for these kinds of proceedings, which is to restrain directorially self-serving misconduct. Such a restraint benefits not only the company but also all corporate constituencies, including the shareholders.

## FINAL CONCLUSIONS

In the final analysis, the book indicates that the ESVA, while attractive as the modern normative standard for corporate objectives under the current corporate law dispensation in Anglo-American jurisdictions, has failed to influence the reform of the corporate legal enforcement regime. This effectively means that the AESVA would be better suited, as it invariably leads to the institutionalisation of the broadly inclusive corporate legal enforcement regime, particularly in derivative legal proceedings.

The book further indicates that the dismal failure of the corporate constituency statutes, particularly in the influence of corporate law developments in the United States, leads to the unavoidable conclusion that the policy wisdom of these statutory measures has been incontrovertibly challenged. It is argued that had these measures been effectively implemented, they would have appropriately put to rest the question of the primary objective of fiduciary obligations and, thus, the possible inclusion of non-shareholder corporate constituencies within the corporate legal enforcement framework. Furthermore, a perfect opportunity to empower non-shareholder corporate constituent groups with a right of action in corporate law remedies was missed during the enactment of benefit corporation statutes, as the recognition of public benefit objectives within those statutes could have justifiably been supplemented by the extension of the right of action to the very beneficiaries of those public benefit objectives, who are, undeniably, non-shareholder corporate constituencies.

The book also questions the continued preference for the conventional shareholder-oriented corporate legal enforcement framework on the basis that only the shareholders are corporate owners and that they are the exclusive beneficiaries of corporate voting privileges and directorial duties. The retention of the conventional corporate legal enforcement framework is also questioned to the extent that it is justified on the basis of the need to curb supposed floodgates of litigation, as there are other measures that can be adopted to deal with such an eventuality.

The book finally demonstrates how recent corporate law developments in South Africa have questioned the continued desirability of the conventional corporate legal enforcement framework by indicating how the new Companies Act of 2008 has addressed the broadening of the legal standing rules in the vindication of personal and collective rights of non-shareholder corporate constituencies in corporate law and in the institution or continuation of derivative litigation proceedings by those non-shareholder corporate constituencies.

The book finally concludes that a broadly inclusive corporate legal enforcement framework is long overdue in Anglo-American jurisdictions and all other jurisdictions with which they share corporate law traditions. This is particularly true as it is indisputable that safeguards against the abuse of corporate law remedies cannot be solely based on the reservation of the remedies to corporate constituencies merely because of the nature of the investment the relevant constituency has made in the public company.

## NOTES

1. In the case of *Haitas & Others v Port Wild Props 12 (Pty) Ltd* 2011 (5) SA 562 (GSJ), the court confirmed that it was vested with an inherent power to regulate its own process. It continued to emphasise that, whilst engaging in this process, the courts should guard against vexatious, reckless and unmeritorious litigation. It further held that each case must be decided on its own peculiar facts, taking into account the interests of justice. In *Boost Sports Africa (Pty) Ltd v South African Breweries Ltd* 2014 (4) SA 343 (GP), the court approved the decision taken in *Haitas*. The court also held that the defendant's defence in the main proceedings and any other pertinent factors should also be taken into account.

2. See also *Haitas & Others v Port Wild Props 12 (Pty) Ltd 2011 (5) SA 562 (GSJ)* and *Boost Sports Africa (Pty) Ltd v South African Breweries Ltd 2014 (4) SA 343 (GP)*.

3. *Haitas & Others v Port Wild Props 12 (Pty) Ltd 2011 (5) SA 562 (GSJ)(Haitas) & Boost Sports Africa (Pty) Ltd v South African Breweries Ltd 2014 (4) SA 343 (GP)*.

4. First, whether a conflict can possibly exist between the interests of those in a horizontal relationship is questioned. Second, if indeed such a conflict can arise, its resolution is not impossible.

5. See, for example, s 157(1)(a) of the South African Companies Act, 2008, which clearly envisages the possible extension of the power to vindicate violations of personal rights beyond just shareholders.

6. As in the case of section 157(1)(b) of the South African Companies Act of 2008.

7. As provided for in section 157(1)(c) of the South African Companies Act of 2008.

8. Which will be the equivalent of section 157(1)(d) of the South African Companies Act of 2008.

9. As in the South African Companies Act of 2008.

10. As was cogently argued in the South African Eastern Cape High Court case of *Ngxuza and Others v Permanent Secretary, Department of Welfare, Eastern Cape & another 2001 (2) SA 609 (ECD)* at 624D – E, this decision was upheld by the Supreme Court of Appeal in *Permanent Secretary Department of Welfare, Eastern Cape Provincial Government and Another v Ngxuza and Others* (493/2000) [2001] ZASCA 85.

11. See *Children Resource Centre Trust and Others v Pioneer Food (Pty) Ltd and Others* 2013 (2) SA 213 (SCA), Para 23.

12. Per Wallis JA (with Nugent, Ponnan, Malan and Tshiqi JJA concurring), Ibid.

13. Ibid., Para 29–34.

14. Ibid., Para 35–43.

15. Ibid., Para 44–45.

16. Ibid., Para 46–48.

17. In particular, ss 165(2)(d), (3), (4)(a), and (5)(b).

18. In Chapter 4.

19. Ibid.

20. See A Global Picture of Business, at 276.

# Bibliography

## JOURNAL ARTICLES


Adams ES & Matheson JH, 'A Statutory Model for Corporate Constituency Concerns' (2000) 49 *Emory Law Journal* 1085, at 1101.

Aguilar LA, 'Shareholders Need Robust Disclosure to Exercise their Voting Rights as Investors and Owners' *The CLS Blue Sky Blog*, Columbia Law School's blog on Corporations and the Capital Markets. Available at https://clsbluesky.law.columbia.edu/2013/02/21/shareholders-need-robust-disclosure-to-exercise-their-voting-rights-as-investors-and-owners/, accessed on 3 May 2024.

Alchien A & Demsetz H, 'Production, Information Costs, and Economic Organization' (1972) 66 *American Economic Review* 777.

Alexander JC, Spivey MF & Marr MW, 'Nonshareholder Constituency Statutes and Shareholder Wealth' (1997) 21 *Journal of Banking and Finance* 417.

Allen WT, 'Our Schizophrenic Conception of the Corporation' (1992) 14 *Cardozo Law Review* 261.

Anderson JA, 'Maine's Non-Shareholder Constituency Statute' (1993) 45 *Maine Law Review* 153.

Armour J, Deakin S & Konzelmann S, 'Shareholder Primacy and the Trajectory of UK Corporate Governance' (2003) 41 *British Journal of Industrial Relations* 531.

Bainbridge S, 'Director Primacy: The Means and Ends of Corporate Governance' (2003) 97 *Northwestern University Law Review* 547.

Bainbridge S, 'In Defense of the Shareholder Wealth Maximization Norm: A Reply to Professor Green' (1993) 50 *Washington and Lee Law Review* 1423.

Bainbridge SM, 'Interpreting Nonshareholder Constituency Statutes' (1992) 19 *Pepperdine Law Review* 971.

Barrett RI, 'Directors' Duties to Creditors' (1977) 40 *MLR* 266.

Baxt R, 'A Senior Australian Court Gives the Thumbs Up to the *Winkworth* Principle' (1989) 7 *C&SLJ* 344.

Baxt R, 'Duties of Directors with Respect to Creditors' (1989) 63 *ALJ* 846.

Berle AA, 'For Whom Corporate Managers Are Trustees: A Note', (1932) 45 *Harvard Law Review* 1365.
Beuthin RC, 'The Range of a Company's Interests' (1969) 86 *South African Law Journal* 155.
Bisconti A, 'The Double Bottom Line: Can Constituency Statutes Protect Socially Responsible Corporations Stuck in *Revlon* Land' (2009) 42 *Loyola of Lost Angeles Law Review* 765.
Black B & Kraakman R, 'A Self-Enforcing Model of Corporate Law' (1996) 109 *Harvard Law Review* 1911.
Blair M & Stout L, 'A Team Production Theory to Corporate Law' (1999) 85 *Virginia Law Review* 247.
Cabot WM, 'The Free Market Promotes Long-Term Efficiency that Benefits all Stakeholders' (1991) 21 *Stetson Law Review* 245.
Calnan RJ, 'Corporate Gifts and Creditors Rights' (1990) 2 *C&SLJ* 91.
Carney WJ, 'Does Defining Constituencies Matter?' (1990)59 *University of Cincinnati Law Review* 385.
Cheffins BR, 'Reforming the Derivative Action: The Canadian Experience and British Prospects' (1997) *Company, Financial and Insolvency Law Review* 227.
Collins H, 'Method and aims of Comparative Law' (1991) *Oxford Journal of Legal Studies* 396.
Committee on Corporate Laws of the Business Law Section of American Bar Association, 'Other Constituency Statutes: Potential for Confusion' (1990) 45 *The Business Lawyer* 2253.
Conn K, 'When School Management Companies Fail: Righting Educational Wrongs' (2002) 31 *Journal of Law and Education* 245.
Dabner J, 'Directors' Duties-The Schiziod Company' (1988) 6 *Company and Securities Law Journal (C&SLJ)* 105.
Dawson F, 'Acting in the Best Interests of the Company – For Whom are Directors Trustees?' (1984) 11 *NZULR* 68.
DeBow ME & Lee DR, 'Shareholders, Nonshareholders, and Corporate Law: Communitarianism and Resource Allocation' (1993) 18 *Delaware Journal of Corporate Law* 393.
Dodd EM, 'For Whom Are Corporate Managers Trustees?' (1932) 45 *Harvard Law Review* 1145.
Easterbrook FH & Fischel DR, 'Voting in Corporate Law' (1983) 26 *The Journal of Law and Economics* 395.
Engel D, 'An Approach to Corporate Social Responsibility' (1979) 32 *Stan LR* 1.
Fama EF, 'Agency Problems and the Theory of the Firm' (1980) 88 *Journal of Political Economy* 288.
Farrar JH, 'The Responsibility of Directors and Shareholders for a Company's Debts' (1989) 4 *Canterbury Law Review* 12.
Finch V, 'Directors' Duties Towards Creditors' (1989) 10 *Company Lawyer* 23.
Fisch J, 'Measuring Efficiency in Corporate Law: The Role of Shareholder Primacy' (2005) *Fordham Law Legal Studies Research Paper No 105*, at 30. http://papers.ssrn.com/sol3/papers.cfm?abstract_id=878391, accessed on 3 May 2024.

Fourie OJS, 'Die Plig van Direkteure Teenoor Maatskappyskuldeisers' (1992) 4 *South African Mercantile Law Journal* 25.

Freeman RE, 'The Politics of Stakeholder Theory: Some Future Directions' (1994) 4 *Business Ethics Quarterly* 409.

Garcia FJ, 'Protecting Nonshareholder Interests In the Market for Corporate Control. A Role for State Takeover Statutes' (1990) 23 *University of Michigan Journal of Law Reform* 507.

Gavis AC, 'A Framework For Satisfying Corporate Directors' Responsibilities Under State Nonshareholder Constituency Statutes: The Use of Explicit Contracts' (1990) 138 *University of Pennsylvania Law Review* 1451.

Grantham R, 'Directors' Duties and Insolvent Companies' (1991) 54 *MLR* 576.

Grantham R, 'The Judicial Extension of Directors' Duties to Creditors' [1991] *JBL* 1.

Greene EF, 'Regulatory and Legislative Responses to Takeover Activity in the 1980s: The United States and Europe' (1991) 69 *Texas Law Review* 1539.

Greenfield K, 'New Principles for Corporate Law' (2005) 1 *Hastings Business Law Journal* 89.

Hale K, 'Corporate law and Stakeholders: Moving Beyond Stakeholders Statutes' (2003) 45 *Arizona Law Review* 823.

Hanks Jr. JJ, 'Non-Stockholder Constituency Statutes: An Idea Whose Time Should Never Have Come' (1989) 3 (12) *INSIGHTS* 20.

Hanks Jr. JJ, 'Playing with Fire: Nonshareholder Constituency Statutes in the 1990s' (1991) 21 *Stetson Law Review* 97.

Hansmann H & Kraakman R, 'The End of History for Corporate Law' (2001) 89 *Georgetown Law Journal* 439.

Hart O, 'An Economist's View of Fiduciary Duty' (1993) 43 *University of Toronto Law Journal* 299.

Hart RM & Degener CM, 'Non-Stockholder Constituency Statutes' (1990) 203 *New York Law Journal* 1.

Harvard Business School, Cashe Study 9-496-037, at 5.

Hawke N, 'Creditors' Interests in Solvent and Insolvent Companies' [1989] *JBL* 54.

Hill J, 'Duties of Directors towards Creditors' (1986) 60 *ALJ* 525.

Ho JKS, 'Director's Duty to Promote the Success of the Company: Should Hong Kong Implement a Similar Provision?' (2010) 10 (1) *Journal of Corporate Law Studies* 17.

Ho VH, '"Enlightened Shareholder Value": Corporate Governance Beyond the Shareholder-Stakeholder Divide' (2010) *SelectedWorks* (From the SelectedWorks of Virginia E Ho). Available at http://works.bepress.com/virginia_ho/3, accessed on 16 August 2014.

Hodes L, 'The Social Responsibility of a Company' (1983) 100 *South African Law Journal* (*SALJ*) 468.

Jensen M, 'Value Maximisation, Stakeholder Theory and the Corporate Objective Function' (2001) 7 (3) *European Financial Management* 297.

Jensen M & Meckling W, 'Theory of the Firm: Managerial Behaviour, Agency Costs, and Ownership Structure' (1976) 3 *Journal of Financial Economics* 305.

Johnson L & Millon D, 'Missing the Point About State Take-over Statutes' (1989) 87 *Michigan Law Review* 846.

Karmel RS, 'Implications of the Stakeholder Model' (1993) 61 *George Washington Law Review* 1156.

Keay A, 'Ascertaining the Corporate Objective: An Entity Maximisation and Sustainability Model' (2008) 71 *Modern Law Review* 663.

Keay A, 'Tackling the Issue of Corporate Objective: An Analysis of the United Kingdom's Enlightened Shareholder Value Approach' (2007) 29 *Sydney Law Review* 577.

Keay A, 'The Ultimate Objective of the Company and the Enforcement of the Entity Maximisation and Sustainability Model' (2010) 10 *Journal of Corporate Law Studies* 35.

Kotz H, 'The Role of the Judge in the Court-room: The Common and Civil Law Compared' (1987) *Tydskrif van Suid Afrikaanse Reg (TSAR)* 35.

Lacovara C, 'Strange Creatures: A Hybrid Approach to Fiduciary Duty in Benefit Corporations' (2011) 3 *Columbia Business Law Review* 815.

Legrand P, 'Against a European Civil Code' (1997) *Modern Law Review* 44.

Legrand P, 'Comparative Legal Studies and Commitment to Theory' (1995) 58 *Modern Law Review* 262.

Legrand P, 'Comparing Legal Cultures' (book review) (1997) 56 *Cambridge Law Journal* 646.

Lipton M, 'Takeover Bids in the Target's Boardroom' (1979) 35 *Business Lawyer* 101.

Luca E & Volpin P, 'Corporate Governance Reforms in Continental Europe' (2007) 21 *Journal of Economic Perspectives*, at 117.

Macey JR, 'An Economic Analysis of the Various Rationales for Making Shareholders the Exclusive Beneficiaries of Corporate Fiduciary Duties' (1991) 21 *Stetson Law Review* 23.

Macey JR, 'Externalities, Firm-Specific Capital Investments, and the Legal Treatment of Fundamental Corporate Changes' (1989) *DUKE Law Journal* 173.

Macey JR & Miller GP, 'Corporate Stakeholders: A Contractual Perspective' (1993) 43 *University of Toronto Law Journal* 401.

Matheson JH & Olson BA, 'Corporate Cooperation, Relationship Management, and the Trialogical Imperative for Corporate Law'(1994) 78 *Minnesota Law Review* 1443.

McDaniel M, 'Bondholders and Stockholders' (1988) 13 *Journal of Corporation Law* 205.

McDonnell BH, 'Corporate Constituency Statutes and Employee Governance' (2004) 30 (4) *William Mitchell Law Review* 1227.

McPherson BH, 'Duties of Directors and Powers of Shareholders' (1977) 51 *ALJ* 460.

Mickels A, 'Beyond Corporate Social Responsibility: Reconciling the Ideals of a For-Benefit Corporation with Director Fiduciary Duties in the U.S. and Europe' (2009) 32 *Hastings International & Comparative Law Review* 271.

Millon D, 'Theories of the Corporation' (1990) *Duke Law Journal* 201.

Millon D, 'Redefining Corporate Law' (1991) 24 *Indiana Law Review* 223.

Mitchell LE, 'A Theoretical and Practical Framework for Enforcing Corporate Constituency Statutes' (1992) 70 (3) *Texas Law Review* 579.

Mitchell LE, 'The Fairness Rights of Corporate Bondholders' (1990) 65 *New York University Law Review (N.Y.U. L. REV.)* 1165.

Norwitz TS, 'The Metaphysics of Time: A Radical Corporate Vision' (1991) 46 *Business Law* 377.

Oswald LJ, 'Evaluating Corporate Constituency Statutes Under the Takings Clause' (1998) *The Journal of Corporation Law* 1.

Page A, 'Has Corporate Law Failed? Addressing Proposals for Reform' (2009) 107 *Michigan Law Review* 979.

Paine LS, 'What Does Stakeholder Capitalism Mean to You? A Guide to the Four Main Types' (2023) *Harvard Business Review* 109–119.

Prentice DD, 'Creditor's Interests and Director's Duties' (1990) 10 *Oxford JLS* 265.

Roe M, 'The Shareholder Wealth Maximization Norm and Industrial Organization' (2001) 149 *University of Pennsylvania Law Review* 2063.

Romano R, 'The Corporate Stakeholder Debate: The Classical Theory and its Critics' (1993) 43 *University of Toronto Law Journal* 533.

Ruder D, 'Public Obligations of Private Corporations' (1965) 114 *University of Pennsylvania Law Review (U.Pa.L.Rev.)* 209.

Salacuse JW, 'Corporate Governance in the New Century' (2004) 25 (3) *The Company Lawyer* 69.

Santow GKF, 'Defensive Measures against Company Take-overs' (1979) 53 *ALJ* 374.

Sealy LS, 'Directors' Duties-an Unnecessary Gloss' (1988) *CLJ* 175.

Sealy LS, 'The Director as Trustee' (1967) *Cambridge Law Journal (CLJ)* 83.

Sealy LS, 'Directors' Wider Responsibilities-Problems Conceptual, Practical and Procedural' (1987) 13 *Monash ULR* 164.

Sheehy B, 'Scrooge – The Reluctant Stakeholder: Theoretical Problems in the Shareholder-Stakeholder Debate' (2005) 14 *University of Miami Business Law Review* 193.

Slaughter CM, 'Corporate Social Responsibility: A New Perspective' (1997) 18 *Company Lawyer* 313.

Smith DG, 'The Shareholder Primacy Norm' (1998) 23 *Journal of Corporate Law* 277.

Sommer AA, 'Whom Should the Corporation Serve? The Berle-Dodd Debate Revisited Sixty Years Later' (1991) 16 *Delaware Journal of Corporate Law* 33.

Springer JD, 'Corporate Constituency Statutes: Hollow Hopes and False Fears' (1999) *Annual Survey of American Law* 85.

Tarver MT, 'The Arrogance of Corporate Power: A study of the Evolution of the Fiduciary Duty Owed by Management to the Corporation or its Shareholders' (1967) 42 *Tulane LR* 155.

Tyler J, 'Negating the Legal Problem of Having "Two Masters": A Framework for L3C Fiduciary Duties and Accountability' (2010) 35*Vermont Law Review* 117.

Vagts DF, 'Reforming the Modem Corporation: Perspective From the German' (1966) 80 *Harvard Law Review* 37.

Van der Weide ME, 'Against Fiduciary Duties to Corporate Stakeholders' (1996) 21 *Delaware Journal of Corporate Law* 27.

Wallman SMH, 'The Proper Interpretation of Corporate Constituency Statutes and Formulation of Director Duties' (1991) 21 *Stetson Law Review* 163.

Walsh JK, 'The Exercise of Powers in the Interests of the Company' (1967) 8 *University of Western Australia Law Review* 176.

Watts PG, 'Directors' and Shareholders' Duties Arising Otherwise Than by Contract' [1990] *NZRLR* 192.

Wedderburn L, 'The Social Responsibility of Companies' (1985) 15 *MULR* 4.

Weiner JL, 'The Berle-Dodd Dialogue on the Concept of the Corporation' (1964) 64 *Columbia LR* 1458.

Werner W, 'Corporation Law in Search of its Future' (1981) 81 *Columbia LR* 1611.

White JB, 'How Should We Talk About Corporations? The Languages of Economics and of Citizenship' (1985) 94 *Yale Law Journal* 1416.

Williams CA & Conley JM, 'An Emerging Third Way? The Erosion of the Anglo-American Shareholder Value Construct' (2005) 38 *Cornell International Law Journal* 493, at 500.

Williamson O, 'Corporate Governance' (1984) 93 *Yale Law Journal* 1197.

Wishart DA, 'Models and Theories of Directors' Duties to Creditors' (1991) 14 *NZULR* 323.

Ziegel JS, 'Creditors as Corporate Stakeholders: the Quiet Revolution---an Anglo-Canadian Perspective' (1993) 43 *UTLJ* 511.

## BOOKS (AND BOOK CHAPTERS), REPORTS AND THESES

Austin RP & Ramsay IM, *Ford's Principles of Corporations Law,* 12th ed. (2005) LexisNexis Butterworths.

Berle AA, *The 20th Century Capitalist Revolution* (1954) Harcourt, Brace & Co.

Blair MM, *Ownership and Control: Rethinking Corporate Governance for the Twenty-First Century* (1995) Washington, DC: Brookings Institute.

Boros EJ, *Minority Shareholders Remedies* (1995) Clarendon Press

Bratton WW, 'Game Theory and the Restoration of Honor to Corporate Law's Duty of Loyalty' in LE Mitchell (ed.), *Progressive Corporate Law* (1995) Westview Press.

Cassim FHI, Cassim MF, Cassim R, Jooste R, Shev J & Yeats J, *Contemporary Company Law,* 2nd ed. (2012) Juta & Co.

Chivers DQC, *The Companies Act 2006: Directors' Duties Guidance* (2007) The Corporate Responsibility Coalition.

Clark R, *Corporate Law* (1986) Little Brown & Company.

Clarke T, 'Introduction' in *Theories of Corporate Governance* (2004) Routledge.

Dallas LL, 'Working Toward a New Paradigm' in LE Mitchell (ed.), *Progressive Corporate Law* (1995) Westview Press.

Davis DM, 'Dealing with Corporate Defaulters: Curbing the Unfettered Exercise of Criminal Law' in TH Mongalo (ed.), *Modern Company Law for a Competitive South African Economy* (2010) Juta & Co.

Dean J, *Directing Public Companies* (2001) Cavendish.

Eisenberg MA, *The Structure of the Corporation: A Legal Analysis* (1976) Washington, DC: Beard Books.

Esser I, *Recognition of Various Stakeholder Interests in Company Management* (2008) Unpublished LLD (UNISA).

Freeman RE, 'A Stakeholder Theory of the Modern Corporation' in TL Beauchamp & NE Bowie (eds.), *Ethical Theory and Business,* 5th ed. (1997) Upper Saddle.

Friedman M & Friedman R, *Capitalism and Freedom,* 40th Anniversary ed. (2002) University of Chicago Press.

Greenfield K, *The Failure of Corporate Law: Fundamental Flaws and Progressive Possibilities* (2007) University of Chicago Press.

Hanks Jr. JJ, *Comparison of the Principal Provisions of the Delaware and Maryland Corporation Statutes* (2011) Venable LLP.

Hansmann H & Kraakman R, 'Toward a Single Model of Corporate Law?' in JA McCahery, P Moerland, T Raaijmakers, & L Renneboog (eds.), *Corporate Governance Regimes: Convergence and Diversity* (2003).

Heydon JD, 'Directors' Duties and the Company's Interests' in PD Finn (ed.), *Equity and Commercial Relations* (1987) The Law Book Company Limited.

Hyland R, 'Comparative Law' in Patterson (ed.), *Blackwell's Companion to Law and Legal Theory* (1999) Blackwell Publishing.

Joubert NL, 'Reigniting the Corporate Conscience: Reflections on Some Aspects of Social and Ethics Committees of Companies Listed on the Johannesburg Stock Exchange' in C Visser and JT Pretorius (eds.), *Essays in Honour of Frans Malan Former Judge of the Supreme Court of Appeal* (2014).

Manning B & Hanks Jr. JJ, *Legal Capital,* 3rd ed. (1990) Foundation Press.

Millon D, 'Communitarianism in Corporate Law: Foundations and Law Reform Strategies' in LE Mitchell (ed.), *Progressive Corporate Law: New Perspectives on Law, Culture, and Society* (1995) Westview Press.

Mongalo T, *Corporate Law & Corporate Governance: A Global Picture of Business Undertakings in South Africa* (2003) Van Schaik Publishers.

Mongalo TH & Scott T, *Corporate Law and Corporate Governance: An Overview of Business Undertakings in South Africa,* 2nd ed. (2022) Van Schaik Publishers.

Mongalo TH, ed., *Modern Company Law for a Competitive South African Economy* (2010) Juta & Co.

Mongalo, Tshepo Herbert, 'Corporate Actions and the Empowerment of Non-shareholder Constituencies' (2015). PhD Thesis submitted at the University of Cape Town. Available from http://hdl.handle.net/11427/16606.

Mongalo T, 'Corporate Governance and the Constitution: A Case for Broadening the Stakeholders' in S Pete & M Du Plessis (eds.), *Constitutional Democracy in South Africa 1994-2004* (2004) LexisNexis Butterworths.

Olson JF, 'South Africa Moves to a Global Model of Corporate Governance but with Important National Variations' in TH Mongalo (ed.), *Modern Company Law for a Competitive South African Economy* (2010) Juta & Co.

Ölter RW, *Interessen und Organisation der Aktiengesellschaft im amerikanischen und deutschen Recht* (1961) Verlag CF Müller, Karlsruhe.

Stein C (assisted by Everingham G) *The New Companies Act Unlocked – A Businessperson's Guide* (2011). Available at https://juta.co.za/catalogue-details/new-companies-act-unlocked-the-a-practical-guide_29287, accessed on 03 May 2024.
Sharrock R, *Business Transactions Law,* 8th ed. (2011) Juta & Co.
Stout LA, *The Shareholder Value Myth: How Putting Shareholders First Harms Investors, Corporations, and the Public* (2012) Berrett-Koehler Publishers, Inc.
Zimpritch JB, *Maine Corporation Law and Practice* (Supp. 1991) Tower Publishing.

## TABLE OF STATUTES, CODES AND BILLS

### Australia

Corporations Act (Commonwealth) 2001.

### South Africa

Close Corporations Act, 1984 (Act No. 69 of 1984).
Companies Act, 1973 (Act No. 61 of 1973).
Companies Act, 2008 (Act No. 71 of 2008).

### United Kingdom

Companies Act, 1985.
Companies Act, 2006.

### United States

Arizona (ARIZ. REV. STAT. ANN. (West 2008)).
California Benefit Corporation Act (2011).
California Corporate Flexibility Act of 2011.
California Corporations Code.
Connecticut (CONN. GEN. STAT. (2008)).
Connecticut Business Corporation Act (Conn Gen Stat (2009)).
Delaware General Corporation Law.
Florida (FLA. STAT. ANN. (West 2007)).
Georgia (GA. CODE ANN. (2003)).
Hawaii (HAW. REV. STAT. (2004)).
HAW. REV. STAT. (*Sustainable Business Corporations*) (2011)).
Idaho (IDAHO CODE ANN. (2008)).
Illinois (805 ILL. COMP. STAT. ANN. 5/8.85 (West 2004)).
Indiana (IND. CODE ANN. (West 2008)).
Iowa (IOWA CODE ANN. (West 1999)).
Kentucky (KY. REV. STAT. ANN. (LexisNexis 2003)).

Louisiana Benefit Corporation Law (2012).
Louisiana (LA. REV. STAT. ANN. (2008)).
Louisiana Revised Statutes of 1950 (LA. Rev. Stat.).
Maine (ME. REV. STAT. ANN. tit. 13-C (2009)).
Maryland Benefit Corporations Act (2011).
Maryland General Corporation Law. (MD. CODE. ANN. CORPS. & ASS'NS. (LexisNexis 2007)).
Minnesota (MINN. STAT. ANN. (West 2004)).
Mississippi (MISS. CODE ANN. (2000)).
Missouri (MO. ANN. STAT. (West 2001)).
Model Business Corporations Act (Official Text with Official Comment and Statutory Cross-References Revised through 2012).
Nevada, (NV. ST. 78).
New Jersey Business Corporation Act (N.J.S.14A) (2011).
New Jersey (N.J. STAT. ANN. (West 2003)).
New Mexico (N.M. STAT. ANN. (LexisNexis 2004)).
New York Benefit Corporations Act (2011).
N. Y. BUS. CORP. LAW (Article 17: Benefit Corporation) (2011).
New York (N.Y.BUS. CORP. LAW (McKinney 2003)).
North Dakota (N.D. CENT. CODE (2007)).
Ohio (OHIO REV. CODE ANN. (LexisNexis 2009)).
Oregon (OR. REV. STAT. (2009)).
Pennsylvania (15 Pa. Cons. Stat. Ann. (Purdon Supp. 1986) (repealed 1986)).
Pennsylvania (15 PA. CONS. STAT. (West 1995)).
Rhode Island (R.I. GEN. LAWS (West 2009)).
South Carolina Benefit Corporation Act (2012).
South Dakota (S.D. CODIFIED LAWS (2007)).
Tennessee (TENN. CODE ANN. (2008)).
Vermont (VT. STAT. ANN. tit. 11A (West 2007)).
Vermont Benefit Corporation Act (2011).
Virginia Benefit Corporations Act (2011).
Virginia Business Corporation Act (2011).
Wisconsin WIS. STAT. ANN. (West 2002).
Wyoming (WYO. STAT. ANN. (2009)).

## TABLE OF CASES

### Australia

*Australian Growth Resources Corporation Pty Ltd v Van Reesema (1988) 13 ACLR 261 268 SC (SA).*
*Australian Metropolitan Life Assurance Co Ltd v Ure (1923) 33 CLR 199 (HC of A).*
*Brunninghausen v Glavanics [1999] NSWCA 199, (1999) 17 ACLC 1247.*
*Castrisios v McManus (1991) 4 ACSR 1 SC (Tas).*

*Darvall v North Sydney Brick and Tile Co Ltd (1987) 12 ACLR 537; (1988) 6 ACLC 154, 176. Darvall v North Sydney Brick & Tile Co Ltd (1989) 15 ACLR 230 248 CA (NSW).*
*Equiticorp Finance Ltd v Bank of New Zealand (1993) 11 ACSR 642 CA (NSW).*
*Galladin Pty Ltd v Aimnorth Pty Ltd (1993) 11 ACSR 23 SC (SA).*
*Glover v Willert (1996) 20 ACSR 182 SC (Qld).*
*Grove v Flavel (1986) 43 SASR 410; (1986) 11 ACLR 116 SC (SA).*
*Jeffree v National Companies and Securities Commission (1989) 15 ACLR 217 SC (WA).*
*Kinsela v Russell Kinsela Pty Ltd (1986) 10 ACLR 395 401–402 CA (NSW).*
*Linton v Telnet Pty Ltd (1999) 30 ACSR 465 CA (NSW).*
*Magafas v Carantinos [2006] NSWSC 1459.*
*In Re New World Alliance Pty Ltd: Sycotex Pty Ltd v Baseler (1994) 122 ALR 531 550 (Fed C of A).*
*Nicholson v Permakraft (NZ) Ltd [1985] 1 NZLR 242 CA(NZ); (1985) 3 ACLC 453.*
*Russell Kinsela Pty Ltd v Kinsela (1983) 8 ACLR 384 402–404 SC(NSW).*
*Standard Chartered Bank of Australia Ltd v Antico (1995) 131 ALR 1; (1995) 18 ACSR 1 SC (NSW).*
*Spies v R (2000) 35 ACSR 500 526 (HC of A).*
*Swansson v R A Pratt Properties Pty Ltd (2002) 42 ACSR 313.*
*Walker v Wimborne (1976) 137 CLR 1 (HC of A).*

## Canada

*Frame v Smith (1987) 42 DLR (4th) 81.*
*Peoples' Department Stores v Wise [2004] SCC 68, (2004) 244 DLR (4th) 564.*

## South Africa

*Aquatus (Pty) Ltd v Sacks and Others* 1989 (1) SA 56 (A).
*Boost Sports Africa (Pty) Ltd v South African Breweries Ltd* 2014 (4) SA 343 (GP).
*Children Resource Centre Trust and Others v Pioneer Food (Pty) Ltd and Others* 2013 (2) SA 213 (SCA).
*Coronation Syndicate Ltd v Lilienfeld and the New Fortuna Co Ltd* 1903 TS 489.
*Director of Education, Transvaal v McCagie and Others* 1918 AD 616.
*Fedsure Life Assurance Co Ltd v Worldwide African Investment Holdings (Pty) Ltd and Others* 2003 (3) SA 268.
*Graaff-Reinet Municipality v Van Ryneveld's Pass Irrigation Board* 1950 (2) SA 420 (A).
*Gundelfinger v African Textile Manufacturers Ltd and Others* 1939 SA 314 (AD).
*Haitas & Others v Port Wild Props 12 (Pty) Ltd* 2011 (5) SA 562 (GSJ).
*Henri Viljoen (Pty) Ltd v Awerbuch Brothers* 1953 (2) SA 151 (O).
*McLelland v Hulett and Others* 1992 (1) SA 456 (D&CLD).
*Moti v Moti and Hassim Moti Ltd* 1934 TPD 428.

*Ngxuza and Others v Permanent Secretary Department of Welfare, Eastern Cape* 2001 (2) SA 609 (ECD).
*Ngxuza and Others v Permanent Secretary, Department of Welfare, Eastern Cape & another* 2001 (2) SA 609 (ECD).
*Organisation Undoing Tax Abuse NPC and Another v Myeni and Another* ((15996/2017) [2019] ZAGPPHC 957).
*Permanent Secretary Department of Welfare, Eastern Cape Provincial Government and Another v Ngxuza and Others* (493/2000) [2001] ZASCA 85.
*R v Mall* 1959 (4) SA 607.
*S v Hepker* 1973 (1) SA 472 (W) 484.
*Sammel v President Brand Gold Mining Co Ltd* 1969 (3) SA 629 (A).
*TWK Agriculture Ltd v NCT Forestry Co-operative Ltd and Others* 2006 SA 20 (N).
*United Watch & Diamond Co (Pty) Ltd and Others v Disa Hotel Ltd and Another* 1972 (4) SA 409 (C).
*Wood and Others v Ondangwa Tribal Authority and Another* 1975 (2) SA 294 (A).

## United Kingdom

*Brady v Brady* (1987) 3 BCC 535; [1988] BCLC 20 (CA); [1988] BCLC 579 (HL).
*Re BSB Holdings Ltd (No 2) [1996] 1 BCLC 155.*
*Charterbridge Corp Ltd v Lloyds Bank Ltd [1969] 2 All ER 1185; [1970] Ch 62.*
*Colin Gwyer v London Wharf [2003] 2 BCLC 153 ChD.*
*Re Forrest of Dean Coal Mining Co (1878) 10 ChD 450.*
*Foss v Harbottle (1843) 2 Hare 461; 67 ER 189.*
*Fulham Football Club Ltd v Cabra Estates plc* [1992] BCC 863;[1994] 1 BCLC 363.
*Gaiman v National Association for Mental Health [1971] Ch 317; [1970] 2 All ER 362.*
*Greenhalgh v Arderne Cinemas Ltd [1951] Ch 286 291; [1950] 2 All ER 1120 (CA).*
*Harris v North Devon Railway Co (1885) 20 Beav 384; 52 ER 651.*
*Re Horsley & Weight Ltd [1982] Ch 442; [1982] 3 All ER 1045 (CA).*
*Howard Smith v Ampol Petroleum Ltd [1974] AC 821; [1974] 1 All ER 1126 (PC).*
*Hutton v West Cork Railway* (23 Ch. D 654, at 672–73).
*Kuwait Asia Bank EC v National Mutual Life Nominees Ltd [1991] 1 AC 187; [1990] 3 All ER 404 (PC).*
*Lee Panavision Ltd v Lee Lighting [1992] BCLC 22* (CA).
*Lee v Lee Air Farming [1961] AC 12.*
*Lonrho Ltd v Shell Petroleum Co Ltd [1980] 1 WLR 627.*
*Multinational Gas and Petrochemical Co v Multinational Gas and Petrochemical Services Ltd [1983] Ch 258; [1983] 2 All ER 563 (CA).*
*Parke v Daily News Ltd [1962] Ch 927 963; [1962] 2 All ER 929 948.*
*Percival v Wright* [1902] 2 Ch 421.
*Prudential Assurance v Newman Industries (1981) Ch 257; [1982] Ch 204 (CA).*
*Runciman v Walter Runciman plc [1992] BCLC 1084.*
*Salomon v A. Salomon & Co [1897] 2 AC 22.*
*Spokes v Grosvenor Hotel Co* 1991 BCLC 279.

*Wallersteiner v Moir* (2) [1975] 1 ALL ER 849 (CA).
*West Mercia Safetywear Ltd v Dodd* [1988] BCLC 250 (CA).
*West Mercia Safetywear Ltd v Dodd* [1988] BCLC 250, at 252–253 (CA).
*Wilson v Lord Bury (1880) 5 QBD 518 (CA).*
*Re Wincham Shipbuilding, Boiler, and Salt Co (Poole, Jackson, and Whyte's Case) (1878) 9 Winkworth v Edward Baron Development Co Ltd [1987] 1 All ER 114 (HL).*
*Yukong Line Ltd of Korea v Rensburg Investments Corp of Liberia* [1998] 2 BCLC 485.

## United States

*Amanda Acquisition Corp. v Universal Foods Corp., 877 F.2d 496 (7th Cir.1989).*
*Ashwander v Tennessee Valley Auth., 297 U.S. 288, 321 (1936).*
*Baron v Strawbridge & Clothier 646 F. Supp. 690 (E.D. Pa. 1986).*
*Blasius Indus. v Atlas Corp., 564 A.2d 651, 663 (Del. Ch.1988).*
*Burwell, Secretary of Health and Human Services, et al. v. Hobby Lobby Stores, Inc., et al. 573 U. S. (2014).*
*Diamond v Oreamun, 248 N.E.2d 910, 914 (N.Y. 1969).*
*Dirks v SEC, 463 U.S. 646, 653 (1983).*
*Dodge v Ford Motor Co* (1919) 170 NW 668.
*Dorfinan v Chemical Bank, 56 F.R.D. 363, 364 (S.D.N.Y. 1972).*
*Essex Universal Corp. v Yates, 305 F.2d 572, 575 (2d Cir. 1962).*
*Georgia-Pacific Corp. v Great Northern Nekoosa Corp.*
*Gerdes v Reynolds, 28 N.Y.S.2d 622, 629–30 (N.Y. Sup. Ct. 1941).*
*Grobow v Perot 539 A.2d 180 (Del. 1988).*
*Guth v Loft, Inc., 5 A.2d 503, 505–08, 510 (Del. 1939).*
*Haberman v Washington Public Power Supply System, 744 P.2d 1032, 1061 (Wash. 1987).*
*Harff v Kerkorkian, 324 A.2d 215, 219 (Del. Ch. 1974).*
*Irving Trust Co. v Deutsch, 73 F.2d 121, 123 (2dCir. 1934), 294 U.S. 708 (1935).*
*Kauffman v Dreyfus Fund, Inc., 434 F.2d 727, 735 (3d Cir. 1970).*
*Klinicki v Lundgren, 695 P.2d 906, 920–21 (Or. 1985).*
*Kusner v First Pennsylvania Corp., 395 F. Supp. 276, 280 (E.D. Pa. 1975).*
*Metropolitan Life Ins. Co. v RJR Nabisco, 716 F. Supp. 1504, 1524 (S.D.N.Y. 1989).*
*Moran v Household Int'l, Inc. 490 A.2d 1059, 1070 (Del. Ch. 1985); 500 A.2d 1346 (Del. 1986).Paramount Communications, Inc. v Time Inc 571 A.2d 1140 (Del. 1989).*
*Moran v Household Int'l, Inc., 500 A.2d 1346, 1356 (Del. 1985).*
*Pepper v Litton 308 U.S. 295 (1939).*
*Perlman v Feldmann, 219 F.2d 173, 174–75 (2d Cir.) and 349 U.S. 952 (1955).*
*Polk v Good,* 507 A 2d 531,536 (Del, 1986).
*Revlon Inc v MacAndrews & Forbes Holdings Inc,* 506 A 2d 173,179 (Del, 1986).
*Revlon, Inc. v MacAndrews & Forbes Holdings, Inc. 506 A.2d 173 (Del.1986).*
*727 F. Supp. 31 (D. Me. 1989).*

*Simons v Cogan, 542 A.2d 785, 791 (Del. 1987).*
*Simons v Cogan, 549 A.2d 300, 304 (Del. 1988).*
*Smith v Van Gorkum 488* A. 2d 858 (Del. 1985).
*Spiegel v Buntrock* 571 A.2d 767 (Del. 1990).
*Stahl v Apple Bancorp, 579 A.2d 1115, 1121 (Del. Ch. 1990).*
*Tooley v Donaldson, Lufkin & Jenrette, Inc., 845 A.2d at 1035.*
*Unocal Corp. v Mesa Petroleum Co.*, 493 A.2d 946, 955 (Del. 1985).
*Zapata Corp. v Maldonado* 430 A.2d 779 (Del. 1981).

## REPORTS AND OTHER SOURCES

ABA (Reg. &L. Rep. (BNA)) Model Act Panel Rejects Other-Constituencies Measures (Aug. 17, 1990).

ALI Principles of Corporate Governance (1988) (Rent. Draft No. 8).

Amodu NA, *Corporate Social Responsibility and Law in Africa: Theories, Issues and Practices* (2020), Routledge.

British Academy, *Policy & Practice for Purposeful Business' The British Academy, Policy & Practice for Purposeful Business: The Final Report of the Future of the Corporation Programme* (2021) The British Academy.

Bruner CM, *The Corporation as Technology: Re-Calibrating Corporate Governance for a Sustainable Future* (2022), Oxford University Press.

Choudhury B and Petrin M, *Corporate Duties to the Public* (2018), Cambridge University Press.

The Company Law Review Steering Group, *Modern Company Law for a Competitive Economy: Developing the Framework* (1999), at 35, Available at https://citeseerx.ist.psu.edu/document?repid=rep1&type=pdf&doi=e8e8bfb4b7ed29eefdaf05e917447a3d21361f2d, accessed on 3 May 2024.

The Company Law Review Steering Group, UK Department of Trade and Industry, *Modern Company Law for a Competitive Economy: The Strategic Framework* (1999), Available at https://citeseerx.ist.psu.edu/document?repid=rep1&type=pdf&doi=e8e8bfb4b7ed29eefdaf05e917447a3d21361f2d, accessed on 3 May 2024.

Corporations and Markets Advisory Committee, *The Social Responsibility of Corporations* (2018), Available at https://treasury.gov.au/sites/default/files/2019-03/c2018-t319861-CAMAC-final-report-2018.pdf, accessed on 03 May 2024.

Delaware Legislation Update, Available at https://kb.bimpactassessment.net/support/solutions, accessed on 3 May 2024.

Department of Trade and Industry, *South Africa: South African Company Law Reform for the 21st Century: Guidelines for Corporate Law Reform (May 2004)*, Government Gazette No. 26493, Notice No. 1183 OF 2004, Available at https://www.gov.za/sites/default/files/gcis_document/201409/26493gen1183a.pdf, accessed on 03 May 2024.

du Plessis JJ, Varottil U and Veldman J (eds.), *Globalisation of Corporate Social Responsibility and its Impact on Corporate Governance* (2018), Springer.

Gibson, Dunn & Crutcher, 'California Adopts Two New Corporate Forms to Advance Social Benefits', Available at http://www.gibsondunn.com, accessed on 03 May 2024.

The Hampel Committee, *Report on Corporate Governance (Final Committee Report)* (1998).

http://www.southafrica.info/business/economy/econoverview.htm, accessed on 03 May 2024.

http://m.state.gov/md2898.htm, accessed on 17 May 2012.

http://www.venable.com/james-j-hanks/, accessed on 03 May 2024.

http://sydney.edu.au/law/slr/slr29_4/Keay.pdf, accessed on 03 May 2024.

http://www.gibsondunn.com/publications/Pages/CAAdoptsTwoNewCorporateForms-AdvanceSocialBenefits.aspx, accessed on 03 May 2024.

http://www.pmg.org.za/files/bills/080925b61b-08.pdf, accessed on 03 May 2024.

http://upetd.up.ac.za/book/submitted/etd-06222007-093702/unrestricted/03part3.pdf, accessed on 03 May 2024.

http://www.arizonalawreview.org/pdf/45-3/45arizlrev823.pdf, accessed on 03 May 2024.

http://www.law.leeds.ac.uk/assets/files/research/cblp/CBLPREPORT0708.pdf, accessed on 03 May 2024.

http://www.law.leeds.ac.uk/leedslaw/webdocs/leedslaw/uploadeddocuments/CBLPAn05.pdf, accessed on 03 May 2024.

https://law.justia.com/codes/hawaii/2011/division2/title23/chapter414d/414d-14, accessed on 03 May 2024.

https://www.jstor.org/stable/23526794, accessed on 03 May 2024.

http://www.alastairhudson.com/companylaw/Directors%20duties%20-%20materials.pdf, accessed on 03 May 2024.

http://www.csringreece.gr/files/research/CSR-1289992271.pdf?user, accessed on 03 May 2024.

http://ir.lib.uwo.ca/cgi/viewcontent.cgi?article=2104&context=etd, accessed on 03 May 2024.

http://www.wipo.int/wipolex/en/text.jsp?file_id=218289, accessed on 03 May 2024.

http://delcode.delaware.gov/title8/c001/sc15/index.shtml, accessed on 03 May 2024.

http://usir.salford.ac.uk/30240/1/Book_(Xiaofan_Wang).pdf, accessed on 03 May 2024.

http://law.unsw.edu.au/Course/laws4010/2005s2/lesleyAndHuang_ReadingMaterials.doc, accessed on 03 May 2024.

http://www.saflii.org/za/legis/consol_act/ca2008107/, accessed on 03 May 2024.

http://www.law.leeds.ac.uk/assets/files/research/events/directors-duties/keay-the-duty-to-promote-the-success.pdf, accessed on 03 May 2024.

http://www.leginfo.ca.gov/pub/11-12/bill/sen/sb_0201-0250/sb_201_bill_20110902_enrolled.pdf, accessed on 03 May 2024.

http://corporate-911.co.za/Corporate-911-act-regulations.pdf, accessed on 03 May 2024.

http://blogs.law.uiowa.edu/jcl/wp-content/uploads/2012/01/Frost_FINAL-SMF.pdf, accessed on 03 May 2024.

http://www.leginfo.ca.gov/pub/11-12/bill/asm/ab_0351-0400/ab_361_bill_20110830_enrolled.pdf, accessed on 03 May 2024.

http://www.legis.state.pa.us/WU01/LI/LI/CT/HTM/15/15.HTM, accessed on 03 May 2024014.

Ingrassia R, 'They Gave and It Hurts', *Daily News*, Sept. 24, 2002.

Institute of Directors in Southern Africa (IODSA), 'King Committee's Report on Corporate Governance' (2002).

Malecki C, *Corporate Social Responsibility: Perspectives for Sustainable Corporate Governance* (2018), Elgar.

Mäntysaari P, *Stocks for All: People's Capitalism in the Twenty-First Century* (2022), De Gruyter.

Mayer C, *Prosperity: Better Business Makes the Greater Good* (2018), Oxford University Press.

Osuji OK and Ngwu FN, *Corporate Social Responsibility Across the Globe* (2021), Cambridge University Press.

Parliamentary Joint Committee on Corporations and Financial Services, Commonwealth of Australia, *Corporate Responsibility: Managing Risk and Creating Value* (2006), at 59, Available at https://www.aph.gov.au/~/media/wopapub/senate/committee/corporations_ctte/completed_inquiries/2004_07/corporate_responsibility/report/report_pdf.ashx, accessed on 3 May 2024.

Reyes J, *Reframing Corporate Governance: Company Law Beyond Law and Economics* (2018), Elgar.

See also the encapsulation of the Shareholder Primacy Theory in the American Law Institute's *Principles of Corporate Governance.*

Sjafjell B, Liao C and Argyrou A (eds.), *Innovating Business for Sustainability: Regulatory Approaches in the Anthropocene* (2022), Elgar.

UK Department of Trade & Industry, Ministerial Statements on the Companies Act 2006 (June 2007), Available at https://www.professorbainbridge.com/, accessed on 03 May 2024.

## FURTHER READINGS

### Books

Amodu NA, *Corporate Social Responsibility and Law in Africa: Theories, Issues and Practices* (2020), Routledge.

Anand AI, *Shareholder-driven Corporate Governance* (2020), Oxford University Press.

Bainbridge SM, *The Profit Motive: Defending Shareholder Value Maximization* (2023), Cambridge University Press.

Bruner CM, *The Corporation as Technology: Re-Calibrating Corporate Governance for a Sustainable Future* (2022), Oxford University Press.

Choudhury B & Petrin M, *Corporate Duties to the Public* (2018) Cambridge University Press.

Du Plessis JJ, Varottil U & Veldman J (eds.), *Globalisation of Corporate Social Responsibility and its Impact on Corporate Governance* (2018), Springer.

Kelly G, Kelly D & Gamble A, *Stakeholder Capitalism* (1997), Springer.

Malecki C, *Corporate Social Responsibility: Perspectives for Sustainable Corporate Governance* (2018), Elgar.

Mäntysaari P, *Stocks for All: People's Capitalism in the Twenty-First Century* (2022), De Gruyter.

Mayer C, *Prosperity: Better Business Makes the Greater Good* (2018), Oxford University Press.

Osuji OK & Ngwu FN, *Corporate Social Responsibility Across the Globe* (2021), Cambridge University Press.

Reyes J, *Reframing Corporate Governance: Company Law Beyond Law and Economics* (2018), Elgar.

Schwab K, *Stakeholder capitalism: A global economy that works for progress, people and planet* (2021), Wiley.

Sjåfjell B, Liao C & Argyrou A (eds.), *Innovating Business for Sustainability: Regulatory Approaches in the Anthropocene* (2022), Elgar.

## Journal Articles

Beck D & Ferasso, M, 'How Can Stakeholder Capitalism Contribute to Achieving the Sustainable Development Goals? A Cross-network Literature Analysis' (2023) *Ecological Economics* 107673.

Freeman E & Liedtka J, 'Stakeholder Capitalism and the Value Chain' (1997) *European Management Journal* 286–296.

Freeman RE, Martin K & Parmar B, 'Stakeholder Capitalism' (2007) *Journal of Business Ethics* 303–314.

Gadinis S & MA, 'A Test of Stakeholder Capitalism' (2021) *Journal of Corporation Law* 50.

Mhlanga D, 'Stakeholder Capitalism, the Fourth Industrial Revolution (4IR), and Sustainable Development: Issues to Be Resolved' (2022) *Sustainability* 3902.

Rock EB, 'For Whom Is the Corporation Managed in 2020? The Debate Over Corporate Purpose' (2021) *The Business Lawyer* 363.

Shahrokhi M, Parhizgari AM, Hashemijoo M, Okafor CE, Nishikawa Y & Dastan A, 'Corporate Governance and Stakeholder Capitalism' (2022) *Insight* 1123.

## Theses and Reports

Bariz H, *From Shareholder to Stakeholder Capitalism: Value Creation by Board Composition, Ownership Structure and Information Disclosure* (2022) Ph.D. thesis, Technische Universität Darmstadt.

Walsh C, *Stakeholder Capitalism: An Investigation of the Linkage between Corporate Social Responsibility and Financial Performance* (2022) College of Business Theses and Dissertations. Available at https://via.library.depaul.edu/business_etd/23.

# Index

Note: The page reference for the figure is italicised

# Index of Commentators

# About the Author

**Tshepo Herbert Mongalo** is a professor of corporate law at the University of the Witwatersrand's School of Law in Johannesburg, South Africa, and a sessional lecturer at Wits Business School at the same university. He is also the chairperson of the Legal Entities' doctrinal study group of the International Association of Law Schools. He is currently the deputy chairperson and member of the Specialist Committee on Company Law in South Africa. His teaching and scholarship focus on corporate law, corporate law regulatory framework design, securities regulation, corporate governance and leadership studies. He is currently the faculty member of the Global Advanced Leadership Academy (ALAC Global), the member designate for the Takeover Regulation Panel in South Africa, the lead consultant and project coordinator for the Namibian Corporate Law Reform Project, and the life member of the Pan African Lawyers Union, based in Arusha, Tanzania. He was recently appointed commissioner of the South African Law Reform Commission.

Prof. Mongalo is the former lead expert and project manager for the South African Corporate Law Reform Project, which culminated in the enactment of the current Companies Act, 2008 of South Africa (Act No. 71 of 2008). He was also the project director and regulatory framework manager for the Business Registration Reform Project in South Africa.

Prof. Mongalo possesses the following degree qualifications: B.Proc (*Summa Cum Laude*), LL.B. (University of Natal, Durban), LL.M. (Commercial Law) (Cambridge University), PhD (Commercial Law) (University of Cape Town), and PGDHE (Wits University). Mongalo is also a recipient of certificates in Legal Writing (UCT), Law, Social Thought and Global Governance (Brown International Advanced Research Institute, Brown University (USA)), and Global Law, Economic Policy & Social Justice (Institute for Global Law and Policy (IGLP, Harvard (USA)). He is the Fellow of the Cambridge Commonwealth Society (FCCS).

Prof. Mongalo is the sole author of the first edition of the book *Corporate Law and Corporate Governance: A Global Picture of Business Undertakings in South Africa* (2003) and the co-author (with Dr Tshepiso Scott) of the second edition, entitled *Corporate Law and Corporate Governance: An Overview of Business Undertakings in South Africa* (2023). He is also the co-author (with Dr Cephas Lumina and Fahreen Kader) of the book entitled *Forms of Business Enterprise: Theory, Structure and Operation* (2004). Mongalo edited the first book to be published on the new Companies Act, 2008, in South Africa, entitled *Modern Company Law for a Competitive South African Economy* (2010). Prof. Mongalo recently contributed a chapter on *Innovating Corporate Governance in South Africa: Social and Ethics Committees* in the highly acclaimed book co-edited by Beate K. Sjåfjell and Christopher M. Bruner, entitled *The Cambridge Handbook on Corporate Law, Corporate Governance and Sustainability* (2019).

www.ingramcontent.com/pod-product-compliance
Ingram Content Group UK Ltd.
Pitfield, Milton Keynes, MK11 3LW, UK
UKHW041835031026
15587UKWH00002B/777

9 781666 922585